SE
INDIA
the MODI WAY

SECURING
INDIA
the MODI WAY

Balakot, Anti-Satellite
Missile Test and More

NITIN A. GOKHALE

BLOOMSBURY

NEW DELHI • LONDON • OXFORD • NEW YORK • SYDNEY

BLOOMSBURY INDIA
Bloomsbury Publishing India Pvt. Ltd
Second Floor, LSC Building No. 4, DDA Complex, Pocket C – 6 & 7,
Vasant Kunj New Delhi 110070

BLOOMSBURY, BLOOMSBURY PRIME and the Diana logo are
trademarks of Bloomsbury Publishing Plc

First published 2017
Revised and updated version 2019

ISBN: 978-93-89000-83-2

2 4 6 8 10 9 7 5 3 1

Printed and bound in India by Replika Press Pvt Ltd

Bloomsbury Publishing Plc makes every effort to ensure that the papers used in
the manufacture of our books are natural, recyclable products made from wood
grown in well-managed forests. Our manufacturing processes conform to the
environmental regulations of the country of origin.

To find out more about our authors and books visit www.bloomsbury.com
and sign up for our newsletters

Contents

MANOHAR PARRIKAR
CHIEF MINISTER, GOA

Foreword

This book by Nitin Gokhale focuses on Prime Minister Shri Narendra Modi's national security policies and some of the steps he has taken to improve India's strategic and national security position.

The Prime Minister's decision to personally reach out to the world and re-energise India's foreign policy approach is by now well known. India's rising global stature is a result of his vision and his government's initiatives. This book documents in detail some of the fundamental changes that are being ushered in by the Prime Minister, his government's efforts to strengthen our military, and the role of our armed forces and intelligence agencies in making India secure.

I have personally benefitted from Gokhale's insights and his long experience as a journalist covering matters of national security. I am confident that this book, written using simple and easy to understand language, will be useful to both military enthusiasts and common citizens alike.

Manohar Parrikar

Panaji
September 2017

Preface

One of the challenges that writers on contemporary issues face is to get the full picture immediately after the events have taken place. And so it has been with me in revising and updating this book. I had a similar experience when I wrote the first edition in 2017. It was released exactly a month after the resolution of the Dolam (Doklam) crisis between India and China was announced.

I just had a week to piece together the story of how one of the most serious border standoffs between the two Asian neighbours in recent years was resolved. Naturally, it was not possible to get all behind-the-scene details of the delicate diplomacy, hard negotiations and the decision-making at the highest level that went into the de-escalation, either because the main protagonists were out of my reach or were unwilling to speak because of the sensitive posts they held. And yet, as an observer of current affairs and author, I thought I had enough material to write an authentic account of how the solution to the Dolam faceoff was found. The book of course had many other insights about the decision-making process on national security matters under Prime Minister Narendra Modi.

In two years since the first edition was released in September 2017, many more significant actions have taken place in the national security space to be ignored. The killing of 40 plus troopers of the Central Reserve Police Force at Pulwama in Jammu and Kashmir on 14 February 2019 and its fallout for instance. When a Jaish-e-Mohammad (JeM) inspired and trained suicide bomber rammed his vehicle into the CRPF convoy, he set off a chain of events that has led to redrawing of several redlines and altered equations not just between India and Pakistan but also forced a rethink—at least on some counts—in the approach of Pakistan's all-weather ally China towards Islamabad's policies of supporting terror groups.

As we now know, in February 2019, Indian war planes struck a JeM terror camp at Balakot in the Khyber Pakhtunkhwa province inside Pakistan (not Pakistan-occupied Jammu & Kashmir, which technically is Indian territory). By deciding to go where no Indian government had dared to go in 48 years after the 1971 war, the Modi government set a new template in tackling terror emanating from Pakistan and has surely forced a rethink in Pakistan's strategy of pursuing a proxy war in J&K, if not completely stopped it.

The Balakot strike and the subsequent support India received globally for its action taken in self-defence, also compelled China to change its decade-old stand on terror and Pakistan. After the Pulwama terror attack, other permanent members of the UN Security Council, led by the US, UK and France had pursued JeM founder Masood Azhar's listing, first issuing a UNSC statement specifically condemning JeM followed by a proposal to designate Azhar as a terrorist at the UNSC 1267 Sanctions Committee. After China placed yet another hold on the designation in mid-March 2019—as it had done since 2008—the three countries advocated a tougher line, threatening China with bringing the proposal to the full UN Security Council.

Nifty diplomacy and India's enhanced status internationally coupled with realisation that supporting Pakistan blindly and shielding Azhar was giving diminishing returns, forced Beijing to finally agree to designate Azhar as an international terrorist.

So the decision-making process leading to the Balakot strike, the meticulous planning by the IAF on the back of real time intelligence inputs from the ground, the daring and professionalism of air force pilots, the subsequent air battle, the capture of Wing Commander Abhinandan that led to an unprecedented tension between India and Pakistan, all form a major part of this revised and updated edition.

The Modi government also took a giant step in ordering the testing of an anti-satellite missile, pre-empting any attempt to keep India out of future rule-making regime on space matters. I have updated the chapter on Middle East (or West Asia as we call it in India) since two important developments needed to be taken note of: One, India's presence at the plenary of the Organisation of Islamic Cooperation (OIC) as guest of honour and two, the increased security cooperation between India and the Gulf countries leading to extradition of Christian Michel James, perhaps the first White British National in history to be extradited to a non-European country, and many more fugitives.

The other big challenge in putting together a book on current events is to decide on a cut off date. When does one stop updating the book when some developments are still on-going? Which information to withhold and which to put in, especially in the sensitive matters of national security? These questions always create conflict in my mind and every time I am confronted with this dilemma, I fall back on the wisdom of my guru MV Kamath, who told me many moons ago: 'Remember, it is more important what you don't write than what you write.' I followed that dictum again since many data points are still secret and should remain so for some more time. May be, at the end of the Modi government's second tenure in 2024, I will add and elaborate on some of the events that I have taken note of only in passing right now.

One important point to note before you start reading this edition. The first six chapters of the book in your hand are fresh and focus on recent important milestones in the national security domain while the seventh is an updated version from the previous edition. Most other chapters have been kept unchanged from the first edition. So they might appear to be out of date or repetitive but remember they were written in the first half of 2017.

This book is based on several insider accounts and hitherto unknown facts about some of the unprecedented steps that the Modi government has taken in the past 22 months. This is by no means an analytical document. In fact, it is mostly factual and narrated from the point of view of those involved—and more importantly, those to whom I had access.

In many ways it is an incomplete account of recent events but it's a start. There is no denying the fact that this book has gained

immensely by the trust reposed in me by people in very sensitive
appointments. Many who spoke to me cannot be named because
they continue to serve in the military and our intelligence agencies.
Their contribution nevertheless is invaluable.

One person I terribly miss is Manohar Parrikar. He had
written the foreword for the first edition which I have retained.
The former defence minister and Goa Chief Minister passed away
recently. I will never forget those 28–29 months he spent in Delhi
as defence minister during which he bestowed his friendship on
me, unreservedly.

A book is never complete without help from friends, family,
colleagues and the very accommodative staff of Bloomsbury,
publishers of my previous four books. I remain indebted to all of
them for the understanding and patience they show with me. In
the end, if as a reader you feel that this book could have had more
details, the fault is entirely mine.

New Delhi   *Nitin A. Gokhale*
July 2019

Pulwama:
Testing Modi's Resolve

February 15, 2019: The morning after the Pulwama incident.

India's Prime Minister Narendra Modi had summoned the meeting of the Cabinet Committee on Security (CCS). The country's highest decision-making body on security and strategic matters was meeting to formulate India's response to the brazen attack that had killed more than 40 soldiers of the Central Reserve Police Force (CRPF) at Pulwama in Jammu and Kashmir the previous day.

Prime Minister Narendra Modi laying wreath on the mortal remains of the martyred CRPF Jawans, at Palam airport, in New Delhi on 15 February 2019

It was by far the biggest terror attack in J&K in a decade and had greatly enraged the nation and particularly the security forces. They wanted to avenge the attack quickly. The common people of the country perceived it to be part of Pakistan's continued perfidy and wanted the government to act decisively.

As senior ministers arrived for the meeting, the mood was sombre and tense. For the ruling National Democratic Alliance (NDA), battling perceptions of under-performance and under-delivery in the five years since it took office in May 2014, the timing of the Jaish-e-Mohammad (JeM)-inspired and organised terrorist strike was awkward.

India was two months away from the start of the general elections 2019 to elect the next government at the Centre.

The ruling alliance could hardly afford not to respond aggressively. In September 2016, the surgical strikes against terrorist camps inside Pakistan-occupied Jammu and Kashmir (POJK) in the wake of the killing of 19 Indian soldiers at Uri, was a path-breaking step. But the outrage over Pulwama needed a stronger and demonstrable riposte.

The CCS chaired by the Prime Minister then comprised Home Minister Rajnath Singh, External Affairs Minister Sushma Swaraj, Finance Minister Arun Jaitley and Defence Minister Nirmala Sitharaman. It was briefed by India's National Security Adviser (NSA) Ajit Doval on the current situation and options that India had before it. They vowed to mount an all-round offensive to pin down Pakistan for its continuing support to JeM in particular and other terrorist groups in general. Several steps, including withdrawal of most-favoured nation status to Pakistan, were discussed. Once the meeting ended, Arun Jaitley and Nirmala Sitharaman, aware of the heightened interest across the country and internationally, briefed the media outside the Prime Minister's residence and declared India's intention to put intense pressure on Pakistan on all fronts. Prime Minister Modi, addressing a function immediately after the CCS meeting, also spoke of a befitting response. Anyone who had tracked the Modi government's approach to national security, was in no doubt that a hard response was coming.

The CCS meeting on 15 February 2019

It was now a question of how and when and not if.

Since a ground assault by Special Forces had already been employed successfully in September 2016, Pakistan would have been ready to face a repetition. So that option clearly ruled itself out.

What else could India do? A coordinated attack on multiple posts all along the Line of Control (LoC) to alter the current status of the de facto boundary? An air strike? Or a naval blockade? No one could say with certainty. The answer was hanging in the air.

Meanwhile, India withdrew the MFN status to Pakistan. Seen largely as a symbolic gesture, the decision nevertheless signaled India's seriousness in putting Pakistan on the back foot and take punitive measures even if the step was small in terms of any substantial impact. On several occasions in the past, New Delhi had resisted the call to withdraw the special status to Pakistan even in the face of extreme provocation like the 26/11 Mumbai attacks that killed over 160 people.

In a meeting called by the NSA of the Foreign Secretary, Home Secretary, Director, Intelligence Bureau (DIB), Secretary Research and Analysis Wing (R&AW), Secretary Revenue, it was also decided to present a new dossier to the FATF or Financial Action Task Force, an international terror finance watchdog to prove Pakistan's support and financing provided to JeM. Pakistan

Satellite picture of a terrorist camp at Garhi Habibullah, KPK
(34.422606N, 73.406578E)

was placed on the grey list of the anti-terror finance watchdog in July 2018 and continues to be there. The FATF currently has 35 members and two regional organisations—European Commission and Gulf Cooperation Council. North Korea and Iran are also in the FATF blacklist.

In addition, India once again sent a detailed dossier listing exact locations of terrorist camps run with full knowledge of the Pakistani establishment. The dossier contained satellite pictures, specific latitude-longitudinal positions and details of number of trainees and trainers present there besides the type of training imparted in the camps. The list of 14 camps run by Lashkar-e-Taiyyaba (LeT), JeM, Hizbul Mujahideen (HM), Harkat-ul-Mujahideen (HuM) and Al Badr, also included the Balakot facility. Indian agencies had satellite pictures of the Tabook and Khyber camps run by LeT in Pakistan's Khyber Pakhtunkhwa (KPK) province too.

However, Pakistan treated the whole exercise lightly. In the week after Pulwama attack it was once again proved that the diplomatic pressure on Pakistan to act decisively and take verifiable action against the terrorists failed to have any impact. JeM, which by this time had become a fully ISI-controlled and run organisation enjoyed near immunity from any government action. Whatever little was done was only for perception management and hoodwink international opinion.

Even as these steps were initiated, speculation mounted on what India could do in retribution since passions over the killing of the CRPF jawans were running high. As days and a week passed without any visible action, criticism over the government's intentions or lack of it was now becoming louder.

Through all this, the Prime Minister however dropped broad hints that India was not about to allow Pakistan's and JeM's Pulwama outrage to go unpunished.

And sure enough, on the morning of 26 February 2019 India, Pakistan and the world woke up to the news of a dozen Indian Air Force combat jets crossing the Line of Control (LoC) and going beyond to hit a JeM training camp at Balakot located in the PKP province. The world was stunned.

There were several firsts in this action: for the first time in 48 years, Indian war planes had crossed the LoC; for the first time, India had struck terrorist camps not located in POJK but on sovereign Pakistani territory and for the first time, no one—not one country, including China—objected to or condemned the Indian action. The strike carried out at the dead of night was largely accepted as India's legitimate right to respond to Pakistan-based terrorist groups' attack on an Indian target.

The official Indian statement, within hours of the IAF action and read out by Foreign Secretary Vijay Gokhale was measured and aptly conveyed New Delhi's decision to take an unprecedented and paradigm-shifting step.

It read in parts: 'On 14 February 2019, a suicide terror attack was conducted by a Pak-based terrorist organization Jaish-e-Mohammad, leading to the martyrdom of 40 brave jawans of the CRPF. JeM has been active in Pakistan for the last two decades, and is led by Masood Azhar with its headquarters in Bahawalpur.

'This organization, which is proscribed by the UN, has been responsible of a series of terrorist attacks including on the Indian Parliament in December 2001 and the Pathankot airbase in January 2016.

'India has been repeatedly urging Pakistan to take action against the JeM to prevent jihadis from being trained and armed inside Pakistan. Pakistan has taken no concrete actions to dismantle the infrastructure of terrorism on its soil.

'Credible intelligence was received that JeM was attempting another suicide terror attack in various parts of the country, and the fidayeen jihadis were being trained for this purpose. In the face of imminent danger, a pre-emptive strike became absolutely necessary.

'In an intelligence led operation in the early hours of today, India struck the biggest training camp of JeM in Balakot. In this operation, a very large number of JeM terrorists, trainers, senior commanders and groups of jihadis who were being trained for fidayeen action were eliminated. This facility at Balakot was headed by Maulana Yousuf Azhar (alias Ustad Ghouri), the brother-in-law of Masood Azhar, Chief of JeM.

'The Government of India is firmly and resolutely committed to taking all necessary measures to fight the menace of terrorism. Hence this non-military preemptive action was specifically targeted at the JeM camp. The selection of the target was also conditioned by our desire to avoid civilian casualties. The facility is located in a thick forest on a hilltop far away from any civilian presence. As the strike has taken place only a short while ago, we are awaiting further details.

'The Government of Pakistan had made a solemn commitment in January 2004 not to allow its soil or territory under its control to be used for terrorism against India. We expect that Pakistan lives up to its public commitment and takes follow up actions to dismantle all JeM and other camps and hold the terrorists accountable for the actions.'

The statement, when analysed closely, conveyed three distinct strands: one, India will no longer be restrained in using its military forces in responding to a terrorist attack by Pakistan-based groups, sponsored and sheltered by the establishment. Two, India took a pre-emptive step to prevent another suicide attack and three, New Delhi had no intention to escalate matters.

With the Balakot strike (*see separate chapter*), Narendra Modi proved once again why he has changed the rules of the game with Pakistan ever since he took over as Prime Minister five years ago. Balakot, in many ways removed the fear in the minds of Indian decision makers about imaginary nuclear red lines in India–Pakistan equation. Mr Modi's two actions—surgical strikes in 2016 and the air strike in 2019—has allowed India to find space for one more mode of response in the spectrum ranging from sub-conventional action to an all-out war under a nuclear overhang.

As NSA Ajit Doval, who has been reappointed for another term co-terminus with the Prime Minister's tenure—and with an enhanced status equivalent to a cabinet minister—elaborates, India under Modi has followed a national security policy that sought to repair the damage it was subjected to in the 10-year UPA reign between 2004 and 2014. 'Only a strong and decisive central government can provide critical leadership at a time when there is growing uncertainty and unpredictability in global affairs,' he said in his speech at the Sardar Patel Memorial lecture organised by the Information and Broadcasting Ministry, which very much sums up this government's approach.

In one of his rare on-record conversations, the NSA told me: 'Nations like India need to have a clear vision about its national interest and take calculated risks. In Prime Minister Modi, India is lucky to have someone who is not afraid to put national interest above political considerations.' Of course the Prime Minister

PM Modi with National Security Adviser Ajit Doval

had picked right advisers like Doval who have a displayed penchant for innovative ideas to implement the Prime Minister's bold vision.

In a way, the Modi–Doval team was convinced that decisive and clear message to Pakistan was necessary for improving our long term bilateral relations. Modi's first choice was a peace offensive. However when within a week of his visit to Lahore in December 2015 there was an attack on the Pathankot air base (*see separate chapter*) with the knowledge of the ISI, Prime Minister Modi felt that the peace process cannot be pursued as long as Pakistan was convinced that India's effort emanates from its weakness.

For years, Pakistan seemed to have employed one of guerrilla warfare's well-known principles first propagated by Ernesto 'Che' Guevara, a Marxist-Leninist revolutionary leader of Argentine origin. In his warfare doctrine, Che Guevera had recommended a way to reduce pressure on the guerilla force. He had said if occupation forces are pinned down to static formations, it retards their mobility and puts them into a defensive mindset. He used to suggest that the guerilla should be on the lookout for any opportunity where he can hit at the soft target which would lead to further accretion of forces on non-offensive deployment. The NSA felt that the Indian security deployment had got into a defensive mindset over the years in Jammu and Kashmir. The more the terrorists attacked, the more ring-fencing of military and security installations took place. This approach allowed the terrorists to attack Indian targets freely without incurring much losses to themselves. The suicide bombers were easy fodder in applying such tactics. The Indian counter-strategy, on the other hand, was not imposing any cost on either the Pakistani establishment or the Pakistani-backed terrorist outfits.

Doval was determined to get India out of this logjam that over the decades had got deeply ingrained in the minds of political leaders, bureaucrats, and security managers. Even senior commanders when they thought differently found their voice too feeble and the initiatives too risky. Modi was the first Prime Minister since India faced the threat of state-sponsored covert action starting in the early 1980s, to realise that India has to extricate itself from this quagmire. He knew this vicious cycle had to be broken. To bring about this transformation, Modi needed to take various steps including appointing someone as his security adviser who had the experience, vision and established credentials to do the job. Doval had impeccable credentials on all the counts and enjoyed wide respect and acceptability among security professionals. This step the Prime Minister had taken in 2014 itself in appointing Doval as the NSA and continuing with him in the second term with an enhanced status.

Thus, the Modi–Doval combination brought in a new approach to national security: taking calculated risks to take the fight to the adversary. It is clear now that the surgical strikes in 2016 and the Balakot operation in 2019 were anchored in this philosophy (*see Plate 1*).

But dealing with Pakistan kinetically was just one aspect. Since 2017 (when this book was first written), India has notched up many foreign policy firsts too. Getting invited as guest of honour to the plenary of the Organisation of Islamic Countries (OIC) in the face of vehement opposition from Pakistan, for instance. External Affairs Minister Sushma Swaraj represented India at the conference in Abu Dhabi to mark a significant milestone in India's relations with the Islamic nations (see updated Chapter *Re-engaging with the Middle East*) in March 2019. Similarly, in February–March 2018, most analysts had written India off in Maldives concluding that China had taken full control of the island nation in the Indian Ocean. Less than a year later, New Delhi helped pro-democratic forces in Maldives to regain a firm foothold. The turnaround in Maldives and restoring balance in some of the other neighbouring countries like Nepal and Bangladesh is a story in itself.

Looking back, a robust, pragmatic and multi-aligned foreign and security policies were the last thing that analysts and commentators expected from Narendra Modi when he took office as India's Prime Minister in the summer of 2014. Five years down the line, it is perhaps time to revise that opinion and concede that India's standing in the world has gone up several notches, thanks to Modi's personal approach to diplomacy and national security based purely on India's national interest and not dictated or influenced by extraneous reasons. The signs of robust, more pragmatic policies were visible in the first three years itself which the first edition of this book recorded when it was released in 2017.

2

Taking the Fight into Pakistan

On the day the CCS met on 15 February, one of the key questions that India's top security managers led by NSA Doval were grappling with, was the magnitude of a counter-strike on Pakistan. They needed to calibrate the quantum of attack and ensure that civilians were not hurt. Coming up with such an option would be tough.

Prime Minister Narendra Modi was clear in his objective. Flagging off the *Vande Bharat*, a semi-high speed train, to Varanasi from Delhi on 15 February less than 24-hours after the Pulwama attack, Modi declared in his first public reaction to the massacre, 'The blood of our people is boiling…Pakistan cannot weaken India through such acts and will have to pay a heavy price…. I have given the security forces complete freedom, a free hand to deal with the situation…this act of terror will not go unpunished.'

Critics however, did not expect the Prime Minister to go beyond the rhetoric. Writing on the options before Modi, columnist Swaminathan Aiyar wrote in *The Times of India*, 'The terrorist attack at Pulwama, killing 40 soldiers, provides Narendra Modi a huge but risky chance to portray himself as the toughest politician in India. Atal Bihari Vajpayee's victory in the 1999 Kargil war helped him win the next general election. Can Modi use Pulwama to do the same? He must avoid military action, which could backfire badly. Far wiser would be new forms of political theatre, similar to his "surgical strikes" in 2016, in retaliation for the attack on our armed forces at Uri. That satisfied the public demand for action without risking dangerous escalation into an all-out war.'

The Prime Minister and his national security team however had other ideas. They factored in possible backlash from Pakistan and also war-gamed escalation and concluded that Pakistan was not in a position to launch any big offensive if India took a bold step. At best it would up the ante on the LoC or activate some of its sleeper cells in Indian cities to carry out terrorist strikes, the NSA and his team assessed.

In both scenarios, India's national security set up was confident enough to handle any possible fallout. On the LoC, the Indian Army has time and again demonstrated its overwhelming firepower. More significantly, between 2014 and 2019, combined efforts of the entire national security system had ensured that terrorists were unable to execute any major action in urban areas. In comparison, more than 1000 people had been killed in 26 major attacks in Indian cities between 2004 and 2014.

As Doval, the three service chiefs and top brass of intelligence agencies put their heads together, several alternatives were on the table. A 2016-like surgical strike by the Indian Army's Special Forces on terrorist camps in POJK, was already ruled out since the known camps across the LoC and in POJK had been either vacated or their security strengthened in the wake of the Pulwama incident.

Besides, the retribution had to be demonstrable and effective to send a message to both terrorists and their backers, the Pakistani Army. A precision air strike on a high value target therefore seemed the most obvious choice. In theory, this was easiest to do too. A couple of planes could go into POJK, bomb a target or two and return in a jiffy, one would think. In real life, it wasn't as easy as playing a video game. There would be huge implications if Indian Air Force (IAF) planes crossed the LoC, an action that India and Pakistan had studiously avoided since the 1971 war.

Much deliberations and planning based on multiple intelligence inputs were needed before taking the big step. So NSA Doval assigned specific tasks to different agencies. India's external spying agency, Research and Analysis Wing (R&AW) which maintains the list of designated terrorist training camps run by JeM and LeT inside Pakistan was asked to get the updates on latest activities at the bigger JeM camps, apart from its headquarter at Bhawalpur in Pakistan's Punjab, not too far from Lahore. The National Technical Research Organisation (NTRO) and Indian Space Research Organization (ISRO), got down to scanning some of the locations provided by R&AW to try and get images with resolutions which would be 50 cm or less. Operatives of these two outfits sat with IAF image specialists as well as pilots to figure out the most suitable targets. Intelligence Bureau (IB) operatives in the meantime were tapping their sources to try and obtain actionable inputs.

Bhawalpur apart, India had identified two more potential targets, a camp at Sawai Nallah near Muzafarabad in POJK (*see Plate 2*) and Balakot, which is located in the Khyber Pakhtunkhwa province, mainland Pakistan. The Bhawalpur HQ of the Jaish was difficult to strike without incurring civilian casualties since it was located in a densely populated area of Punjab. Sawai Nallah in POJK would have been easier to hit but having ordered a surgical strike on camps in POJK post the Uri attacks in September 2016, the Prime Minister and his security team were keen that this time the target be more significant to make a bigger statement than just another operation across the line of control. So the option was narrowing down to Balakot.

Balakot in many ways was an ideal choice for at least two reasons. One, it was located in mainland Pakistan in the Khyber

Sign board of the Markaz at Manshera–Balakot road leading to the main camp

Pakhtunkhwa province. The Markaz Syed Ahmad Shaheed, as the training facility was known, was set up in the early 2000s and is located on the crest of ridge called Jaba top. Isolated from civilian zones, it was accessible only to those who needed to go to the camp. Indian intelligence agencies had kept a close watch over the Balakot facility for a long time.

The main complex had several facilities divided to house Jaish members based on their seniority. There was a dormitory type accommodation for the junior lot while the senior leadership like chief trainer Yusuf and his senior colleagues stayed in various single rooms. On the top floor were the new arrivals mingled with some of the hardened terrorist who had undergone at least six months focused training in weapons and explosives handling.

Indian intelligence operatives had already put together details of different training courses of the Jaish that were conducted at the Balakot camp. There were religious courses (Daura-e-Owais Karni; Daura-e-Aalim; Daura-e-Khair and Dars-e-Nizam). And there were courses for fidayeen. They included:

- *Daura-e-Tarbiyah:* Seven to 14 days course for selected cadres, primarily for motivation and indoctrination.
- *Daura-e-Tafseer:* A 40-day course on interpretation of particular verses of the Quran with reference to jihad.
- *Daura-e-Asasiyah:* A 14-day foundation course focused on basic knowledge of jihad.

The armed training courses included:

- *Daura-e-Zarar:* A 40-day course. Cadres are taught to handle explosives and grenades, pistols, AK-47 rifles, LMGs, rocket launchers and Under Barrel Grenade Launchers. Also taught radio and mobile communication skills.
- *Daura-e-Al Araad:* An advanced four-month course for honing basic skills besides 10-days firing practice and Quranic lessons.

Communications training:

- Handling electronic and communications equipment.

- Advance communications course combined with use of GPS, code words, map reading and IED making.

Basically, the fidayeen or suicide bombers were trained like any other armed group but their selection was rigorous and they were motivated purely on the basis of religion. At any given time there were always more than 200 occupants at the camp.

The Army and the Indian Navy were meanwhile doing their bit to keep Pakistan guessing. All along the LoC, the Army had stepped up its retaliatory operations, responding to even the slightest Pakistani provocations with ferocity and keeping the Pakistani deployment under constant pressure.

The Indian Navy, which was in the middle of its war game since January 2019—done every two years—called Theatre Level Operational Readiness Exercise (TROPEX)—immediately redeployed in an operational mode to prevent movement of Pakistani naval assets a couple of days after the Pulwama attack. As a result, over the next three months the Pakistani Navy was virtually bottled up in the Karachi harbour or is limited to patrolling near the shores, fearing Indian ingress.

Two Pakistani ships—PNS Saif and PNS Moawin—scheduled to visit Qingdao in China to join the 70th anniversary celebrations

Indian naval ships during Tropex 2019 which got converted to an operational deployment post-Pulwama

of the PLA Navy, cancelled their planned visit although the Pakistani Navy Chief attended the ceremony slated on April 24. On the other hand, India sent two ships to join the celebrations.

The Indian Navy later revealed how it quickly transited from a training exercise to an operational deployment in the wake of the Pulwama attack. 'The major combat units of the Indian Navy including the Carrier Battle Group with INS Vikramaditya, nuclear submarines and scores of other ships, submarines and aircraft swiftly transited from exercise to operational deployment mode as tensions between India and Pakistan escalated. A clear and resolute message regarding the operational posture of the Indian Navy to prevent, deter and defeat any misadventure by Pakistan in the maritime domain was conveyed...' the Navy said.

INS Arihant, India's indigenously designed, developed and manufactured nuclear submarine, was also part of the deployment.

Following the deployment, Pakistan also cancelled the visit of its ship PNS Aslat to the Langkawi International Maritime and Aerospace Exhibition (LIMA) held at Langkawi in Malaysia between March 26 and 30 and the visit of PNS Shamsheer to Bahrain. To add insult to injury, the Government of Maldives on its own called off a scheduled port call of PNS Aslat to its country en route to Langkawi even before it was known that the Pakistanis had decided not to participate in the Langkawi exhibition.

The pressure created by the presence of a large number Indian naval assets in the area had clearly forced Pakistan to make changes to its scheduled programme of overseas deployments.

As the Indian Navy said in its press note: 'About 60 ships of the Indian Navy, 12 ships of the Indian Coast Guard and 60 aircraft were part of TROPEX 19. Amongst the key attributes of naval forces are the "Versatility" to change roles, "Mobility" and "Poise". Availability of such a large number of combat-ready assets in the theatre of operations for TROPEX 19 allowed the Indian Navy to expeditiously respond to the developing situation in synergy with the three services. The overwhelming superiority of Indian Navy in all three dimensions forced the Pakistan Navy to remain deployed

close to the Makran coast and not venture out in the open ocean'
(*see Plates 3 and 4*).

Outgoing Navy Chief Admiral Sunil Lanba in his last interview
to me before leaving office, confirmed the India Navy's role. 'We
were in the throes of our annual exercise TROPEX. When Pulwama
happened, we pulled out some units and forward deployed them
towards the northern Arabian Sea. When we were given clear-
cut directives that we were going to do an action in Balakot, we
terminated TROPEX, redeployed our forces to the northern part of
the Arabian sea-different task groups including the CBG (Carrier
Battle Group) and submarines. We were aggressively poised to
prevent any action being taken by our enemy.'

Pointing out that the asymmetry between the Indian and
Pakistani armed forces is the maximum between the Pakistan and
Indian Navies, Admiral Lanba said: 'If push had come to shove we
would have decimated the Pakistani Navy.'

The all-round pressure being brought to bear on Pakistan
should have left the establishment in Islamabad in no doubt that
India was serious about retaliation. However, it was difficult for
Pakistan to guess where and how the retribution would come.

For all the talk about the likelihood of a precise air strike
on terrorist camp(s), the IAF top brass was seemingly busy with
its once-in-two years Air Show called Aero India at Bengaluru.
Original Equipment Manufacturers, Indian defence companies,
the entire defence hierarchy—everyone seem to be at the air show.
Little did anyone know that this was a façade.

Behind the scene, the IB and R&AW operatives had started
feeding their agents who have links inside Pakistan with bits and
pieces of information hinting at India's intention to target the
Bhawalpur complex of the Jaish. Around 20 February, India's on-
ground sources reported significant movement of Jaish members
from Bhawalpur to Balakot.

Now it was up to the IAF to devise and execute the plan. By
the time the Aero India show ended in Bengaluru on 23 February,
the Air Force brass was already back in Delhi and their respective
headquarters. Air Force stations in Rajasthan, Gujarat and Punjab,

already on a higher alert, were now flying sorties almost round-the-clock. Pakistani air defence and Pakistan Air Force formations also went on a high alert along the border with India as the intensity of the IAF flying tempo kept rising.

Simultaneously, India prepared a detailed dossier about the activities of the JeM and once again provided specific locations of different camps, including Balakot operated by the outfit to Pakistan. The Ministry of External Affairs (MEA) officially handed over the dossier to Pakistan and sought credible action.

NSA Doval assigned different tasks to the members of the core team. While the Air Force got down to plan the strike mission, India's intelligence services tapped several of its assets, including technical resources, to get the latest updates from inside Pakistan and collate terrorist movements. An elaborate contingency plan involving all other components of the Indian security apparatus was prepared and pressed into service. It was a silent and discreet exercise but executed with precision and in record time.

Meanwhile, the IAF continued flying several sorties, both in the day and at night along India's western border. Several fighter jets across bases spread in Rajasthan and Punjab carried out specific missions to create an impression that India was gearing up for a major air action. The Pakistanis, because of multiple messaging by the Prime Minister who publicly announced several times his intention to avenge the outrageous attack at Pulwama, unless it took immediate, verifiable and visible actions against the perpetrators of the Pulwama attack thought an air strike on the JeM's headquarter at Bhawalpur was imminent.

An intelligence operation of disinformation synchronised with actual movements on the ground and air, reinforced Pakistan's assessment that JeM HQs at Bhawalpur was the most likely target. The Pakistanis moved Masood Azhar and others from their known locations to safer destinations under ISI protection.

In Delhi, envoys of important friendly nations were briefed by Foreign Secretary Vijay Gokhale that India intended to avenge the Pulwama attack. Of course without going into details. The Cabinet Committee on Security (CCS) in its regular weekly meeting on

20 February also discussed the possible retaliation. It authorised Prime Minister Modi to take the appropriate decision. NSA Doval was also in constant touch with his counterparts without from prominent global powers giving any indication of the target, type of operation or likely time.

Specialists from the National Technical Research Organisation (NTRO) meanwhile on continuing basis were obtaining latest satellite images of Balakot and its surroundings via ISRO satellites and analysing them along with the IAF's satellite image interpreters to map the area precisely, breaking it down to the last detail about the layout of the buildings in the campus, matching the inputs with information from the ground obtained by the intelligence agencies to arrive at the importance of each structure to narrow down the targets. The most important inputs however came from two IB and R&AWs sources within the JeM who managed to get inside the Balakot facility for three days between 19 and 22 February and send information backed by pictures which clinched the decision to hit the camp. The photos showed the training camp was alive and

A – Hall, residence, hostel
B – Mosque (34.464, 73.318)
C – Guest house/residence of trainers
D – Big hall/hostel for cadres
E – Canteen area
F – Residence of Yusuf Azhar and
      abandoned school
G – Main entrance
H – Swimming pool
I – Hijama, dispensary and canteen
J – Tailoring facility

*The Balakot camp as seen in satellite pictures a day before
the strike on 26 February 2019*

kicking and was in fact getting ready to welcome 200 more trainees from 25 February.

The two sources managed to document the entire facility visually and identify important buildings and their occupants (*see Plate 5*). Spread over few acres, the camp had 8 major buildings or complexes devoted to various kinds of activities. Most importantly, the camp was run by Masood Azhar's brother-in-law Yusuf Azhar, who resided in an abandoned school complex on the campus. Tragically, both the sources are believed to have been killed in the IAF strike on 26 February. The invaluable information and confirmation about the layout of the camp and movement of important personnel in the compound helped India in precisely target specific structures.

For instance, the sources confirmed Yusuf Azhar, the chief trainer used to stay in Room No. 1. Senior Jaish trainers Mufti Umar and Maulana Javed, Maulana Aslam and Maulana Abdul Gafur Kashmiri, Maulana Ajmal and Maulana Zubair, occupied rooms adjacent to Azhar's in the descending order of their importance. The top floor of the complex was allotted to the 100-odd fidayeen who were undergoing training at that moment. The sources had also obtained photographs of the entrance where flags of USA, UK and Israel had been printed on the steps so that new recruits could feel that they were stepping on the enemy's flags (*see Plate 6*).

At the northern end of the camp was another large complex with a hostel, dining room and a big hall that housed as many 150 recruits of various categories. The agencies even had information on the number of recruits and the hierarchies they were grouped under as per the Jaish organisational structure (*see Chapter 1*). By 25 February, a new course with 200 more recruits began, taking the total number of occupants at the complex to over 350.

The mosque complex was slightly away from the residential quarters. Indian operatives had managed to obtain pictures from inside the mosque. Photographs showed its walls lined with portraits of so-called shaheeds or martyrs, the terrorists who died fighting in Kashmir. Another building, adjacent to the mosque served as temporary accommodation for those who came for short visits.

Maulana Yusuf Azhar and his vehicle. Azhar was killed
with others in the air strike

In the third week of February, three top trainers Maulana Junaid, Maulana Qudratullah, and Maulana Qasim of Lahore, declared absconders under Pakistan's Anti-Terrorism Act, had arrived at the Balakot complex. They had not returned to their respective homes for years. Qudratullah is regarded as a special mentor while Qasim imparted martial arts skills to the new recruits.

Time was now ripe to strike at the camp.

By 23 February, the core team had enough actionable intelligence to undertake an intelligence driven strike mission at Balakot. Doval, held a final meeting with Air Chief Air Marshal BS Dhanoa and Secretary R (as the R&AW head is known officially), Anil Dhasmana. Final instructions were given to all concerned and the countdown began. Within hours Doval held another meeting with all the three service chiefs to finalise contingency plans should there be any escalation. The Indian plan was to only hit at the terrorist and not cause any civilians casualties or collateral damage to the extent possible.

Next day, the NSA took the entire findings to Prime Minister Modi and briefed him about the target and its locations and outlined the risks involved. The Prime Minister listened patiently, asked a couple of probing questions about the possibility of IAF planes being intercepted and the backup plan for such an eventuality. He was also told that hitting Balakot had an inherent risk since it was located in mainland Pakistan's Khyber Pakhtunkhwa province. Not since 1971, when India helped create

Bangladesh out of East Pakistan, Indian war planes had been allowed to cross the Line of Control (LoC) because of an unspoken fear of triggering an unintended military escalation. After mulling over the scenario, and going into various details, the Prime Minister gave the final go ahead to Doval.

This was not the first time that such information (about existence of camps) was being given to the Pakistanis (*see Plate 7*). Earlier too they were provided with details of not just camps but also about the terrorists leaders and prominent criminals like Dawood Ibrahim. India had given specific locations, names, details of their movements. But Pakistan consistently denied presence of any such persons. That has been their standard formulation. This time, when Pakistan showed no sign of taking action, India wanted to send a message: that it was not given to false bravado or empty threats. In the past, the Pakistanis were used to seeing India talking big but taking no action. 'Our past utterances were treated as a joke. So when we took action, they were utterly surprised,' recalls one top official.

Speaking to me in one of his rare on-record interactions, NSA Doval said: 'Table top analysts think and believe that coercive or deterrent power of the state is directly proportionate to the size of its army and lethality of its arsenal. They presume that a country with a strong security apparatus will invariably have an edge over its adversaries. However, if a nation-state possesses all the instruments and assets to protect itself but fails to muster the courage to use it, it starts losing credibility. India had fallen into this trap as evident prominently in the wake of the Mumbai attack in November 2008. We had to convince our adversaries that we had both the will and the ability to take necessary actions when required.'

Doval went on to add: 'We wanted to show the world that India's Prime Minister has to be taken seriously. When the Prime Minister says India will take action, that action must be taken. However a Prime Minister like Modi will not declare his intentions unless he has got both the capability and intention to do so, unlike politicians in the past. For both surgical strikes in 2016 and the

Balakot operation in 2019, our Prime Minister said India will take action and it did.'

There was intent and the Air Force assured the leadership that it had capacity.

The countdown for a historic mission had started.

Now it was up to the Air Force, its planning, the skills and daring of the pilots to translate the audacious plan into action.

It was also time to re-establish India's credibility.

3

The Action Phase

Once the political clearance came, it was left to the IAF to decide on the composition of the force package. The brass decided to use deception, low altitude flying, and terrain masking to catch PAF and its air defences by surprise. These three elements actually determined which aircraft will be deployed, from where they will take off and what weapons they will use.

This is where the Gwalior-based Mirage squadron came into play. Considering the terrain, the distance and the requirement to have pin-pointed accuracy in bombing the target, the IAF leadership honed in on the French-origin Mirage 2000 combat jets for the task.

The Mirage, with their versatile capability was best suited to carry out the important task. So 16 of the best aircraft were chosen to be part of the strike mission.

Mirage-2000s: The versatile war machine

Out of the 16 Mirages, six were fitted with the Israeli-made SPICE (Smart Precise Impact and Cost Effective) 2000 bombs and six others with Crystal Maze bombs (as a back up). There were chosen after careful deliberation and keeping the mission target in mind (*What is SPICE BOMB, What does it do? See box*). Four aircraft were earmarked for air defence (in case the force package encountered any challenge during the mission) or escort role.

It is to be noted that for any mission the IAF plans, force-packaging is done on the basis of objectives that are given. As an air force officer involved in the planning the Balakot strike revealed, 'You require X-number of aircraft to destroy the target. Why do have the force-packaging? The force-packaging is based on threats that we envisage from the adversary. The threats could come from surface-to-guided missiles, air-to-air interceptors, depending on the routes we choose, air bases in and around the target area. For instance, if I'm attacking Peshawar, I can't have interceptors coming from Karachi, it is one-hour away. So you take the number of air fields which are there to have general intelligence about what are the airfields with what aircraft—how much counter-strike capability they can muster in a hurry. The force packaging is done based on all these factors: how many aircraft will be in a decoy role, how many in actual strike role. Therefore, the number of aircraft that are part of the package are many times more than the actual strike aircraft. The aim is singular: Successful mission to achieve the main objective.'

At the Air HQ and Western Air Command, both located in Delhi, the operations were being given the necessary support. The leadership was looking at two dates—26 and 29 February. The two days between these two were ruled out because of bad weather. Even the night between 25 and 26 February was estimated to have a very small window of clear weather over Balakot. There was another complication. The then Western Air Command (WAC) Chief, Air Marshal C Hari Kumar was to retire on 28 February. So, a week before his retirement, the IAF and Air Force had to name Hari Kumar's replacement.

THE ACTION PHASE 25

The choice fell on Air Marshal Raghunath Nambiar, who was heading the Eastern Air Command, headquartered in Shillong at the time. He was drafted in and brought into the Air HQ to be part of the planned operation to strike Balakot, before he took over WAC on 1 March.

On the night of 25 February, the IAF top brass told the Mirage Squadron at Gwalior that the mission was a go. To maintain total secrecy and normal appearance however, the entire brass—the Air Chief, his Commander-in-Chiefs, the Principal Staff Officers at the Air HQ—hosted a farewell dinner for Hari Kumar. As the dinner broke up, it was back to work for the Air Chief and his Operations Staff.

Now it was hours away from rolling out the mission.

By 8 PM, the Western Air Command—which stretches from Bikaner in Rajasthan to Ladakh and up to Sarsawa in Uttar Pradesh—ordered intensified sorties along the western border with Pakistan. Fighter jets were taking off one after the other from all air bases that night. 'The idea was to keep the Pakistani air defence system busy and guessing,' a senior IAF official revealed. The deception plan was underway.

Meanwhile in Gwalior, the 16 Mirages were ready and primed.

What Is SPICE Bomb, What Does It Do?

As Air Marsha SBP Sinha, who retired as Commander-in-Chief of Central Air Command in December 2018 and has had long experience in both operations and procurement, explained, 'SPICE is qualified with 4 words. First is Smart, next is Precise, then Penetration, and fourth is Standoff. Smart because the aircraft after delivering the weapon can turn back and the bomb can continue its journey towards the target on its own guidance. The weapon has a mid-course guidance system too which is un-jammable because its precision code and CPNC codes are controlled Israel and US, who don't disclose it. The weapon is therefore very precise.'

SPICE Bomb

Those who know say the terminal guidance of SPICE is done by digital SIM correlation and picture matching. This means that if you take satellite imagery of the area, the head of the bomb, fitted with electro optical and infrared sensors, picks up the image and digitally matches it with the pictures which are already fed in the bomb. The head is always looking. As it comes closer, it starts picking up the target distinctly and starts matching picture correlations. That is why it is very accurate.

As Air Marshal Sinha added, 'The accuracy of SPICE is governed by the quality of the picture/images that are fed. Therefore, the resolution of the pictures that the satellites obtain is important. If you feed 100 cm resolution—that means each pixel is 100 cm by 100 cm—the accuracy is half of that pixel. For the Balakot attack, the Air Force obtained pictures with 60 cm resolution. That means the accuracy was 30 cm.'

The next great attribute of SPICE is its penetration ability. For that, this bomb is specifically designed to penetrate thick, blast-proof structures, especially roofs on important buildings. It not only ensures penetration but also a blast once it enters a building with pin pointed accuracy. With a weight of 2,000 pounds, the bomb's metal body is very strong. When it is released at .95 Mach (or 17–18 km per minute speed), the bomb impacts the target with the speed of 780 to 850 km. Once the bomb penetrates a building, it will explode depending on the pre-programmed time fed into it. The delayed timing for the bomb to explode is set depending on the penetration depth. So the explosion takes place after the bomb has entered the building and not before. Otherwise only the rooftop will blow up. Plus, if the bomb explodes at the entry of penetration, it will not generate the requisite pressure and blast effect.

With its 90 kg warhead, the blast has a devastating effect in a closed room, creating pressure waves, flames and fire which will raise the temperature to anything beyond 1,000 to 2,000 degrees. So whatever or whoever is in the room, will be decimated. Which is exactly what happened once the six SPICE bombs hit the target at Balakot.

Air Marshal Sinha, who was also Deputy Chief of the IAF, in charge of procurements, says SPICE 2000s were bought mainly to enable the IAF to target the adversary's command and control structures which are heavily fortified and hidden under reinforced structures. This and for precision strikes to have least collateral damage.

'That's why in the pictures which I was showing you, it is important to know when and where the bomb has entered. Now the entry point is very important. The width of the bomb is 50 cm where it enters and makes hole of 50–60 cm only. The bomb is designed to create that "pin hole" effect so that the big burst explosion does not escape from the point of entry and instead is effective inside the confined room.'

As Air Marshal Sinha points out, 'Normally, people except an earthquake-like devastation after every bombing. But it is good to remember that the earthquake does not kill, collapsing buildings do and yet, there are many survivors. So if people have to be eliminated, a burst effect with very high temperatures has to be created which is what a SPICE 2000 bomb does and did at Balakot. The buildings won't fall but the occupants would either be burnt to death or die because of the blast effect, which is exactly what happened at the JeM camp.'

So post-midnight on 25 February, the mission took off from Gwalior at around 1.30 AM, went north and then flew west along the Himalayan boundary to avoid detection by Pakistani Airborne Warning And Control System. According to Air Marshal SBP Sinha, the Pakistanis use two types of AWACS. One is the 360 Chinese-built ZDK-03 Karakoram Eagle AWACS aircraft version and the other one is rotating dome type. The other is *Saab-2000* Airborne Early Warning & Control (AEW&C) equipped with the Erieye radar system. 'When I was in service I used to monitor their activities. I find that that the Chinese version was used for the southern sectors towards Rajasthan, Gujarat sides and the Erieye was used in Rawalpindi, Lahore sectors, because that is more important for them.'

So, as the Mirages took off northward and then towards the west undetected, they topped up their fuel tanks over Himachal Pradesh through the mid-air refuellers that the IAF has bought exactly for such a purpose. The entire strike package flew over Srinagar and crossed the LoC into POJK, after climbing over 30,000 feet to rush towards Balakot. Four Mirages, which were assigned the role of escorts, penetrated the POJK airspace first, followed by the 12 carrying bombs. Once they were about 50 km into POJK, six SPICE-carrying Mirages, released the bombs and turned back. Because of bad weather, the other six aircraft carrying Crystal Maze weapons decided against using them since the pilots were not sure if the Crystal Maze would have achieved its intended objectives. Even as the SPICE 2000s were cruising towards the intended targets, the 16 Mirages turned back, re-entered Indian airspace and landed at Adampur in Punjab.

The mid-air refuelling that had happened less than an hour previously was to make sure the Mirages had the requisite extra fuel even if they had to travel further to Ambala or back to Gwalior as the entirety of northern India was experiencing bad weather that night/early morning. It took less than eight minutes for the 16 Mirages to go into POJK, release the payload and turn back, giving little time to a surprised Pakistani air defence to react. By the time the PAF could get two of its F-16s in the air, the Indian strike

Another satellite picture of the Balakot camp

package was already on its way back. Moreover, the two F-16s realised they would be outnumbered by the number of Indian escorts and refrained from pursuing the returning Indian airplanes, the IAF assessment concluded.

Meanwhile on ground, the bombs went and hit the four designated targets. It was all over in less than three minutes. As two of the pilots who were part of Operation Bandar, as the Balakot Strike was codenamed, told the media at Gwalior during the 20th anniversary of the Kargil conflict—in which Mirages had played a vital part too—the Indian air strike was 'over within 90 seconds'. The mission was carried out with such secrecy that not even close family members of the assault team knew nothing about the developments. 'It was over in 90 seconds; we released the weapon and we turned back,' said one of the Mirage 2000 fighter pilots. 'No one, not even my close family knew,' the unnamed IAF pilot told media persons at the Gwalior airbase. 'Next day, when news broke, my wife asked me whether I was part of the attack. I kept quiet and slept off,' he added.

As mentioned earlier, targets were different buildings in the Balakot complex. The time was also chosen with care because at

3 in the morning most people are sleeping no matter what kind of work they do.

The SPICE-2000 bombs hit the targeted buildings, penetrated the rooftops easily and went in to explode and kill all the occupants. While the IAF has refused to put a number to the death toll, considering that there were close to 300 people in the four targeted buildings and that SPICE bombs are devastatingly accurate and effective, the number of deaths, estimated by Indian intelligence agencies after cross-checking with on-ground sources, is between 250 and 280 people.

Pulwama was avenged.

The world was stunned, and Pakistan predictably was in denial.

Prime Minister Modi had forever redrawn the self-imposed red lines with Pakistan, breaking out of decades-long timidity that had pervaded the minds of the decision-makers.

4

Strategic Shift

Ironically, the first acknowledgement of IAF's strike over Balakot came not from India but from the spokesman of Pakistan's Inter-Services Public Relations (ISPR), Maj Gen Asif Ghafoor who tweeted as early as 5.40 AM on 26 February. Social media users in India and Pakistan woke up to his tweet, 'Indian Air Force violated Line of Control. Pakistan Air Force immediately scrambled. Indian aircrafts (sic) gone back. Details to follow.' His second tweet in succession confirmed the location of the camp. It read: 'Indian aircrafts intruded from Muzaffarabad sector. Facing timely and effective response from Pakistan Air Force released payload in haste while escaping which fell near Balakot. No casualties or damage.'

All hell broke loose.

Media, security analysts and common citizens were frantically looking for more information. As we looked up the map, Balakot showed up in mainland Pakistan's Khyber Pakhtunkhwa province and not in POJK. As all of us in the media and security circuit—me included—started dialling our contacts and even official spokespersons on the Ministry of Defence and Ministry of External Affairs for more and authentic information.

There was a sense of disbelief. Indian war planes had not crossed the LoC since 1971. The Indian decision-makers, indeed even the Indian military leadership had assumed the LoC as a sacrosanct line, not to be breached lest the situation escalated. Pakistan had often spoken about bringing nuclear weapons into play if India dared attack Pakistan's mainland (not so much POJK).

By 6.45 AM I had managed to get through to some of the top sources with the knowledge of what had transpired overnight. So at 6.58 AM, I remember tweeting, 'Multiple Indian Air Force planes went right up to Balakot and hit Jaish camp(s) can be confirmed...'

The rest of the day went by in a blur. Like it had happened on 29 September 2016 for instance (after the surgical strike inside POJK), I was shuffling between one TV appearance to another and from one conference call for foreign investors to another. Worldwide, the Indian air strike in Pakistan was leading the news. After all, this was the first time that a nuclear-armed nation had struck with its air force inside another nuclear power's territory.

In one stroke, Prime Minister Narendra Modi's decision to use air power inside Pakistan had redrawn the so-called redlines in the India–Pakistan equation. As well-known analyst, Col Anil A Athale wrote on rediff.com: 'The Balakot strike in response to the Pulwama attack was indeed a "game changer" in India-Pakistan relations...analysts like me and many others have been crying hoarse for several decades that India needs to embrace the strategy of "counter terror" and not just anti-terror.

'Let me explain it in plain terms. All through the 1980s to the 21st century, after every terror attack traceable to Pakistan, India responded with anti-terror measures.

'We increased CCTV coverage, created counter terror special forces, fenced the border and tried to tackle Pakistan diplomatically. This was true after the 2006 Mumbai train bombings as well as the 26/11 Mumbai attacks.

'Even earlier, India's response even to the Kargil intrusion was "defensive" in nature. We recovered our lost territory, but did not cross the LoC.

'Although a grave provocation like the December 2001 attack on Parliament by Pakistan-based Jaish-e-Mohammad terrorists evoked a strong response and we mobilised the armed forces for a conventional war, India did back out ultimately.

'If we are to understand the Pakistani strategy as proxy war, then we are essentially confined ourselves to "defense" only. It is well understood by all students of war that one can never win a war with a purely defensive strategy. But that is precisely what India has been doing for the last 30 years.

'Pakistan has been successfully using the strategy (called the "Mad Mullah" by the *Washington Post*) of deterring India by threatening "irrational" responses and invoking the spectre of nuclear war.

'With the air strike on the Balakot terror camp in mainland Pakistan (not just the disputed territory of Jammu and Kashmir) India has called the Pakistani bluff.

'Irrespective of the damage done at Balakot, the air strike has established a new red line in the sub-continent.'

Concurs Air Marshal SBP Sinha, 'This is the first time that an anti-terror airstrike was launched against an adversary who also has a formidable air force. This is a very significant milestone for the Indian Air Force because we are the fourth largest air force but Pakistan isn't very far behind, they're like the 8th or 9th largest air force. A lot of people talk about Israel and its air force and its daring acts but essentially the Israelis keep pounding the Gaza strip, or Lebanon but there is no opposing air force to speak of. Even in the Afghan war or campaign against ISIS in Iraq and Syria, there is no real threat to the US aircraft carrying out the operations,' he pointed out.

Sinha also avers that redlines are in the political domain. 'The armed forces are always prepared to go across because that is our job; that is what we train for, that is why our capabilities are developed.' The ultimate decision has to come from the political leadership. 'That is why the resolve shown by Prime Minister Modi and the political risk he took must be applauded,' Air Marshal Sinha added.

As a government functionary quipped: 'Suppose the air strike had failed, let's say an aircraft was shot down inside Pakistan during the air raid, Mr Modi would have lost enormous political capital just a couple of months ahead of the general elections. Most others would have therefore played safe under the circumstances.' This is in keeping with the Prime Minister's philosophy that national interest must always be placed above everything else.

Former foreign secretary Kanwal Sibal has noted in an interview: 'We have been reluctant to cross the LoC in Jammu and Kashmir by air as we saw during the Kargil War when our air force was under strict orders not to do so. On land, exchange of fire and limited incursions across the LoC have been going on for a long time. The 2016 surgical strikes in response to the Uri attack was the official announcement of a new policy decision. The Balakot air strike raises the level of our riposte much higher, especially as we have gone beyond POJK and have hit Pakistan proper. We have opened up a lot of strategic space for ourselves because we have signalled our willingness to attack anywhere in Pakistan against a terrorist target. We have also overcome our concern that striking at Pakistan conventionally could escalate matters to the nuclear level. With Balakot, we have called Pakistan's nuclear bluff.'

Going further back, history tells us that in every war or conflict with Pakistan since 1947, India has always reacted to a Pakistani-initiated attack, except perhaps Operation Meghdoot under which India outsmarted its adversary to gain control of the passes on the Saltoro ridge overlooking the Siachen glacier (For details read my book Beyond NJ 9842: The Siachen Saga). In 1947, Pakistan sent civilian raiders to try and seize control of Kashmir, repeated the tactics in the 1965 war by pushing in a large number of infiltrators. In 1971, the humungous refugee influx from East Pakistan in the wake of a brutal and inhuman crackdown on Bengali Muslims by the Pakistani army, pushed India into a war that it won decisively. Exactly 20 years ago in 1999, Gen Pervez Musharraf tried to cut off the Srinagar–Leh highway by plonking intruders on the icy heights of Kargil, Drass and Batalik.

In each instance, the Indian military reacted to Pakistani attempts at either altering the territorial boundary or keeping one of its provinces under control. And invariably emerged victorious, albeit at a great cost of losing thousands of its soldiers. As a bigger and responsible country, India has never shown any interest in attacking Pakistan. But, as explained elsewhere in this book, the reactive approach, also engendered a defensive mindset, especially since the early 1980s when Pakistan-sponsored covert action (sometimes referred to as insurgency or militancy in Punjab and J&K) began. The Indian security establishment became cautious in its outlook to security rather than being pro-active.

However, the cross-border raids in Myanmar and POJK in 2015 and 2016 respectively and more particularly after Balakot, it can be said that under the Modi–Doval combine, India's mindset has shed the timidity in dealing with Pakistan just because it is a nuclear power. When we look back maybe 20 years later we will realise how significant this milestone has been as far as the strategic calculus between India and Pakistan is concerned. The rest is a matter of detail and nitty-gritty. The IAF proved its worth by carrying out an operation assigned to it with precision and with professionalism and got the desired results that the political leadership desired.

5

The Air Battle

As the world was coming to grips with India's audacious attack on Balakot and contemplating its consequences, the Pakistani Army and Pakistani Air Force was plotting revenge. It had no choice. To maintain its credibility and standing among Pakistani citizens, the military had to demonstrate a retaliation against India and yet make sure it didn't get out of hand.

All along India's western front, meanwhile, the IAF and the Indian Army was on highest alert expecting the Pakistani revenge strike. At the LoC, Army units were primed for heightened fire exchange or even multiple infiltration attempts by terrorists into Jammu and Kashmir.

Various combat air patrols (CAPs) of the IAF were on 24×7 duty in various sectors along the western front. A combat air patrol literally means a group of fighter jets patrolling a designated area in the sky, looking to counter any intrusion by the adversary's planes. On 27 February Standing (airborne) CAPs in the northern sector (practically the entire skies over Jammu and Kashmir (excluding Ladakh) consisted of two aircraft which were getting replaced every couple of hours by a fresh pair since two hours of constant flying would render the aircraft low on fuel. And then there were other aircraft ready on ground to take off at short notice, ranging from two to 15 minutes.

On ground, the radars and flight control centres were also keeping a close watch on the Pakistani air space to detect any unusual activity. In fact, all air fields near the borders and the second tier ones have operational readiness platform (ORP) aircraft ready all the time. Says Air Marshal Sinha, 'These aircraft are weaponised and are in complete readiness. Depending on the type of aircraft and number of engines (one or two), these aircraft can get airborne between 2 and 6 minutes. All the ground radars are operationalized and networked through the IACCS (Integrated Air command and Control System). This includes the radars of Indian Air Force, several radars of Army and also the coastal radars of the Navy. So the entire picture taken by any radars of India is available centrally through this IACCS.'

However, for more than 12 hours after India struck at Balakot, Pakistan was in shock and trying to understand the implications of the most daring intrusion into its airspace. If the American SEALS embarrassed the Pakistanis when they came in undetected, eliminated Al Qaeda leader Osama bin Laden under the nose of the Pakistani Army at Abottabad, the IAF humiliated them by going in deeper than ever before and coming out unscathed after hitting the JeM camp at Balakot. The PAF could not get more than two F-16s in the air to try and intercept the Mirage 2000 package that day.

The insult had to be avenged or at least seen to be avenged. Otherwise, the Pakistani military's stock would take a severe beating in the eyes of the ordinary citizens.

So as 27 February dawned, almost the entire PAF fleet was cranked up. Pakistan first closed its civilian airspace and disallowed any commercial traffic around 8:45–9 AM.

At 9 AM IST, Indian flight controllers, sweeping the Pakistani skies sitting at Ambala in Haryana, noticed a Pakistan International (PIA) commercial flight on its way to Skardu in POJK turning back midway. However, it wasn't until 9.45 AM or so that the Indian radars noticed almost two dozen PAF aircraft getting airborne simultaneously. Taking off from different airports spread from north to south, these aircraft were grouped into smaller packages as they approached the LoC. According to the IAF's own assessment, four Chinese-made JF-17 aircraft were coming towards the LoC from Muzaffarabad sector towards Srinagar, 12 aircraft (four F-16s, four JF-17s and four Mirage IIIs) were coming straight from Islamabad and nearby airports and were headed towards Poonch–Rajouri–Nowshera (described as central sector by aviators who have studied the battle), while eight more aircraft (four Mirage III/IVs and four F-16s) were approaching from the southern sector opposite Suchetgarh–Anupgarh in Rajasthan. A Swedish-manufactured ERIEYE AEW&C (airborne early warning and control) aircraft was right behind these aircraft providing surveillance and radar control.

All the 24 aircraft appeared headed towards Jammu and Kashmir. As it turned out the main attack was to be carried out by the 12 aircraft in the central axis (*see Plate 8*).

As luck would have it, exactly around the same time when the PAF aircraft were about to enter the Indian airspace, the 'standing' Indian CAP in the above-mentioned northern sector was witnessing a change over which meant that two Su-30s, running low on fuel were preparing to leave to be replaced by two Mirage 2000s.

Meanwhile at Ambala, an alert and calm woman fighter controller noticed the massive PAF package clearly headed towards Nowshera. As she alerted the control centre, for a moment there was panic and chaos as her seniors tried to get a grip on the situation. But before they could get their act together, Squadron Leader Minty Agarwal, had taken charge. The Indian flight controller, aware of the danger, quickly alerted four fighters—two Su-30s and two Mirage-2000s—deployed on combat air patrol in the area south of Pir Panjal and simultaneously ordered eight MiG-21s Bisons, based in Srinagar and Awantipura to scramble. Seven of the MiGs took off in no time. In fact, because of the highest state of alert, one MiG each was stationed at two ends of the runaway to take off at two minute's notice.

One of those MiGs was piloted by Wing Commander Abhinandan Varthaman. The MiGs flew south to assist the freshly arrived Mirages and departing Su-30s (low on fuel by then). At Ambala, Sqn Leader Agarwal—relatively junior in rank and with limited experience—quietly took charge at the consoles and fired rapid instructions to the Indian pilots tasked to defend the impending attack.

According to Sameer Joshi a former fighter pilot, 'In central axis, the F-16s climbed to 40,000 feet and went supersonic. The JF-17s and Mirage IIIs released their payloads out of range due the threat of the Mirage 2000s flying in the zone north east of them, whom the JF-17s coming from south had failed to check effectively.' The F-16s, it should be noted, are armed with the Advanced Medium-Range Air-to-Air Missiles or AMRAAM Missiles—generally considered the most advanced and sophisticated air dominance weapon.

The next few minutes witnessed an air battle that the sub-continent had not seen since the 1971 war between the IAF and PAF.

As the F-16s tried to target the Su-30s and the Mirages with their AMRAAM Missiles, the alertness of the flight controller and their superior training helped Indian pilots to 'turn cold', that is, stay out of the adversary's missile envelope until they (F-16s) turned back to return into Pakistani territory. Air Marshal Sinha (retd) has analysed the air battle in detail. He explains: 'They (the F-16s) were engaged in a BVR (Beyond Visual Range) combat with Su-30. In this combat there is something called hot and cold state. Whenever pilots face an adversary they go through several manoeuvres. One of them is called turning hot and going cold. When a fighter plane takes on an enemy plane, it is called turning hot and when it takes evasive action and turns back it is called going cold. So the process of hot and cold carries on till you get the advantage. This process was going on when the F-16 launched the AMRAAM which never hit a Sukhoi or the Mirage. It showed poor BVR training of PAF pilots.'

Meanwhile as the cat and mouse game between F-16s and Su-30s continued, the two MiG-21 BISONS, one of them piloted by Wing Cdr Abhinandan, arrived on the scene. The F-16s, busy in dealing with the Sukhois, did not notice the MiGs hot on their trail. Since the radars at the control centre are capable of seeing the big picture in the sky unlike the individual planes (which have visibility of 60 degrees or thereabouts), the directions of the on-ground fighter controllers became the byword for the Indian pilots. And sure enough, as the PAF package advanced towards the LoC, momentarily it appeared that the Indians were outnumbered but the woman officer and her colleagues at the flight control centre noticed that only three F-16s made a shallow ingress across the LoC, dropped a few laser-guided bombs on military targets close to the LoC and scrambled back without hitting their targets even as they tried to engage with the Su-30s.

As the Pakistani fighters turned back, Indian interceptors including Wing Cdr Abhinandan were in hot pursuit. Abhinandan reported a 'lock' on the F-16 and fired the R-73 short-range air-to-air missile fitted on the MiG-21 Bison. Even as he did that, the woman officer noticed the F-16s changing direction and turning back into an offensive position or turning hot. Aware of the dangers posed by the AMRAAM missiles integral to the Pakistan planes, taking a split second decision, she alerted both MiG-21 Bison pilots about the impeding threat. Wing Commander Abhinandan's colleague took instant evasive action and initiated counter-measures and manoeuvred his way out of harm of the AMRAAM missile. Abhinandan, however, was not so lucky. Even as he fired the R-73 and hit an F-16, the AMRAAM hit his plane too. Abhinandan was forced to eject. He landed in enemy territory and was captured. Meanwhile, the F-16 also went down and two other parachutes were seen drifting inside Pakistani territory. The fate of the two

Parts of recovered AMRAAM missile being displayed outside South Block, Indian Ministry of Defence headquarter

Pakistani pilots is shrouded in mystery so far. Parts of AMRAAM missile fell in the Indian territory, was recovered and displayed by IAF officials in Delhi.

An Indian analysis has also shown that when Pakistan launched the short retaliatory strike only three or four aircraft including three F-16s barely crossed the LoC. They were challenged by the IAF interceptors. As a senior IAF officer puts it: 'While three or four aircraft briefly came into Indian territory in an offensive mode, 21 aircraft were in the total package only for support. They were all trying to protect those three F-16 aircraft.'

A post-event analysis of the air-to-air combat shows that besides the highest standard of training and discipline displayed by the pilots, the contribution of the woman ground fighter controller in Indian pilots winning the dog fight was significant. As former fighter pilot Sameer Joshi analyses, 'The approach of the 2 MiG-21s was missed by the F-16s who were busy scanning for the Su-30 MKIs, but a Saab 2000 ERIEYE Airborne Early Warning & Control (AEW&C) operating in depth near Islamabad, spotted the MiG-21s over Nawshera, warning the F-16s. The IAF's ground controller saw the defensive manoeuvring of the F-16s, warning the MiGs in turn. While his number 2, who was lagging behind, turned "cold" or away from the F-16s which were going "hot" or facing the MiGs, *Abhinandan chose to ignore this threat and continued towards the F-16s.*

'Both the IACCS & the Phalcon AWACS registered the radar signature of one MiG-21 piloted by Wing Commander Abhinandan Varthaman cross the Line of Control and engage a F-16 with a R-73 missile. *His call on R/T of a missile launch was monitored by the AWACS.* Abhinandan was 8–10 km away from the F-16, which was turning towards him—*aiming for a frontal aspect launch with high closing speed between the missile and the incoming F-16.* The R-73 is a heat seeking air to air missile with a sensitive, dual band cryogenic cooled seeker with a substantial off-boresight capability. The seeker can see targets up to 40° off the missile's centreline. Minimum engagement range is about 300 meters, with maximum aerodynamic range of nearly 30 km at altitude.

'*Abhinandan fired his R-73 well within the range and tracking capabilities of the R-73 missile*, with a high closing speed of more than 3500 kmph between the missile and the F-16, which was at 15,000 feet. *At those ranges, the missile would have closed into the target in less than 20 seconds*, its proximity fuse activating the 7.4 kg warhead to explode and engulf the F-16 in frontal quarters with flame and high velocity shrapnel—*in all probability grievously injuring the pilot*. The "splashed" F-16 fell towards the earth post that, with the pilot ejecting out of the stricken aircraft as reported by eyewitnesses.

'The F-16 "kill" was noticed by the Phalcon's radar—*with the said blip vanishing from the radar scope in the radar picture processed*—8 seconds after the previous one, which had shown the blip in place,' Joshi and avid blogger and military aviation analyst concludes.

A MiG-21 BISON shooting down an F-16 created a sensation across military aviation circles around the world. But Abhinandan's capture by locals inside POJK who later handed him over to soldiers of Pakistan's Northern Light Infantry (NLI) overshadowed the feat.

Abhinandan's capture also heightened the tension between India and Pakistan and for 24 hours on 27 and 28 February. The world watched with bated breath as India warned Pakistan of dire consequences if Abhinandan was not released immediately.

There were mistakes on ground as well. As the air defence machinery went into emergency mode, a panic reaction in an air defence unit wrongly targeted IAF's own Mi-17 helicopter. Described as 'blue on blue' kill, the unfortunate death of IAF personnel and a civilian, showed poor judgement on part of the air defence unit. At the time of writing a military court of inquiry is on in the incident. Several lessons have been derived from the actual dog fight: the unfortunate fratricidal downing of the IAF chopper and the panic in the flight control centre which showed up many seniors in poor light, have all been noted for corrective measures to be implemented internally by the IAF.

A CRISIS IS DEFUSED

By noon on 27 February, two facts had emerged from the sequence of events that occurred between 9.30 and 10.30 AM earlier that morning: one, Wing Commander Abhinandan had shot down a Pakistani Air Force F-16 even as his MiG-21 BISON was hit by a Pakistani AMRAAM Missile. Since he had crossed the LoC while chasing the F-16, Abhinandan ejected at least four km inside POJK, landing at Horan Kotla village. His back must have been hurting badly as ejection from a fighter jet throws pilots out of the airplane with such a force that pilots have known to be rendered unfit for flying forever.

But his future in flying was far from Abhinandan's mind. Right then he had to think of survival. Villagers started surrounding him. Even as he unbuckled himself from the parachute, Abhinandan, asked if he was inside India. One of the young men who had reached the crash site apparently said yes. But a suspicious Abhinandan shouted 'Bharat mata ki Jai (Victory for Mother India),' to test waters. That's when the crowd shouted back 'Pakistan zindabad (long live Pakistan)'. Alarmed, Abhinandan managed to take out his service revolver and fire a few shots in the air even as he started running towards what he thought would be the LoC. The villagers chased him. Some threw stones. After running nearly 500–600 metres, an exhausted Abhinandan, his back hurting, got cornered as he neared a small pond. Villagers pounced on him. Some started beating him with bare hands. But before things could get out of hand, some village elders intervened. Media reports in Pakistan quoted some of them as saying they wanted to capture him alive.

'My objective was to capture the pilot alive. I had seen the Indian flag on his parachute and knew he was Indian,' said Mohammad Razzaq Chaudhry, the head of Horan Kotla village. Speaking to BBC, Chaudhry said, 'The boys chased him until he fell into a stream and one of my nephews who was also armed shot him in the leg. My nephew asked him to drop his pistol, which he did. Then someone else caught him and pinned him down to prevent him from using any other weapon that he might have.'

Chaudhary said the pilot then pulled out papers from his pocket and tried to stuff them all in his mouth to destroy them. But the villagers were able to snatch some of the papers from him, which they later gave to the army.

'Our boys were angry and continued to force their way closer to him to punch and slap him, though some of them tried to stop the aggressors. I also told them not to harm him, to leave him alone until the army officers arrived.'

He was then handed over to Pakistani Army authorities who had arrived on the scene promptly. In Pakistani Army's custody, the Indian pilot was treated for his injuries and was given tea as his captors tried to elicit information from Abhinandan.

On the other side of the border, Pakistan's (in)famous Inter-Services Public Relations (ISPR) went into an overdrive to milk Abhinandan's capture. Videos shot on mobile phones started circulating on social media showing a slightly injured and blindfolded (*see Plate 9*) but poised, calm and composed Abhinandan providing just the bare essential information about himself, giving out his rank, name and number. When pressed for more, he is heard saying 'I am not supposed to tell you anything else.' In another video filmed inside a jeep, a soldier asked the blindfolded Abhinandan his views about the Pakistani Army. Abhinandan replied, 'I hold the Pak army in very high regard and I was hoping there would be a Pak army officer who would get me... I know the Pakistani army is also of soldiers...that is why the first question I asked you was 'Are you from the regular army?'

Before he could reach Rawalpindi however, Major General Asif Ghafoor—the Director-General of ISPR tweeted on the ISPR handle that two Indian jets had been shot down by the PAF in POJK, *with one pilot arrested by the Pakistani Army and two still in the area*. As if on cue, Pakistani handles on social media started talking about the shooting down of two IAF jets and the arrest of two Indian pilots.

An hour later, addressing a press conference, Maj Gen Ghafoor said that another pilot had been arrested. 'Our ground forces arrested two pilots; one of them was injured and has been shifted to CMH (Combined Military Hospital) and, God-willing, he will be taken care of,' and that, 'The other one is with us.' In a blatant lie, uttered with an absolutely straight face, Maj Gen Ghafoor also assured all that no F-16 of the PAF had been shot down, since the F-16s were 'not' used in combat in that sector at all. Post that press conference, the ISPR chief informed all that the pilot in their custody in the military hospital had died!

This is where, the ISPR's expertise on obfuscation and propaganda came into full play. Realising that only one Indian pilot had ejected since only a MiG Bison had been shot down, Ghafoor had to cover up the fact that Pakistani civilians in the Sabzkot area of POJK had assaulted an injured a PAF pilot, who had ejected from the F-16 that Abhinandan had hit. The villagers had mistaken the Pakistani pilot for an Indian and had severely beaten him up. That pilot subsequently died at the CMH because of the beating. Now the GHQ could not acknowledge the Pakistani pilot's demise for two reasons: one, it would have meant accepting an unpalatable fact that an F-16 had been bested by an older generation MiG Bison and two, that a Pakistani fighter pilot had been killed by their own citizens. Also, the Pakistanis would have had to explain to the Americans why F-16s were deployed when their use against India is prohibited by the terms and conditions imposed by USA

Video grabs of Wing Commander Abhinandan and tweets by DG, ISPR immediately after his capture inside POJK

during the sale of the fighter jets. Their use in an offensive role violated the end use agreement on many counts, including use of the AMRAAM missile which had been given to Pakistan to be used against its war on terror.

This elaborate cover up attempt is not surprising since Pakistan is known to have disowned death of at least 1,000 of their own officers and men killed in action in the Kargil conflict exactly two decades ago. It is noteworthy that in today's age and world where mobile phones are omnipresent and in a country where the Pakistani Army has an overwhelming presence, it is hard to believe that its all-powerful spokesperson could not get details from the ground or ascertain how many pilots had been killed/captured in Pakistan's own territory. Based on the DGs inputs, Pakistan's Prime Minister, cricketer-turned-politician Imran Khan, also told the country's Parliament that Pakistan had two Indian pilots in custody. It was only towards late evening that the ISPR corrected itself to say it had only one Indian pilot—Wing Commander Abhinandan—in its custody.

After ascertaining that no other Indian plane or pilots apart from Abhinandan was missing, the MEA summoned Pakistan's acting High Commissioner in Delhi to convey India's 'strong protest', at what it called Pakistan's 'unprovoked act of aggression', including violation of Indian airspace and 'targeting of Indian military installations'. The Pakistani envoy was told that, 'India reserves the right to take firm and decisive action to protect its national security, sovereignty and territorial integrity against any act of aggression or cross-border terrorism.' The MEA also said that India 'strongly objected to Pakistan's vulgar display of an injured personnel of the Indian Air Force in violation of all norms of International Humanitarian Law and the Geneva Convention'. It was made clear that Pakistan would be well advised to ensure that no harm comes to the Indian defence personnel in its custody. 'India also expects his immediate and safe return,' the MEA said. The MEA's statement was typical diplomat speak, courteous and polite. It doesn't really convey what followed that night.

As darkness fell over the sub-continent, tension rose with every passing hour. Pakistan seemed to be gloating over Abhinandan's capture. In contrast, the mood in India was down, especially compared to the euphoric feeling amongst the population on 26 February, just the day before, in the wake of the Balakot strike that morning. There was heightened speculation and rumours about possible escalation between the two neighbours who have fought four wars since 1947. Western nations were especially worried over the fact that India and Pakistan are both nuclear states and Pakistan has frequently invoked its nuclear status when faced with adversity from India.

In New Delhi, Prime Minister Modi and his security managers were not worried about the N-factor. NSA Doval and his team had anticipated possible Pakistani response to the Balakot strike and had concluded that GHQ was in no position to launch any military attack against India given Pakistan's precarious economic condition and its Army's pre-occupation with the western front abutting Afghanistan. However, Abhinandan's captivity had complicated the situation a bit.

As Doval met the three service chiefs, Dhasmana and other key members of the security establishment, it was decided that Pakistan must be told in no uncertain terms that India would not hesitate to escalate matters if Abhinandan was either harmed or not released immediately. Dhasmana opened a channel with the then head of the Pakistani spy agency Inter-Services Intelligence (ISI), Lt Gen Asim Munir. The Secretary R told the ISI Chief that the Indian Army had primed its battery of missiles aimed at high value targets inside Pakistan if the Indian pilot was not handed back forthwith.

NSA Doval, who had been speaking to his counterparts in important capitals since the Pulwama attack, once again reached out to them and conveyed India's resolve to ensure Abhinandan's release at any cost. The Indian NSA had particularly lengthy conversations with the Secretary of State, Mike Pompeo, John Bolton, the American NSA, Russian President Vladimir Putin's closest security adviser Nikolai Patrushev and the heads of the security establishment in the UAE and Saudi Arabia. He had just one message to all of them: India had not initiated the current round of hostilities and had only taken action against a terrorist group when it was easy to target military installations inside Pakistan. The PAF, he pointed out, had however, deliberately targeted Indian military bases in J&K. Abhinandan had unfortunately been captured after an air battle in the wake of the blatant Pakistani attack. Now India reserved the right to retaliate if Abhinandan was not released immediately or was harmed in any manner. The NSA did not speak of any specific threat that India held out to Pakistan but his message was loud and clear.

The Pakistani reaction was mixed. Lt Gen Munir was noncommittal. However, top officials in the Pakistani foreign office establishment told their American counterparts that Pakistan had no desire to climb the escalatory ladder. By late night on 27 February, Washington, Abu Dhabi and Riyadh were on the phone line with GHQ and Islamabad, telling the Pakistanis to make sure Abhinandan was released the next day. Perhaps sensing the mood around the world in India's favour, the Pakistani Army (which anyway calls the shots on foreign and security policies) conveyed to the foreign interlocutors that Abhinandan would be released the next day and that Prime Minister Imran Khan would make the announcement in the Parliament to that effect.

As phone lines burned through the night, India held back its offensive intent. By dawn on 28 February, India had received enough inputs from different world capitals that Abhinandan would be returned soonest.

Ordinary Indians and Pakistanis of course did not know this as they woke up on 28 February. Tension was palpable and the air of uncertainty over 'what next' was all pervasive.

The tension was however defused by noon that day after Imran Khan made a speech in Pakistan's National Assembly to declare that Abhinandan would be released as a 'peace gesture'. Khan also went on to admit to the reports of a possible attack by India. 'I know last night there was a threat there could a missile attack on Pakistan, which later got defused,' Khan said in his speech.

'I also know how our military was prepared to retaliate to such an attack... So I am telling India from this platform, don't take this any further. Because whatever you do, Pakistan will be forced to retaliate,' he added. The Pakistani Prime Minister also said he tried to call Prime Minister Narendra Modi on the evening of February 27 as he wanted to make it clear Pakistan didn't want any type of escalation.

Hours before Imran Khan got up in Parliament to announce Abhinandan's release, President Donald Trump announced at a press conference in Hanoi, at the conclusion of his failed summit with North Korea's Kim Jong-un, that he had some 'reasonably attractive news from Pakistan and India', 'some reasonably decent news'.

The latest crisis between India and Pakistan was clearly winding down as fast as it had escalated.

More than a month later, Prime Minister Modi also obliquely referred to the events on the night on 27 February. Addressing an election rally in late April 2019 Modi said he had warned Pakistan of consequences if it did not return Abhinandan. 'We held a press conference and warned Pakistan that if anything happened to our pilot, you will keep telling the world what Modi did to you.' A senior American official said on the second day that Modi has

A hero's welcome for IAF pilot Wing Commander Abhinandan (right)

kept 12 missiles ready and might attack and the situation will deteriorate. Pakistan announced return of the pilot, or else it was going to be a 'qatal ki raat' (night of massacre), he said. 'This was said by America, I have nothing to say about this now, I will speak about it when the time will come,' the Prime Minister said.

It however took another day and a half for Abhinandan to walk across the Attari-Wagah border. Dressed in civilian clothes—a dark jacket and khakhi trousers—walking proudly toward the gates that separated his captors' country from his homeland, Abhinandan was reunited with his colleagues, friends and family as he was flown in to Delhi. Commissioned into the IAF in 2004, Abhinandan is a second generation fighter pilot. His father, Air Marshal Simhakutty Varthaman also flew MiGs and retired as a three star Air Marshal in the IAF.

'Wing Commander Abhinandan has just been handed over to us. He will be taken now for a detailed medical check-up. This check-up is mandatory as he had to eject from an airplane which would have put his entire body under stress,' said Air Vice Marshal RGK Kapoor to reporters in a brief statement in Attari, near Amritstar.

As he was treated medically at Delhi's military-run Research and Referral Hospital, Abhinandan recounted his 48-hour captivity. What emerges from his story is a tale of quiet courage in the face of great adversity.

He was not provided any medical treatment during the initial hours after ejecting from his MiG-21 following a dogfight with PAF's aircraft on February 27. Beaten, choked, deprived of sleep and subjected to mental and physical harassment by Pakistani interrogators, Abhinandan stuck to his guns about not giving any information to his captors besides the basic details of his name, rank and commission number. The Pakistani interrogators tried to extract crucial information on Indian troop deployment, sensitive logistics and high-security radio frequencies within the first 24 hours of capturing him.

He was constantly moved around and was largely in the custody of the Pakistani army although PAF officers also were part of the team questioning him. Abhinandan's biggest achievement was to hold back critical information on high-security radio frequencies that the IAF uses to transmit messages, troop and fighter jet deployment and sensitive logistics.

All Indian fighter pilots are tutored to hold back information as long as they can in the event that they get captured so that the deployment and frequencies can be changed within the first 24 hours to thwart any attempt by the adversary to leverage the information. All IAF fighter pilots undergo regular survival training courses at Kasuali near Shimla among other places.

Abhinandan's safe return allowed the Indian sub-continent to pull back from the brink that week but it is anybody's guess what would have happened if he was not released quickly.

6

ASAT: Breaking into an Elite Club

On 27 March 2019, around 11.45 AM, Prime Minister Narendra Modi, an avid social media user, made a cryptic announcement on tweeter: 'Today I would be addressing the nation at around 11:45 AM–12.00 noon with an important message. Do watch the address on television, radio or social media.' The nation and the world went into a tizzy.

Social media was instantly abuzz with excitement and speculation. The theories ranged from: has India executed another surgical strike or an air raid on Pakistan? Is there some big breakthrough with China; or has India managed to capture/extradite one of its most-wanted, Dawood Ibrahim? No one had a clue. The stock market held its breath; TV studios hastily assembled in-house experts or makeshift commentators (it was difficult to get real specialists since the subject of the PM's announcement was yet unknown).

Away from the public gaze, Modi was briefing his Cabinet Committee on Security (CCS) in his South Block Office. The members of the CCS—ministers of Home, External Affairs, Defence and Finance—were being told that India had successfully tested an anti-satellite missile becoming only the fourth country to do so. Messrs Rajnath Singh, Arun Jaitley, Sushma Swaraj and Nirmala Sitharaman were briefed on what the test meant and how the announcement would be made. A brief backgrounder and FAQs was to be released by the MEA after the PM made the announcement. As the beaming—and slightly

Prime Minister Modi addressing DRDO scientists immediately after the announcement of the successful ASAT test

bewildered—members of the CCS trooped out of the PMO, Modi went on national television to announce to the world the big breakthrough moment for India.

'Some time back (this morning), our scientists have hit a live satellite 300 km away in the low earth orbit. This was a pre-determined target which has been brought down by an anti-satellite missile. The operation was completed in three minutes. Mission Shakti was a very difficult operation in which very high quality technical capability was required,' Modi said in his televised address.

He assured the country and the world that, 'Our newly acquired capability is not targeted at anyone. This is a defence capability of an India which is progressing at a rapid pace. India has always been opposed to weaponisation of space, and today's test does not alter that position. Today's test does not violate any international law or treaty.' As he watched the Prime Minister address the nation and congratulate the scientists, DRDO Chief Satheesh Reddy's mind went back to September 2016. That month, he had accompanied NSA Doval for a highly classified 15-minute briefing to the Prime Minister outlining the need to conduct an anti-satellite missile test and the ways to do it. A week after the briefing, Reddy, then

Scientific Adviser to the Raksha Mantri (Defence Minister) and Director General, Missiles and Strategic Systems (MSS)—he was yet to become DRDO Chief—got a final go ahead to undertake Mission Shakti.

It was imperative to keep the mission secret so Reddy had to tread cautiously and bring in only absolutely essential personnel on board. 'For the first six months after the green signal came, I co-opted just a couple of key scientists in the project. Besides the PM, NSA and me, only four people had the full picture of the proposed mission. Otherwise, everyone was working in water-tight compartments on a need-to-know basis, not aware of the actual objective,' Reddy remembers. Gradually, as different aspects of the mission started coming together and the road map evolved, then the chairman of Indian Space Research Organisation (ISRO), Kiran Kumar, was briefed by Reddy. As Kiran Kumar made way for Kailasavadivoo Sivan, the current head of ISRO, Reddy's team had made considerable progress in its mission. So by early 2018, ISRO was told to build a satellite specifically for Mission Shakti.

By January 2019, most building blocks of Mission Shakti were in place. On 24 January ISRO launched a specially designed for DRDO micro satellite called Microsat-R, into low earth orbit. The satellite, would have been hurtling at a speed of more than 27,000 km per hour until it was hit by the missile on the morning of 27 March.

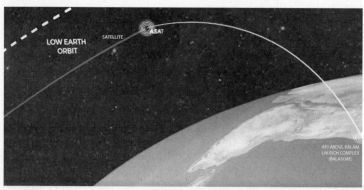

The ISRO built satellite was hit kinetically by a DRDO-designed missile to demonstrate India's newly-developed capability

The entire operation, from the launch to the hit, took just three minutes, the Prime Minister told the nation in a special televised address, calling it 'an unprecedented achievement'. In a tweet later, Modi said: '#MissionShakti is special for 2 reasons: (1) India is only the 4th country to acquire such a specialised & modern capability. (2) Entire effort is indigenous. India stands tall as a space power! It will make India stronger, even more secure and will further peace and harmony.'

India had joined USA, Russia and China as countries that have the strategic capability to hit and destroy satellites.

After the Prime Minister's announcement, a DRDO statement said the BMD Interceptor was a three-stage missile with two solid rocket boosters. 'Tracking data from range sensors has confirmed that the mission met all its objectives. The test has demonstrated the nation's capability to defend its assets in outer space. It is a vindication of the strength and robust nature of DRDO's programmes,' the DRDO said (see Plate 10).

The 27 March test was the culmination of the quest that actually began in 2010. The then DRDO Chief, VK Saraswat, now a member of the NITI Aayog, had in fact announced India's intention to conduct such a test. However for various reasons, not the least of which was lack of a categorical political clearance, the test took more than nine years to fructify. It was left to PM Modi to take the plunge.

As a former controller of research and development in the DRDO, Dr W Selvamurthy observed, 'The final decision to test is no doubt a political call. It is not a technological decision.'

Saraswat and others concur. Sarswat in fact revealed that he had made an informal presentation to the then NSA Shiv Shankar Menon during the UPA II government's regime but there was no clear-cut directive to take the project forward.

Prime Minister Modi however was determined to harness the technological prowess that exists within DRDO, ISRO and other arms of the government to further India's national interest. As the MEA underlined in its statement, 'The test was timed according to the degree of confidence that the country could build, to ensure success in the mission and with no intention of entering into an arms race in the outer space.'

'India has always maintained that space must be used for peaceful purposes and that outer space is the common heritage of humankind. The test does not violate any International law or treaty and also supported UNGA resolution 69/32 on No First Placement of Weapons on Outer Space,' the MEA pointed out.

India has so far undertaken 102 spacecraft missions consisting of communication satellites, earth observation satellites, experimental satellites and navigation satellites apart from satellites meant for scientific research and exploration, academic studies and other small satellites. The March 27 test was done to verify that India has the capability to safeguard its space assets as it is the responsibility of the Government of India to defend the country's interests in outer space, an MEA release added.

The MEA was chosen to issue details about the test and its objectives because India anticipated the world to react negatively if not in horror like it did post the nuclear tests in 1974 and 1998. However, major powers, including China were restrained in commenting on the Indian ASAT test. The Chinese Foreign Ministry simply said, 'We have noticed reports and hope that each country will uphold peace and tranquillity in outer space.'

China had conducted an ASAT in January 2007 that was capable of shooting down satellites at an altitude of over 800 kilometres in the lower earth orbit. USA was the first country to acquire the ASAT technology in 1958 which was followed by USSR in 1964. USA had a mixed response to the Indian test.

First, a State Department spokesperson said, 'The issue of space debris is an important concern for the US government. We took note of Indian government statements that the test was designed to address the debris issues.' And the spokesperson went on to say that the US would continue 'to pursue shared interest in space and scientific and technical cooperation, including collaboration and safety and security in space.' However, NASA, which has a partnership with ISRO was undiplomatic. It not only appeared to suspend cooperation with ISRO on human spaceflight project but also launched a scathing attack on India. The NASA Chief said, 'It is a terrible, terrible thing to create an event that sends debris at an apogee that goes above the International Space Station…That kind of activity is not compatible with the future of human spaceflight that we need to see happen… It is not acceptable for us to allow people to create debris fields that put at risk our people.' However, the suspension of human spaceflight cooperation was reversed a week later at the direction of the White House.

Others like important think tank members or research fellows had a more nuanced understanding. Daniel Porras, the space security fellow at the United Nations Institute for Disarmament Research, said, 'The Chinese demonstration was carried out at 800 kilometers and was widely condemned because of the resulting space debris, which will likely stay in orbit for decades or longer. India's demonstration was conducted at 300 kilometers, so the debris will likely be out of orbit in months. For this reason, the reaction has been much less.' ISRO's long-term partner, Planet Labs, condemned the test and advised that the space environment should be used purely for peaceful purposes.

However, India was undeterred and went ahead perhaps because it did not want to be left behind in any future regulatory regime that might come into existence. By joining the exclusive club, India is now in a position to be a rule maker rather than a follower.

Frank A Rose, Senior Fellow for Security and Strategy at Brookings, commenting on India's test had this to say, 'First, India probably wanted to ensure it had demonstrated a military capability to destroy a satellite before international prohibitions on testing were put in place. Indeed, Prime Minister Modi specifically said in his March 27 statement, "Today's test does not violate any international law or treaty obligation to which India is a party." This is largely shaped by India's experience with nuclear weapons. For example, when India tested a nuclear device in 1974, the Treaty on the Non-proliferation of Nuclear Weapons had already entered into force, and India was thus left outside the club of recognized nuclear powers under the treaty.'

In the past, India has made its stand clear on Prevention of an Arms Race in outer Space (PAROS). India has said during the conference 'it believes that Outer Space should not become an arena of conflict, but a new and expanding frontier of cooperative activity. This places a responsibility on all space-faring nations to contribute to international efforts to safeguard outer space as the common heritage of humankind and preserve and promote the benefits flowing from advances made in space technology and its applications for all. We are against the weaponisation of Outer Space and support international efforts to reinforce safety and security of space based assets.'

A statement by DB Venkatesh Verma, Ambassador and Permanent Representative of India to the Conference on Disarmament had stated that, 'India is a party to all the major international treaties related to Outer Space. We believe that this international legal framework needs to be strengthened to enhance the security of space assets for all space users and to prevent the weaponisation of Outer Space. Thus, India supports the substantive consideration of the item on Prevention of an Arm Race in Outer Space.'

Despite various concerns, the fact is different countries actively pursue technologies to develop military capabilities in order to deny the use of space in times of conflict, as detailed below:

CHINA

An Anti-satellite missile test was conducted by China on 11 January 2007. A Chinese weather satellite, the FY-1C polar orbit satellite of the Fengyun series, at an altitude of 865 kilometer, with a mass of 750 kg, was destroyed by a kinetic kill vehicle (Hit-to-Kill). The test created a huge cloud of debris which can last for centuries in the heavily used orbit. On 11 January 2010 the PRC destroyed a medium-range ballistic missile using the same systems as the one used in the ASAT test, which is considered to be a continuation of the PRC's ASAT testing in the guise of BMD. In October 2015, China first tested Dong Neng-3, which was also masked as anti-missile interceptor test, with another in December 2016. On

5 February 2018 DN-3 successfully destroyed a DF-21 missile in a Hit-to-Kill mode.

China is also pursuing the development of active co-orbital ASAT capabilities. In the year 2010, two satellites (SJ-12 and SJ-06F) carried out on-orbit docking experiments that can potentially lead to the co-orbital ASAT capability. Subsequently, China launched three satellites (CX-3, SJ-15 and SY-07) to conduct experiments on orbital manoeuvres. These have been conducted since then, presumably to test space based ASAT capability.

USA

Starting in the late 1950s, USA began the development of anti-satellite weapons. In May 1963 the 'Nike Zeus' missile armed with a nuclear warhead destroyed an orbiting satellite. Subsequently, efforts were re-directed to develop systems that did not require the use of nuclear weapons. On 13 September 1985, ASM-135 destroyed the Slowind P78-1 satellite at an altitude of 555 km.

On 20 February 2008, USA carried out a successful ASAT exercise and destroyed a non-functioning USA satellite at a much lower altitude (247 km) than the Chinese test. USA claimed that the strike was not a military test but a necessary mission to remove the threat posed by the decaying orbit of a faulty spy satellite with hydrazine fuel. Since the test was carried out at a lower orbit, post interception debris lasted only for a month. There was hardly any criticism from the international community against the test as it was categorised as a protective measures.

RUSSIA

In the early 1980s, the Soviet Union had developed two MiG-31D 'Foxhounds' as a launch platform for a potential anti-satellite weapon system. After the collapse of the Soviets Union, this project was put on hold due to reduced defence expenditures. However, in August 2009, the Russian Air Force had announced the resumption of this program. Further reports in May 2010 indicate that Russia is 'developing a fundamentally new weapon that can destroy potential targets in space'. In the year 2015, Russia reportedly completed initial of new generation robotic spacecraft designed to inspect and destroy enemy satellite.

As per open source information, Russia's PL-Nudo, focused primarily on Anti-satellite missions were successfully tested twice in 2018. 23 December 2018 was the seventh test of the system.

There have been several attempts to lay down codes of conduct, rules and regulations for space activities. Here's a brief description and timeline:

Prevention of an Arms Race in Outer Space (PAROS)

It has been on the agenda of the Conference Disarmament (CD) since 1982. However, CD has not been able to commence negotiations. USA has argued that there are no arms in outer space.

Prevention of the Placement of Weapons in Outer Space (PPWT)

In February 2008, a joint Russia-China draft of a treaty on the Prevention of the Placement of Weapons in Outer Space, the Threat or Use of Force against Outer Space Objects (PPWT), was presented to the CD. It was based on the Working Paper presented in June 2002 by Russia, China, Vietnam, Indonesia, Belarus, Zimbabwe and Syria. USA dismissed the proposal, characterising it as 'a diplomatic ploy by the two nations to gain a military advantage.'

A Revised draft of PPWT was introduced by Russia in June 2014, which has been rejected by USA since it does not cover direct ascent ASAT weapons, lacks provisions for verification and does not prohibit the possession, testing, and stockpiling of weapons that could be placed in outer space. Some countries like Egypt, Iran, and Algeria support PPWT. Pakistan has argued that there is a need for comprehensive legal instruments on PAROS; it has not openly supported PPWT. South Africa favours a balanced approach.

International Code of Conduct (ICoC) for Outer Space Activities

In 2008, the European Union (EU) initiated a procedure to develop non-legally binding ICoC, comprising a set of principles and guidelines, including transparency and confidence-building measures (TCBMs). Western countries led by USA, including Australia, Japan and South Korea support TCBMs. Brazil has opposed ICoC. BRICS voiced its concern in 2014 that the ICoC was being developed out of CD.

No First Placement of Weapons in Outer Space

Russia has been through its resolution in UNGA since 2014, calling for a political commitment on no first placement of arms in outer space. 18 countries so far, including Argentina, Armenia, Belarus, Brazil, Cuba, Indonesia, Kazakhstan, Kyrgyzstan, Russia, Sri Lanka, Tajikistan and Vietnam have made such a commitment. China has not made such a declaration, even though it co-sponsored the resolution.

UN Resolutions on PAROS

- **Prevention of arms race in outer space:** Sponsored by Egypt and Sri Lanka; since mid-1990s, it enjoyed near unanimous support. In 2018, USA and Israel opposed it.
- **Measures to promote transparency and confidence-building in outer space:** Introduced in 2005, it was unanimously adopted till 2017. In 2018, USA and Israel opposed it.
- **No first placement of weapons in outer space:** It was introduced in 2014 by Russia. It was opposed by 12 countries (mostly Western Group) in 2018.
- **Further practical measures for the prevention of an arms race in outer space:** Introduced in 2017, it established a Group of Governmental Expert (GGE) on PAROS. It was opposed in 2018 by USA, Ukraine and Israel with 49 abstentions.

There is thus, at present, no legally binding space or development and possession of ASAT weapons, whether based in space or terrestrial.

Other Chinese ASAT Tests

USA alleged that China conducted a 'non-destructive' test of an ASAT weapon on July 23 2004 and called for China to end the development of such capabilities. The State Department said that, in the test, China had used the same missile system (SC-19) as in the 2007 test.

In the First Committee of the UNGA, the US expressed concern about the continued development, testing, and ultimately, deployment of destructive anti-satellite (ASAT) systems. It noted that although some States had advocated for space arms control measures to prohibit the placement of weapons in outer space, their own development and testing of destructive ASAT capabilities was de-stabilising, could trigger dangerous misinterpretations and miscalculations and could be escalatory in a crisis or conflict.

According to Xinhua, the Chinese Defence Ministry called the test a 'land-based anti-missile technology experiment', suggesting that it was a test of a missile defence system rather than an ASAT weapon. China claimed that subsequent tests of its SC-19 missile in 2010 and January 2013 were part of an effort to develop and understand missile-interceptor technology, not to develop ASAT capabilities.

The question is: can India's anti-satellite missile test be a trigger to advance the development of norms of behaviour for outer space?

While many people may have been surprised by India's decision to conduct the ASAT test, those who have watched Prime Minister Modi and the NSA since 2014 know that space has been at the top of their minds for use in different fields. Within about a month after becoming Prime Minister, Modi had addressed ISRO scientists at Sriharikota as I had mentioned in the first edition of the book as described as follows.

Date: 30 June 2014
Place: Satellite Launch Centre, Sriharikota

Just a month into office, Prime Minister Narendra Modi had travelled to the ISRO (Indian Space Research Organisation) facility to witness the launch of the PSLV-C23 satellite. In his speech after the successful launch, Modi praised the ISRO scientists for their stellar work and then stunned them into momentary silence by posing a challenge. 'Today, I ask our Space community to take up the challenge of developing a SAARC Satellite that we can dedicate to our neighbourhood, as a gift from India. A satellite that provides a full range of applications and services to all our neighbours. I also ask you to enlarge the footprint of our satellite-based navigation system, to cover all of South Asia.'

Initially, the assembled scientists did not know what to say. 'We had never done such a thing,' remembers an old ISRO hand. Modi reinforced this idea five months later, speaking in Kathmandu at the SAARC Summit on 26 November. He said, 'India's gift of a satellite for the SAARC region will benefit us all in areas like education, telemedicine, disaster response, resource management, weather forecasting and communication.'

In less than three years after the Prime Minister challenged the ISRO scientists, they came up with the answer. On 5 May 2017, the SAARC Satellite' was launched from Sriharikota, opening a new chapter in space diplomacy.

The Prime Minister addressing ISRO scientists

The 2,230 kg GSAT-9 is a Geostationary Communication Satellite. Communication services from it will be shared with five neighbours (Bhutan, Nepal, Sri Lanka, Bangladesh, and Maldives). It will help to meet the growing telecommunications and broadcasting needs of the region. All participating nations will have access to at least one transponder using which they can telecast their own programming. The countries will develop their own ground-level infrastructure. The satellite is expected to provide communication channels between countries for better disaster management. Afghanistan is also expected to join the group soon. As a scientist in ISRO says, 'For smaller countries, this is a dream come true. To lease a transponder, a lot of money has to be spent. But here India has gifted them a permanent asset.' Apart from the obvious use (telecommunication, broadcasting), leaders of these six

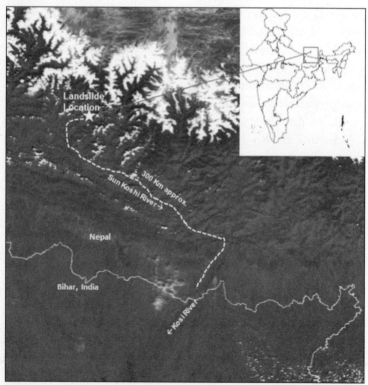

Location map of the Nepal—landslide on Sun Koshi river

countries can have secure dedicated one-on-one communication through the VSAT facility that the satellite provides, explained ISRO officials. The leaders can also have a video conference between themselves if they so wished, thanks to the South Asia satellite.

In a way, by dedicating a separate satellite for the neighbourhood, Modi has taken his favourite theme of *Sabka Saath, Sabka Vikas*, beyond India's physical boundaries. An early example of helping neighbours through satellites came in Nepal. In August 2014, a massive landslide blocked Sun Koshi river in Northern Nepal indicating the possible formation of a lake. This created a flood threat for several villages downstream in Bihar (*see photo*).

ISRO immediately swung into action, acquired the images and in consultation with India's National Disaster Relief Agency (NDMA), ascertained the exact location of the landslide, computed the extent of debris due to landslide and came with a solution for controlled release of blocked water slowly, averting possible flash floods in Bihar. This operation was made possible because ISRO now coordinates closely with Inter-Ministerial Group for Emergency Management at the Centre. IMEG helped coordinate the relief operations in Nepal and later in September 2014 in Srinagar too.

ISRO has also successfully launched CARTOSAT 2 Series of satellites that can provide sub-meter images (spatial resolution of 65 cm) for monitoring purposes. ISRO is also building on capabilities to acquire images from as far as 36,000 km up in the space and yet give a resolution of about 55 cm, at frequent intervals, empowering Indian security agencies like the National Technical Research Organisation (NTRO) and other intelligence arms to monitor real time activities of India's adversaries. Such a capability would also help in effective monitoring of major national disasters in the country. The Special Projects Division dealing with all strategic requirements of the armed forces and intelligence agencies has been reinvigorated. A senior scientist in charge of the Division works in close coordination with the Deputy National Security Adviser to meet all their requirements in quickest time possible. ISRO's assets are now used for various strategic, security and defence purposes. Some of the data acquired by the space agency is so classified that only a handful can access it. Suffice it to say that ISRO's data acquisition has helped Indian armed forces in some of their operations in the past few years.

ISRO has in fact been continuously launching a series of satellites, mainly for cartographic purposes. Called the Cartosat series, these satellites are mainly used for cartographic mapping of the earth. Hence, they are useful for dual purposes—military as well as civil. Through the Cartosat 2 series of satellites programme for instance, ISRO is helping derive 1 × 4000 scale maps for better urban planning. As Kiran Kumar says, 'the beauty of this technology is that it is continuously available. One can take an image today, one can take an image again, 15 days later, compare and monitor the progress of a project, a building or whatever else. With two-time data, say between 2007 and 2017, we can calculate the difference in height of a given building through stereo imaging and three-dimensional mapping and calculations to establish building heights, mining related works or even new constructions.'

K Kasturirangan, former chairman of ISRO, says 'The space agency has a formidable suit of technologies and all are suitably deployed with each user agency utilising the assets to their best advantage.'

So while high resolution imaging satellite can help in urban planning, it can also monitor terrorist camps across the border. Kasturirangan says a satellite image does not distinguish between friend and foe, the interpretation rests with the users.

Kiran Kumar says, 'The Indian space agency will not be found lacking in helping secure India's national interests now and in future.' No wonder, the number of missile tests have increased significantly in the past few years as mentioned in *Appendix I.*

7

Re-engaging with Middle East

It took 50 years to correct the wrong but on 1 March 2019, when External Affairs Minister Sushma Swaraj stood up to deliver a talk to the plenary session of the Organisation of Islamic Cooperation (OIC), events had come full circle for India and Pakistan, half a century later. As Swaraj spoke, Pakistan's Foreign Minister, Shah Mohammed Qureshi, boycotted the session in protest. Pakistan was miffed because Swaraj was invited by hosts United Arab Emirates (UAE) to be the guest of honour.

This was in complete contrast to events in 1969 at the inaugural conference of the OIC at Rabat in Morocco. According

India's External Affairs Minister Sushma Swaraj addressing the plenary session of the OIC. India was a guest of honour, a rare gesture

to former diplomat Gurbachan Singh, then India's Ambassador to Morocco, India was first not invited, then invited and then forced to skip the final session of the foundation of the OIC. According to Singh's account in the Oral History Section of the Ministry of External Affairs, Morocco's then foreign minister personally called the Indian Ambassador to tell him that King Faisal of Saudi Arabia and the host, the King of Morocco, had got all members including Pakistan to invite India at the last moment to the inaugural conference since India had a large Muslim population. As Singh made arrangements after taking due clearance from New Delhi and attended one session as interim leader, it was decided that India's then Minister for Industrial Development, Fakruddin Ali Ahmed, would lead the official delegation sent from Delhi.

However on the final day, the conference went into a tizzy as Pakistan's President Yahya Khan refused to attend the session until India was 'disinvited'. Trying to find a middle path the King of Morocco and King Faisal of Saudi Arabia tried to smoothen matters by requesting India to accept the status of an 'observer' at the conference. The Indian delegation refused and chose instead to return to Delhi. Pakistan had won the day.

In the five decades since then, OIC kept India out of the grouping until March 2019 when UAE and Saudi Arabia ignored Pakistan's tantrums and stuck to their original decision of making the Indian external affairs minister the guest of honour at the plenary session in March 2019.

This single event signifies India's changed status in the Middle East. From being denied entry to the inaugural session of the OIC, India was now being honoured, overriding Pakistan's objections.

Speaking at the plenary, Swaraj spelt out India's approach and vision for the world and how it looks at terrorism as a threat to humanity and not just India. 'This is not a clash of civilisations or cultures, but a contest of ideas and ideals. As Prime Minister Shri Narendra Modi has often said, it is a struggle between the values of humanism and the forces of inhumanity.'

The OIC Conference was being held at the backdrop of heightened India–Pakistan tension following the Pulwama terrorist attack and India's air strike on a JeM terrorist camp in Pakistan. However, Swaraj, refrained from naming Pakistan and yet made it a point to drive home the dangers posed by state-sponsored terrorism. 'If we want to save the humanity then we must tell the states who provide shelter and funding to the terrorists, to dismantle the infrastructure of the terrorist camps and stop providing funding and shelter to the terror organisations, based in their countries. At the same time I would like to say that this menace could not be fought, only through military, intelligence or diplomatic means.

'It is also a battle that must be won through the strengths of our values, and the real message of religions. This is a task that states, societies, sages, scholars, spiritual leaders, and families must pursue, through personal contacts and on social media. And, for this:

- Faiths must speak to faiths.
- Cultures must engage cultures.
- Communities must build bridges, not erect walls.
- The youth must shape the future, not destroy lives.

I am particularly pleased to participate in a conference, whose theme is a road map for prosperity and development.

However, I may enter a caveat: the young are not going to be content, with only road maps. They want roads as well. They also want them to be built fast. Terrorism and extremism bear different names and labels. It uses diverse causes. But in each case, it is driven by distortion of religion, and a misguided belief in its power to succeed. The fight against terrorism is not a confrontation against any religion.

'It cannot be. Just as Islam literally means peace, none of the 99 names of Allah mean violence. Similarly, every religion in the world stands for peace, compassion and brotherhood.

At 50, Organisation of Islamic States is making a new beginning. The choices you make, the direction you set, will have a profound impact on humanity.

The OIC has a huge responsibility and a great opportunity to lift humanity to a higher level of peace and prosperity, and to make this planet a better place, not just for your people, but for rest of the world.'

Swaraj's speech was well received in the Islamic world and former diplomats who have dealt with the Gulf monarchies—the main driving force of the OIC—say there were two or three important points made in the invitation to India. Talmiz Ahmad, India's former Ambassador to Saudi Arabia and a specialist in India's relations to the Arab countries said: 'One, the invitation was a tribute to India's status, two its role in international affairs and three the fact that it has contributed significantly to the Islamic civilisation. All three are very important and relevant factors.'

The ties have of course been on the upswing for over a decade but under the Modi government, the momentum picked up spectacularly.

One indicator of improved relations was increased intelligence cooperation between India and the Gulf countries. India's National Security Adviser (NSA) Ajit Doval, who has had excellent connections to the intelligence czars in the Gulf region, has used his old network very effectively. The extradition of Christian James Michel, the main accused in the Rs 3,600 crore Agusta Westland helicopter bribery scandal, through correct legal means has brought into focus the improvement in India–UAE relations, especially with regard to Abu Dhabi handing over wanted criminals sought by New Delhi.

But it isn't just the UAE alone. Over the past four years, New Delhi has managed to persuade many other countries to hand over or quietly deport several wanted criminals, radicalised youth, militant leaders and even half a dozen Dawood Ibrahim gang (D-gang) members absconding from as far back as the mid-1990s.

According to multiple sources, over 100 Indian nationals of different hues have been brought back to the country, thanks to the excellent intelligence and law enforcement cooperation between New Delhi and other world capitals. These countries include Thailand, Nepal, UAE, Saudi Arabia, Singapore, Myanmar, Bangladesh, Turkey, Oman, Qatar, Afghanistan and France, among others. Since 2014, the UAE alone is reported to have traced at least 30–35 radicalised youth who wanted to or had joined ISIS.

Most of them were either born or raised in Gulf countries where they had gone in search of employment.

Intelligence sources say while the freshly radicalised ISIS members of Indian origin were relatively easy to trace in the Gulf countries, the bigger success was in nabbing 'high value' members of the Indian Mujahideen (IM) group. The case of Abdul Waheed Sidibappa is particularly illustrative of India's improved standing in the Gulf. Sidibappa who had become a key linkman for the IM leadership for facilitating their hawala transactions, was arrested by the Dubai police in March 2014 but despite 61 days of detention, the Dubai authorities could not be convinced by Indian agencies to hand him over. He walked free until Indian intelligence agencies once again tracked him down and convinced the UAE government in May 2016 to hand him over. According to standard practice, he was deported from Dubai and was arrested at Delhi's Indira Gandhi International (IGI) Airport. He is currently facing trial.

India has also had a better success rate in getting members of the older Sikh militant groups such as the Babbar Khalsa International (BKI) and the Khalistan Liberation Front (KLF) from countries such as Thailand and Nepal. For instance, KLF Chief Harminder Singh Mintoo was arrested at Delhi's IGI Airport by the Punjab Police in November 2014 after he was deported from Thailand. Reports at that time said that Mintoo was using Thailand as his base to mobilise funds for the banned organisation. Using a fake Malaysian passport and identity card, Mintoo travelled extensively across Europe and South East Asia in order to develop contacts. He is also believed to have frequently made trips to Pakistan, where he was reported to have acquired funds to support the cause.

After his arrest, Mintoo escaped from Nabha jail in Punjab in November 2016 where he was being kept before he was recaptured. He died in April this year following a cardiac arrest in a jail in Patiala.

It was a similar case with the D-gang members. Living under assumed identities in different countries in the Gulf they were not easy to detect, but constant prodding by Indian intelligence agencies and the willingness of several of their counterparts in the

UAE, Saudi Arabia and Qatar to act on various leads resulted in many of them being handed over to Indian authorities in the past four years.

Take the example of Yasin Manzoor Mohammed Farooq alias Farooq Takla. A key member of the D-gang and an accused in the 1993 Mumbai serial blasts, he had escaped to Dubai in the immediate aftermath of the blasts and lived there under the assumed identity of Mushtaq Mohammed Miyan. Subsequently, Farooq travelled to Pakistan several times and had helped other members of the D-Gang with logistics and money. He had obtained an Indian passport using a false identity in Dubai in 2011. In 2017, Indian intelligence tracked down Farooq and managed to get him back to India in March earlier this year, thanks to the cooperative Dubai police. He is now under trial in a Mumbai TADA court.

India's rising stock in the Gulf countries would have been hard to imagine in 2014, when Modi became Prime Minister. If resounding electoral victory in the 2014 general election was unexpected for many, his focus on recalibrating and rejuvenating India's foreign policy has surely come as a major surprise to the world.

However, one of his most trusted team members, NSA Doval has a different take on Modi's interest in international relations. 'Contrary to what many people think, Prime Minister Modi had a very deep understanding of the interplay of power in the international arena. Even before assuming office in May 2014, he had visited a large number of countries and built a network of personal relationships at various levels that included politicians, people in business and trade, members of the Indian Diaspora, as well as scientists and professionals in various fields. A keen observer, Modi closely followed the trends in international relations, possible areas of cooperation with other countries, and their relevance to India in the larger geo-strategic context,' Doval told me.

According to the NSA, India's national security is an important ingredient of the Prime Minister's vision for India and central to his thinking and interactions. His experience in Gujarat of leveraging hisexternal goodwill to attract investments also came in handy.

Doval says the Prime Minister strongly believes that if India has to unleash its potential power and convert this potential into real power, it has to ensure peace, stability, and security within the country and in the neighbourhood.

As noted analyst Cleo Paskal wrote in an article in 2015: 'Modi began by openly consolidating India's regional base...the photos of the SAARC leaders together on the dais to welcome India's new Prime Minister not only showed to the region, but also to the world, that 'India is back,' and that Modi's India was going to be very different than the one the world had seen in recent decades.'

Since Day One, all his decisions have been focussed on achieving stability and peace in the region. It is another matter that neither Pakistan nor China—both known and old adversaries in the region—have reciprocated Modi's hand of friendship. Three years into his tenure, the Prime Minister however continues to raise the bar higher in the realm of international relations. His outreach to the middle- east and the Central Asian Republics are but small examples. The Indian Ocean initiative, the renewed focus on the neighbours in the Indian sub-continent, South-East Asia, and most strikingly, his visits to America, stand out as examples of outstanding achievements in Modi's foreign policy.

Admittedly, all Prime Ministers in the past have driven India's foreign policy, leaving the execution of the policy to the Ministry of External Affairs (MEA) and External Affairs Ministers.

However, no other Prime Minister, with perhaps the exception of Indira Gandhi, had used personal goodwill and charisma in achieving foreign policy objectives as Modi has managed to do. As one of his senior-most colleagues, Arun Jaitley remarked: 'In the fast-changing multi-polar world to which India is intricately connected, no Indian leader has shown such remarkable understanding to simplify an otherwise complex situation. By surveying, responding and where possible, moulding the international environment, Prime Minister Modi is finding answers to the questions of India's national interests.'

As is well known by now, Modi is perhaps the most frequently travelled Prime Minister in recent years. What is remarkable however is his focus on the immediate and strategic neighbourhood. Comparative figures show that Modi has visited South-East and Central Asian countries the most in the three years that he has been in office. Similarly, in keeping with his neighbourhood first policy, the Prime Minister made 20 trips to South Asian nations. But what has surprised foreign policy watchers is Modi's focus on the Islamic countries of the Middle East. Almost everyone expected him to visit Israel immediately after assuming office but in a crafty move, the Prime Minister opted to visit all the other major players in the region—UAE, Saudi Arabia, Qatar and Iran—before becoming the first Indian Prime Minister to visit Israel in July 2017. In fact, available data indicates that Modi has already made half a dozen trips to the Middle East in less than 40 months that he has been Prime Minister. By contrast, Dr Manmohan Singh managed to visit the Middle East only thrice in his 10-year long tenure!

One illustration of Modi's personal interest in starting unexpected initiatives dates back to July 2015.

That day, Air India One, the Prime Minister's special aircraft was on its way to Turkmenistan from Ufa in Russia.

Modi had just finished an important meeting with his Pakistani counterpart Nawaz Sharif on the side lines of the Shanghai Cooperation Organisation (SCO) summit. The two Prime Ministers had agreed to institute a dialogue mechanism at the level of National Security Advisers (NSAs) of the two countries, among a couple of other important decisions to build mutual confidence. It was quite a feather in the PM's cap to get Sharif to agree on the new mechanism, especially after India–Pakistan ties had hit a roadblock over India's insistence on keeping the Kashmir separatists out of the bilateral dialogue.

Moreover, for the first time, New Delhi had managed to keep any overt reference to Kashmir out of the joint statement and instead succeeded in including 'talks on terrorism', in the final text. Both Modi and Doval should have been happy to have broken the deadlock.

But the Prime Minister's mind was already working on another outreach.

'The PM was satisfied with the meeting (with Sharif), but he was thinking ahead. As we made our way to Turkmenistan, he mentioned the need to improve our ties with countries in the Middle East. "Why don't we make special efforts to reach out to important people in that region",' Doval remembers Modi suggesting to him on the flight to Ashgabat (capital of Turkmenistan).

The Prime Minister felt, Doval recalls, India was not doing enough to engage leaders of the Gulf countries. 'We have a large Indian Diaspora there, the region is vital for our energy security and the developments there impact our geo-strategic interests. Besides, there is great scope of economic cooperation, as India enjoys the advantage of old historic ties and geographical proximity. But, we don't seem to have made concerted efforts to develop rapport with the rulers there,' the Prime Minister mentioned to his National Security Adviser.

Doval had come to realise in the previous one year that they had spent working together that a suggestion from the Prime Minister was like an informal directive. Moreover, his operational mind was quick to comprehend the high potential and import of the Prime Minister's directive. As soon as they landed in Ashgabat, Doval and Jaishankar, already aware of the importance of the region to India's internal and external security challenges, quickly set up the visit to reboot New Delhi's outreach to the Gulf countries. The NSA wanted to carry personal messages from Modi to the movers and shakers in the region.

The PM's whirlwind tour of the Central Asian Republics ended with his meetings in Tajikistan on 13 July (the visit to the CARs itself was in many ways significant). Air India One began its journey back to Delhi, but Doval was not on the return flight. He was on his way to Dubai, exploring the possibility of operationalising the Prime Minister's vision on the ground.

'The Prime Minister was determined to take our relations with the Middle East to a much higher level and willing to invest his own goodwill and energy to achieve that,' says a Ministry of External Affairs official. The secretive mission was so low profile that even the Indian Mission in UAE was unaware of the NSA coming in and

Prime Minister Modi with UAE's leader

going out of the UAE. Only S Jaishankar, India's Foreign Secretary was in the loop. What transpired at their meeting is not a part of public knowledge. Doval also made quiet trips to other capitals in the region, CharuKasturi reported for The Telegraph in September 2015. And that is how one of India's most successful foreign policy initiatives under the Modi government was conceived and rolled out.

Sure enough, in just over a month after Doval's secret parleys with the Dubai Prince, Prime Minister Modi became the first Indian Prime Minister in over 34 years to visit the UAE, kick-starting a new phase in India's relationship with the Gulf countries.

As the Prime Minister remarked in his pre-departure statement at Delhi, 'UAE is a valued partner, and the extent of our ties indicate the vibrant relations India and UAE enjoy-India is UAE's 2nd largest trading partner and UAE is India's 3rd largest trade partner. There are over 2.5 million Indians who have made UAE their home. They have contributed immensely to the progress of UAE and also given back to India on every occasion. India and UAE are closely connected be it via air or through the sea.

'During my visit, I seek to enhance cooperation in energy and trade, and will talk to investors on why India is an attractive destination for investments. I am certain my visit will boost people-to-people ties between our nations.'

Modi had correctly assessed that India's regional, economic, and increasingly, security interests, are closely interlinked with events in the Middle East, and more particularly with the Gulf.

'So far, like with other Gulf States, India's relations with UAE have focused almost exclusively on commercial matters. In the future, India will need to take a more strategic approach,' observed Dr Kadira Pethiyagoda, a visiting Fellow in Asia–Middle East Relations at the Brookings Doha Centre, who was quoted by the Gulf News on the day Modi arrived in Abu Dhabi.

That he chose UAE for his first visit to the Middle East and not Israel after openly acknowledging his affinity to the latter surprised many, but doing the unexpected has been the hallmark of the Modi decision-making style. He realised that the Emirates hosts 2.6 million Indian workers, which constitutes 30 per cent of the population, making Indians the largest nationality group. Clearly, the expats provided Delhi a strategic advantage in bilateral relations.

To be fair, Modi's predecessor, Dr Manmohan Singh had also spoken of a 'Look West' policy, and cited the importance of the Middle East in India's energy security. During the second term of the UPA, the idea of a 'Look West' policy surfaced once again, but with very little productive outcome. Dr Singh eventually failed to translate his wish into action. He barely travelled to the Middle East during his 10-year stint at the helm of affairs. He visited Egypt and Iran because they were hosting Non-Aligned summits. Dr Singh's only bilateral visits were to Saudi Arabia, Oman, and Qatar. As mentioned earlier, no Indian Prime Minister had visited the UAE for over three decades until Modi decided to start his Middle East engagement with an outreach to Abu Dhabi.

As Nicolas Blarel, an assistant professor of international relations at the Institute of Political Science at Leiden University noted in a piece entitled 'Recalibrating India's Middle East Policy', 'the reality is that the Middle East was not an important policy priority for the Modi government during its first year in office. In spite of Modi's important diplomatic activism, which led him to visit more than twenty-five countries in his first fourteen months in office, he did not stop over in any of the region's capitals. This changed in August 2015 when he chose to travel to the United Arab Emirates, and not Israel, as his first destination in the Middle

Modi with Indian workers in UAE

East. That trip, along with the April 2016 visit to Saudi Arabia, demonstrated that there are various long-term and more immediate factors that can account for a renewed focus towards the Gulf.'

The initiative has started earning rich dividends. The Prince paid a return visit to India in 2016. He was also the Chief Guest at the Republic Day parade in 2017. The only other Gulf dignitary to be given the honour of being the chief guest at the Republic day was the Saudi King in 2006.

While the big ticket items are witnessing a surge, expatriates see small gestures like the UAE allotting land for building a temple for the Indian community in Abu Dhabi as a big breakthrough.

There was of course the bigger picture. As Khaleej Times, a leading newspaper in the Gulf noted in its editorial in August 2015, 'The UAE can gain from rapid strides made by India in space and software as it seeks to grow into a knowledge economy. The Indian Prime Minister is keen that the UAE invests more in his country—in sectors like tourism, infrastructure, tourism and retail. "Prosperity should be shared", is the mantra. UAE companies can, therefore, "Make in India" and Indian firms can "Make in the UAE". There are opportunities to grow together and joint investments propel the powerhouses. In this regard, the two countries have agreed to set up a joint $75 billion investment fund to boost infrastructure projects.'

Economic cooperation apart, both India and UAE agreed to step up their partnership in countering extremism and radicalisation. The joint statement at the end of Modi's visit reflected the new pragmatism that marks the relationship. It was significant on at least three counts.

One, it went beyond the usual energy and economic cooperation and elevated the relationship to a strategic level. Two, it concentrated, in large measure, on security cooperation (dialogue between National Security Advisers every six months), and three, also mentioned defence and maritime cooperation.

That the joint statement called on all countries to dismantle the terrorism infrastructure where they exist and bring perpetrators of terrorism to justice was significant, especially since Pakistan is the unnamed country in this common stance. Therefore, while the two countries condemned other countries who use religion to justify terrorism, or support and sponsor such activities against others, India and the UAE decided to coordinate efforts to counter radicalisation and misuse of religion by groups within their own purview.

More importantly, Modi's outreach to the blue-collar skilled workers in the UAE—2.6 million in number—sent the right message. His visit to the Indian workers' camp in Abu Dhabi and the community address in Dubai was meant to invoke pride in India.

As a result of the high level visit, some of the lingering disputes have also been resolved quickly. For example, with Qatar, India had a 25-year contract for buying LNG. Signed between Petronet and RasGas, India was not honouring the terms of the contract because of the lower prices of gas in other markets. When India did not buy its quota of 7.5 million tonnes in 2015, RasGas imposed a penalty of $1.5 billion. During Prime Minister Modi's visit, the issue was resolved with RasGas agreeing to waive the penalty and slash the LNG price to $6–7 per mmBtu from $12–13 mmBtu in keeping with the dip in global price. It was seen as a significant diplomatic

Prime Minister Modi visits TCS all women IT and ITES Centre in Riyadh

success for India and an indication of its growing prestige in the Gulf. Similarly, recognising India's quest to build 'strategic oil reserves,' UAE, Saudi Arabia and Iran have agreed to supply crude oil for the strategic reserve facility at Mangalore.

Modi's visit to the UAE also went further than mere bean counting. It widened India's acceptance in the region as a rising power and allowed greater engagement with the Middle East. Following his UAE sojourn, Modi has visited all major countries in the region including Turkey (14–16 November 2015 for G-20 summit), Saudi Arabia (2–3 April 2016), Iran (22–23 May 2016) and Qatar (4–5 June, 2016). As senior diplomat and India's former High Commissioner to Pakistan, G Parthasarathy points out: 'We are the only power in the world to have the best of relations with all major powers to our west. And in the process, Modi has by-passed Pakistan. In the Islamic world, he has rendered Pakistan impotent by his extraordinary outreach to the Islamic world.

An important trilateral initiative:
The India–Iran–Afghanistan agreement at Chabahar

Moving forward, India's vital interests and the changing regional dynamics will require it to deepen relations with all important actors in the region, preserving its careful balancing act while stepping up to play a more active regional role.'

With Iran, India's strategic partnership witnessed an important development with the signing of the Chabahar port agreement. Moreover, India signed a trilateral transit agreement with Iran and Afghanistan for the Chabahar port, underlining its importance not only for bilateral trade, but also its significance for Indian interests in Afghanistan and Central Asia.

Speaking at the signing ceremony, Modi underlined the importance of the Chabahar port and the trilateral agreement: 'The Agreement on the establishment of a Trilateral Transport and Transit Corridor signed very recently can alter the course of history in this region. It is a new foundation of convergence between our three nations. The corridor would spur unhindered flow of commerce throughout the region. Inflow of capital and technology could lead to new industrial infrastructure in Chabahar. This would include gas based fertilizer plants, petrochemicals, pharmaceuticals and IT. The key arteries of the corridor would pass through the Chabahar port of Iran. Its very location at the mouth of the Gulf of Oman, is of great strategic significance. Afghanistan will get an assured, effective, and friendlier route to trade with the rest of the world... In my vision, the full spectrum of connectivity agenda between Iran, Afghanistan and India should span: from culture to commerce; from traditions to technology; from Investments to IT; from services to strategy; and from people to politics.'

Given the rising tide of terrorism and use of Gulf countries as safe havens by some of the fugitives, India has worked toward enhancing security cooperation and intelligence-sharing with the Gulf States and beyond. India signed MoUs with financial intelligence units of Saudi Arabia and Qatar to counter money-laundering and terror financing. As a paper on India's policy towards the Middle East noted, 'This defence and counterterrorism cooperation with the Gulf states partly continues the policies of previous UPA governments. The strategic partnership signed with

Saudi Arabia in 2010 included robust anti-terror cooperation measures. Additionally, Saudi Arabia's 2012 deportation of Indian terrorist Sayed Zabiuddin Ansari, also known as Abu Jundal and who was involved in the 2008 Mumbai terrorist attacks, had already signalled a willingness to increase counterterrorism cooperation, even if doing so clashed with Pakistani interests.

Around the time when the Modi government took over, the ISIS phenomenon had created an intense turmoil across the world, particularly in the Middle East and African countries. Though ISIS is now on the back foot after being driven out of its strongholds in northern Iraq and Syria, threat of isolated and dispersed attacks from some of the remaining 21,000 foreign fighters in their home countries looms large.

The Gulf region, home to nearly 70 lakh people of Indian origin could not have remained unscathed from the ISIS phenomenon. Under these circumstances, the Modi government took proactive and concerted measures to rescue its kidnapped and trapped nationals abroad. The efforts were monitored at the highest political levels. The combined efforts ensured the safety and security of a large number of Indian citizens abroad, who have greatly contributed towards deepening ties with the Islamic world. NSA Doval personally led the initiatives with the help of some of his officials with extensive ties in the Middle East.

When asked about his role, Doval confirmed that he did travel to Iraq and other Middle East countries. The then Chief Minister of Kerala Oommen Chandy, who had known Doval for over four decades had profoundly thanked him for his role in rescuing nurses and other Malayalee detainees from the clutches of ISIS. How the rescue operation was executed and ISIS allowed the nurses to be taken from their captivity will remain a mystery till the NSA decides to reveal all. People who know him assert he never will.

'The Prime Minister was very clear about one thing: No effort should be spared to extricate Indians from difficult situations anywhere in the world,' Doval told me. Except the disappearance of some Indians in Mosul that happened in June 2014, when the new government was just settling down, Indian lives have been saved in all other cases. All this was due to the timely collection of operational intelligence, quick and effective intervention by the intelligence agencies and improved security cooperation. This was in sharp contrast to the tragic fate of thousands of others that have fallen victim to ISIS' brutal executions. Many officers of India's intelligence community gave credit for it to the high professional credibility in the global intelligence community that the NSA enjoys on one hand and dedicated hard work and commitment of former RAW chief Rajinder Khanna on the other.

Since June 2014 and September 2017, 55 Indian nationals, trapped and kidnapped by dreaded terrorist groups like ISIS, were rescued from their clutches in Iraq, Libya, Nigeria, South Sudan and Afghanistan.

Additionally, the concerted operations of Indian intelligence agencies resulted in the deportation of several terrorists, their sympathisers and recruiters associated with the ISIS, anti-India Jihadi groups, and insurgent groups. The development of real-time and precise intelligence in tracking anti-India elements, living under various assumed identities and frequently shifting their places of residence, was an uphill task. Synergised efforts with foreign intelligence agencies helped in unearthing these cells. Since 2014, Indian intelligence operatives, with the help of Gulf countries, have pre-empted potential attacks by detecting over 20 Indians associated with ISIS modules, having them arrested and deported from different countries in the Gulf region.

PM Modi and Israeli PM Nethanyahu at a demonstration of a mobile seawater desalination unit in Israel

And yet, as in the past, India has to balance its relations with different Gulf actors. The government has been careful. So while Modi visited Saudi Arabia, he also made trips to Iran, the Saudi Kingdom's arch rivals, and Israel. However, it is interesting to note that Modi visited Israel after having made his trips to all other key players in the region. Indeed, his government hosted the Palestinian President in Delhi before Modi embarked for Tel Aviv, breaking a taboo that had held back successive Indian Prime Ministers from going to Israel although full diplomatic relations were established a quarter century ago. As Dhruva Jaishankar, Fellow, Foreign Policy at Brookings India, noted: 'Even as India attempts to 'Act East', it is increasingly 'Thinking West'. And, notwithstanding Modi's decision to skip Ramallah, New Delhi has discovered that a better relationship with Israel does not necessarily mean that it should distance itself from Palestine. The recent visit to India of Mahmoud Abbas, President of the Palestinian National Authority, was ample demonstration of this.'

Clearly, this is Modi-led India has demonstrated that it is possible to balance ties with all the major players to render the old notion that New Delhi has to choose sides in the quagmire that is the Middle East, ineffectual.

8

Removing the Cobwebs: 2014–2017

Thursday, 29 September 2016, was like any other weekday in the country's capital, New Delhi. The scorching summer had given way to cooler mornings, although the political heat was rising on the Narendra Modi government. In the previous week, 19 soldiers had died in Uri. The government was on the back foot, with critics questioning its policy against Pakistan. A sense of despondency hung over the country.

At sunrise that day, Modi's National Security Adviser (NSA), Ajit Doval, driving in his own car, arrived at the residence of the Prime Minister at 7 Race Course Road (now Lok Kalyan Marg) bearing important news.

Neither the Prime Minister nor the National Security Adviser had slept much through the night. Both of them were aware of a Special Forces operation that had been launched across the Line of Control (LoC) by the Indian army the previous evening.

Now, after a suspense-filled 12 hours, Doval came bearing the good news.

India's Special Forces had hit several terrorist camps and returned safely, delivering a tight, hard slap to the Pakistan Army and its proxies in Pakistan Occupied Kashmir (PoK). At least 70–75 occupants in multiple camps—both to the south and north of the Pir Panjal ranges—had been killed. Among the dead was a mix of Pakistani regulars and terrorists waiting to cross over into J&K. Post a short conversation with the Prime Minister, Doval rushed home and then quickly returned to the South Block on Raisina Hills.

The highest seat of power in India was astir earlier than usual that morning. Defence Minister, Manohar Parrikar and Army Chief General, Dalbir Singh had already arrived. Doval informed them of his conversation with the Prime Minister and the directions that he had issued as a follow-up to India's unprecedented action.

Modi too reached his office in South Block by 0800 hours. Finance Minister Arun Jaitley and Home Minister Rajnath Singh—both members of India's highest national security decision-making body, the Cabinet Committee on Security or CCS—also made their way to South Block. External Affairs Minister Sushma Swaraj was unable to attend since she was unwell. At that hour, it was still too early for the prying eyes of the media to notice the unusual gathering of top ministers and other security honchos.

By 0900 hours, the CCS had begun its unscheduled meeting. In attendance were Army Chief General Dalbir Singh and his Director General, Military Operations (DGMO), Lt General Ranbir Singh, the Foreign, Home and Defence secretaries, besides the chiefs of the intelligence agencies.

Right at the beginning, General Dalbir briefed the CCS about the counter-terrorist strike carried out by the Indian Army across the LoC inside PoK and its successful outcome.

*This was the crucial CCS meeting that decided to go public
with the surgical strikes*

Once the briefing concluded, the Prime Minister announced his decision to go public with the raid across the border. Modi told his senior colleagues: 'We must now let the world know what our brave soldiers have achieved to send an unambiguous message to the terrorists and their mentors.' Foreign Secretary S Jaishankar was asked to prepare a press release. It was decided that the DGMO, Lt Gen Ranbir Singh, would read out the succinct press note in the presence of Vikas Swarup, then the Ministry of External Affairs (MEA) Spokesperson and Joint Secretary, External Publicity Division.

Within an hour, the press note was readied.

At precisely 1130 hours, Lt Gen Ranbir Singh, a strapping Infantry officer, announced to the world that India had carried out 'counter-terrorist strikes' on terrorist camps located inside PoK and inflicted heavy damage to both men and material. 'Based on very specific and credible information the Indian army conducted surgical strikes last night. during these counter-terrorist operations, significant casualties have been caused to the terrorists and those who are trying to support them,' the DGMO said, reading from a prepared text, with Vikas Swarup sitting beside him.

The rather anodyne statement did not do justice to what the raid had achieved.

Then DGMO, Lt Gen Ranbir Singh (left) announcing
India's surgical strikes in PoK

For one, never before in India's troubled history with Pakistan had the government taken responsibility at the highest level of an unprecedented step such as cross-border strikes. By taking the onus of the decision on himself—and announcing it too—Prime Minister Modi once again demonstrated why he is capable of thinking beyond the norm, and surprising rivals and supporters alike.

For another, the trans-LoC strikes carried out on multiple locations broke the shackles that the Indian Army had been forced to impose upon itself because of timid political leadership in the past. Now, by exercising the option that had always existed but had never been authorised at the highest level for fear of escalation, it had managed to create an uncertainty in the minds of the Pakistan Army that had become used to predictable responses at the border.

By personally authorising a surgical strike, and then announcing it to the world, Prime Minister Modi was truly living up to his growing reputation as a 'risk taker'. Surgical strikes inside PoK were indeed a massive political and diplomatic gamble.

A number of things could have gone wrong. The advancing parties could have been attacked, or ambushed, leaving Indian soldiers injured or killed in the area occupied by Pakistan. If the information regarding the targeted areas and routes had been found to be inaccurate, the mission could have failed to achieve its objectives. Most importantly, the success of the operation depended upon precise intelligence about the terrorist camps, their presence in those camps, and safe routes to access them which would be free from landmines. The precision and accuracy of intelligence therefore played a vital role.

It is imperative to note that if the trans-LoC raids had failed, the Indian PM would have lost face, as well as huge political capital. A setback in the raids would have further constricted India's room to manoeuvre its policy against Pakistan, and politically, Modi would have been hobbled in domestic affairs. However, he went for the jugular, precisely because no one expected him to. Of course, the Prime Minister could take the risk because he had built a national security team led by Doval that had the requisite operational experience, and the ability to be meticulous in preparation of a plan and execution, based on precise real-time intelligence. The troops too were highly motivated and well trained. Over and above everything else, Modi had confidence in the ability of the forces to carry out the mission.

The Prime Minister's critics have variously described this and some of his other unconventional decisions since coming to power as rash, thoughtless, gimmicky and even dangerous.

Modi has nevertheless charted his own course.

The surgical strikes was just one such example. In the past 40 months, Modi has shown the ability to stay ahead of the curve and catch almost everyone off guard on many occasions.

In fact, Modi began his tenure with a highly unusual move on the day of his assuming office as India's fifteenth Prime Minister.

On the hot dusty evening of 26 May 2014, when Modi took oath of office in the forecourt of the imposing Rashtrapati Bhawan, the colonial era palace that has been home to successive Indian Presidents, over 4,000 guests—politicians, Bollywood celebrities, top bureaucrats, some of India's richest industrialists and common citizens—witnessed the ceremony. The focus was however on the heads of states from seven nations in the neighbourhood who had especially flown in at the personal invitation of the new leader of India, yet to be sworn in. The Prime Ministers of Pakistan, Bhutan, Nepal, and Mauritius and the Presidents of Afghanistan, Sri Lanka, and Maldives, were at hand to witness the tectonic shift in India's political landscape that day.

That they came at less than 24 hours' notice was the first glimpse of the 'shock and awe' technique that Prime Minister Modi would come to employ during his three years plus in office so far. Mandarins of the MEA normally find even a few months too short a notice to arrange visits of the Heads of Government. They are perhaps still wondering how Team Modi organised the whole event, within twenty-four hours, and executed it with clock-work precision. Not only did Modi catch the usually staid MEA off guard by directly reaching out to the heads of states in India's immediate neighbourhood, he broke a long standing taboo of not inviting representatives of the Tibetan government-in- exile and that of Taiwan to official functions, lest Beijing felt offended. The Prime Minister of the Tibetan Government-in-exile and Taiwan's trade representative in New Delhi were among the select invitees to the oath-taking ceremony that summer evening, setting the tone for a more robust foreign policy that has been practiced by Delhi in the past three years. A new regime had indeed made a fresh beginning on Raisina Hill that summer.

The very fact that Prime Minister Nawaz Sharif of Pakistan, India's implacable adversary, flew into New Delhi at Modi's invitation—he was officially still not Prime Minister—spoke highly of the expectations that India's new leader had generated. The enthusiasm would not be misplaced.

Modi had swept to power riding an unprecedented wave of popularity, winning, for the first time in three decades, a clear majority in Parliament, and leaving behind the legacy of shaky, compromised coalition governments that India had been subjected to since the mid-1990s.

He was not about to be constrained by the 'hesitation of history'. Nor was he willing to be weighed down by the precedence or lack of it. In his mind, no decision was impossible just because something had not been done before.

As the well-known strategic affairs columnist and author C Raja Mohan has noted: 'The massive electoral majority that Modi won in the 2014 general elections suggested that an era was coming to an end in India's domestic politics...an empowered government under a strong political leadership with proven experience in administration, which did not carry the ideological burdens of the past and was unabashed about India's great power aspirations, seemed all set to unveil a new age in the nation's evolution since the middle of the 20th century...'

Indeed that was the case as is evident from the bold, unconventional and swift moves in diplomacy, security, and administration, which has marked the Prime Minister's tenure so far, often leaving his opponents stunned and supporters asking for more. One common thread across the spectrum in his approach has been the realisation that it has to be 'India first'. Every decision that is taken and implemented is aimed at making India safe, stable, and prosperous.

Modi's bold move to invite heads of states in the neighbourhood for his own swearing in was not a one-off 'out of the box' decision. The Prime Minister has repeatedly demonstrated his ability to break out of the status quoist mind-set.

Take the example of inviting leaders of the BIMSTEC countries to hold a parallel summit with BRICS in Goa in 2016.

BIMSTEC or the Bay of Bengal Initiative for Multi-sectoral Technical and Economic Cooperation is a grouping of nations that holds immense significance in the South and South-east Asian region. Its members are: Bangladesh, Bhutan, Myanmar, Sri Lanka, Thailand, Nepal, and India.

He not only called the BIMSTEC leaders for a Summit in Goa, but also gave it a substance and new direction by organising a successful meeting of National Security Advisers or equivalent rank officials of the BIMSTEC countries in Delhi. This meeting was conducted under the Chairmanship of Doval within six months of the main BIMSTEC meeting in Goa.

The conference, a first of its kind, proved to be highly successful and is now likely to be institutionalised as a regular forum. As an

Giving a leg upto BIMSTEC

innovator, Modi could see the long term importance of multi-faceted cooperation with BIMSTEC countries, not only on an economic front, but also in the domain of security.

There was a reason why India adopted this approach.

Except Thailand and Myanmar, all other members of BIMSTEC are also part of SAARC or the South Asian Association for Regional Cooperation that counts Pakistan among its members. In 2016, India wanted to limit its diplomatic engagements with Pakistan because of its continued support for cross-border terrorism. New Delhi had in fact led the boycott of the SAARC summit that was supposed to have been held in Pakistan that year. Most other countries supported India's stand.

However, India wanted to keep its engagement with other neighbours on an even keel. So, in one stroke, the Prime Minister facilitated interaction between BRICS nations (Brazil, Russia, China, and South Africa, besides India) and BIMSTEC members, and simultaneously isolated Pakistan.

While India's closer relationship with the US has been a continuous process since the beginning of the 21st century, Modi took it to a higher level by striking a personal rapport with President Barack Obama between 2014 and 2016. After the surprise election of Donald Trump as Barack Obama's successor, there were worries in New Delhi that the growth trajectory of the Indo–US relationship will be cut short given the temperamental nature of the Trump administration. All the apprehensions however vanished once Modi and Trump had a one-on-one meeting in Washington in June 2017.

The two established a working relationship and charted out a practical road map.

That the Trump administration regards India as an important player in South Asia was evident when President Trump unveiled his new Afghanistan policy in August. He wanted India to do more in assisting the war-torn nation even as Trump recognised—and articulated clearly—a stand that India has been advocating vis-à-vis Pakistan in the context of Afghanistan. Washington clearly understood that the problem of terrorism in Afghanistan emanated from Pakistan and that Islamabad must demonstrate its commitment to act against terrorist groups which get sanctuaries and support in Pakistan.

'We welcome President Trump's determination to enhance efforts to overcome the challenges facing Afghanistan and confronting issues of safe havens and other forms of cross-border support enjoyed by terrorists. India shares these concerns and objectives. We are committed to supporting the Government and the people of Afghanistan in their efforts to bring peace, security, stability, and prosperity in their country. We have been steadfast in extending reconstruction and development assistance to Afghanistan in keeping with our traditional friendship with its people. We will continue these efforts, and in partnership with other countries,' MEA noted within hours of Trump's public statement.

Modi's national security team has also not neglected old friendships that New Delhi has had over decades even as it set out to capture new ground. So the Prime Minister made special efforts to reach out to Russian President Vladimir Putin since an impression had gained ground that India was abandoning Moscow in favour of Washington. Modi and Doval made special efforts to not let Russia feel neglected. India continues to source over 60 per cent of India's military hardware from Russia. India's decision to buy S-400 missiles from Russia for its vital air defence needs is one example of the continuing robust New Delhi–Moscow relationship.

Several other instances come to mind. Stepping up the outreach to Middle East countries across the board (from Saudi Arabia to Iran and from the UAE to Israel) has been a deliberate, well-thought out plan for instance. Then there is the decision to move away from the stereotype of addressing the annual conference of Director Generals of Police in the capital. Traditionally, the two-day conference has always been held in Delhi and had a set agenda for years. Usually, the Prime Minister spoke at the inaugural function, followed by the interaction with the Home Minister.

Modi however, decided to take the unusual step of holding this annual meeting away from Delhi.

Hence in 2014, Guwahati, Assam's capital and the biggest city in India's north–east, was chosen as the venue. The police chiefs— of all the states, and the Central Armed Police Forces—travelled to Guwahati that year. In 2015, the conference venue shifted west, to the Rann of Kutch, and then in 2016, it was held in Hyderabad. But the change in venue was only one out of many factors that were different. There has been a paradigm shift in the way in which the police chiefs now come for the annual gathering as the Prime Minister gives his full attention to suggestions and presentations by the DGs, in tackling increasingly complex challenges faced by law enforcers.

For three years running, Modi has spent two to three full days listening to presentations by the heads of police forces from across the country, trying to understand their challenges, demands, and shortcomings. The retreat, participants reveal, is business-like and starts with a common yoga and PT session early in the morning, followed by day-long deliberations on different topics, and finally ending with dinner.

In between the formal deliberations, Modi makes it a point to meet the DGs in groups. So, as a police chief reveals, during breakfast, he may ask DGs of states that are facing the problem of Left Wing Extremism to join his table; at lunch he may meet the heads of police forces from all the eight north-eastern states and dinner could be with a group drawn from states facing the threat of radicalisation. 'This format, of discussion in a smaller group over meals, allows us to speak a little more freely. The PM is also more focused,' reveals a serving DG.

However, the discussion on the dining table just doesn't remain there. As another police chief says, 'After discussion over meals, we have to follow up on the points we had made on the dining table by sending official inputs to both Ministry of Home Affairs and the Prime Minister's Office. Often, within months, we are asked for a follow up report.'

Clearly, apart from the obvious team building it fosters, these retreats have allowed the Prime Minister to understand the internal security situation in the country first hand. Prakash Mishra, who

Police chiefs with the Prime Minister and the Home Minister

PM Modi and his colleagues taking a stroll in Rann of Kutch

retired as DG, CRPF in 2015, says the Prime Minister's attention to detail and ability to be a good listener is remarkable. 'He engages on a broad spectrum of issues ranging from policing philosophy for a new India to the intricate workings of the police force. His emphasis on technology, modernisation, morale of the forces, and so on, can possibly be considered the first attempt at the highest level to bring about a paradigm shift in police working,' he adds.

Giving an example of how Modi's mind works, a police chief recounted: 'In one of the conversations, he asked some of us why is it that senior police officers no longer seem to have any communication with citizens and then he answered the query himself. Perhaps many senior police officers have forgotten to inter-mingle with common people. Perhaps they should make it a point to walk through crowded streets, in the markets in peak hours, to establish a rapport with people. Perhaps they should leave behind their official vehicles and let only a minimum staff accompany them during these interactions, letting people feel less intimidated and more open about the problems faced by them,' the Prime Minister gently suggested.

There is no matrix to measure if his suggestions have been followed in any way, but clearly, Modi has the ability to think of even seemingly mundane methods to improve the efficiency and acceptance of the much-maligned police force. A police chief recalls the Prime Minister's suggestion to take steps to honour hundreds of policemen martyred on duty. During one of the meetings, Modi's suggestion was to put up a simple photograph of such figures with a brief description of his/her deeds in all the schools in the village/town the policeman or woman belonged to, which could go a long way in inspiring children to take up the policeman's profession. These initiatives apart, Modi will however have to crack the whip on implementing long pending police reforms in the coming years.

TRANSFORMATION

It has been a remarkable transformation for someone who was essentially a local leader, efficiently running a state and not wasting his time on what was not his domain then. Perhaps because Modi did not take office with any pre-conceived ideas about national security and foreign policy, he has been able to chart a new course.

As a long-time government watcher remarked, 'Starting with a clean slate has allowed him to escape the usual timidity that has come to symbolise some of our decision-making at the highest level.'

His approach to global affairs is based on interlinking foreign policy with strong internal growth. He envisions a secure India that is confident of its place in the world and capable of dealing with its peers and competitors from a position of confidence and strength.

His handling of China—extending a hand of friendship first but then acting tough when Beijing started playing truant on various issues—and taking a plunge in signing the Logistics Exchange Memorandum of Agreement (LEMOA) with the United States, is testimony to Modi's confidence in dealing with tricky foreign policy issues.

Modi also looks at the vast Indian diaspora as a national asset and makes every effort to engage with them during his foreign visits. Most of them feel that Modi's statesman-like image of a strong and decisive leader has changed people's perception of India. People of Indian origin today are looked upon with greater respect and deference in countries of their domicile. As veteran diplomat G Parathasarthy says, 'Prime Minister Modi has courted the Indian community abroad more aggressively than anyone else in my memory. And is also the first person to have the guts to do it in Arab countries like the UAE and Saudi Arabia. The Indian community abroad swears by him. He has been able to mobilise the Indian community in a manner no other leader has done.' So I asked Partha (as he is fondly known by friends and admirers alike)what advantage that brings to India. 'Ah, the advantage! In the US for example we can now move Indians to organise bi-partisan support. And because the Indian community is politically organised on both sides, there is a big advantage. Similarly, in the UK. Given the money and influence the Indian community has in many countries, Modi is using their reach strategically.'

One of the first examples of the deft use of the diaspora's influence was the presence of three dozen members of the US Congress including Senate Foreign Relations Committee Chair Democratic Senator, Bob Menendez and the Indian American Republican Governor of South Carolina Nikki Haley, on stage with Modi's grand Madison Square Garden event in New York in September 2014. Cleo Paskal, Associate Fellow at Chatam House, the Royal Institute of International Affairs, London, in a chapter in his recent book on Modi's foreign policy writes, 'This was Modi's first visit to the US as Prime Minister and media inimical to the changes in India were looking for reasons to call the visit a failure... The US politicians were there because Indian–Americans are coveted supporters. They are not permanently tied to any party and are well above the US average in wealth and education. They are potentially influential voters and donors.'

Vijay Chauthiawale, in-charge of BJP's department of foreign affairs since 2015 and the man entrusted with organising the Prime Minister's public interactions abroad wherever possible, reveals the thought behind the exercise that allows Modi to leverage the strength of the Indian community abroad.

'The idea to organise a civic reception began in 2014 just before Modi made his first visit as Prime Minister to the US. We don't have any set structure in various countries, but there are influential individuals, and of course, organisations like Overseas Friends of BJP who help in managing these events. For example, there is Dr Bharat Barai in Chicago—a popular, influential doctor with ties across the political spectrum in the US—who took the initiative in setting up the Madison Square Garden event in September 2014. There was no set template available when we began. But now we have a precedent, having organised public meetings for the PM even at places like Singapore and Dubai,' Chauthaiwale revealed.

Initially, there used to be a lot of chaos, lot of jostling for credit, infighting, but the now the system has settled down. So Chauthaiwale, a PhD in microbiology and a former vice-president at Torrent Pharmaceuticals, travels weeks in advance to a country

The Prime Minister amidst ecstatic supporters in MSG

where the Prime Minister is scheduled to visit and sets up his public outreach to the diaspora.

'The first thing I tell everyone that this is not about the BJP or the OFBJP (Overseas Friends of BJP), but about the entire community. I give that message loud and clear in the very first meeting with the Diaspora outfits. The organising committees, which we set up, consist of representatives from all communities, linguistic and professional groups of the Diaspora,' Chauthaiwale told me.

The aim, close aides of the PM say, is to make India acceptable everywhere. That is why the Prime Minister has chosen to tour smaller countries like Fiji, Sychelles, Mauritius, and Mongolia, countries as diverse as they can get.

Chauthaiwale points out, 'By interacting with Indians abroad and solving their issues, the PM sends a message that he cares for them and is concerned about their well-being. Take for example, the issue of land for a temple in the UAE. It was a longstanding desire of the community there. The PM personally intervened and had the land allotted to them. These are small issues, emotive issues, but they add substantially to the comfort of the community. Moreover, the Prime Minister's visits and his addresses to the Diaspora have increased their stature in their own country.'

The larger strategic aim of course is to project India as the rising power with a booming economy, democratic ethos, and vibrant culture. It is with this singular focus that Modi tours the world. Between 15 June 2014—when he visited Bhutan for his first official trip as Prime Minister—and May 2017, Modi had undertaken visits to 49 countries. By contrast, the PM's predecessor, Dr Manmohan Singh, in his first three years in office had toured 27 countries, according to records available on the MEA website. As former diplomat Amit Dasgupta wrote recently: 'If we assume that the essence of foreign policy lies in furthering a nation's vital interests through policies that are principled, pragmatic, strategic and outcome-driven, the approach is as important as the objective. The means, in other words, reflect how the end would be perceived and are, thus, equally important.

'To achieve his strategic vision, Modi opted for his own distinctive approach: first, he chose to place greater emphasis on personal equations and second, he opted to be disruptive and unpredictable and, if required, unhesitatingly forceful. Both depart dramatically from the approach adopted by his predecessors.

'The results, so far, have been encouraging. India's sagging international image during the UPA 2 tenure has, undoubtedly, seen a dramatic revival. The Prime Minister's personal outreach and strategically designed approach in establishing personal equations with world leaders has been reciprocated substantially. Both, with US President Barack Obama and more recently, with President Trump, this was visibly apparent, as was his disruptive initiative in reaching out to Israel. These were paradigm shifts in approach.'

But what of Modi's security policies? What is his approach?

At one level, because of his record as a no-nonsense administrator and his nationalistic views, it was a given that Modi would adopt a more robust security policy with respect to both Pakistan and China. Breaking years of status quo and hesitation have not been easy. Inevitably, there have been setbacks—in

Kashmir and the Maoist-dominated areas—but in each case, the national security apparatus under Modi's premiership has bounced back and reconfigured itself.

Ambassador Satish Chandra, seasoned diplomat and former deputy national security adviser, sums it up succinctly: 'Modi is not looking at the past as a inhibiting factor. The Prime Minister will do what he thinks is right. He is not inhibited by lack of precedence. Every Prime Minister gets bogged down by countervailing forces within the well-established system. But Modi has been able to break out of the iron clad framework because he is a complete outsider. He is not part of the Delhi Durbar and can therefore think out of the box on most vital issues like foreign policy and national security.'

The results may not be immediately apparent, but many far-reaching changes, ushered in over the past three years, will strengthen national security, as the subsequent chapters will argue.

However, according to NSA Doval, it is difficult to comprehend Modi's security policies without understanding his vision for the

PM Modi and NSA Ajit Doval: Effective combination

nation. Groomed and nurtured ideologically in a strong nationalist mode, he has both a civilisational awareness and a long-term strategic vision of India's security. He believes that a strong economy, transformed human capital of India, technological excellence, and powerful national consciousness of the Indian people are the guarantors of Indian security. His emphasis on human resource development, indigenisation of defence production, and emphasis on technology in defence, are all aimed at making India strong and secure. A careful analysis of all his speeches and utterances make it clear that he considers the will of the nation as the main ingredient of its Comprehensive National Power (CNP). He wants the Indian people to be proud of their past, resolute in their present, and imbued with high hopes for the future. Most Indians credit him for raising the national consciousness to a much higher level.

With those objectives in mind, the Prime Minister wanted to build an effective and efficient team around him. The team members also needed to share his vision and jointly resolve to secure India, and to make it powerful, potent, and prosperous. Modi therefore, needed to have a team leader with experience, knowledge, integrity, and high credibility in the security domain.

He found that man in Ajit Doval, the old security czar, a legend in the highly competitive and covert world of intelligence, but more importantly someone, who like Modi, was uninhibited by personal biases and did not harbour a private agenda, except making India strong and secure. Doval had served for long years in the Intelligence Bureau and dealt with crucial matters of national security before retiring in 2005 as Director of the IB.

Indeed Doval's appointment as National Security Adviser (NSA) was one of the first official decisions that Modi took after assuming office on 26 May 2014.

Modi and Doval had a nodding acquaintance when Doval was in service, but they came to know each other better after 2005 when the NSA retired as head of the Intelligence Bureau. By that time, Modi was a well-established and undisputed leader in Gujarat. Gradually, Doval, who founded the Vivekananda International Foundation (VIF), a think-tank on strategic affairs after retirement, developed a great deal of admiration and saw in Modi a leader who could transform India. Modi roped him in to establish the Raksha Shakti University in Gujarat. A one of its kind training institution, the Raksha Shakti University has a vision to 'impart customised education to the youth of the country in all vital aspects of internal security to ensure that specialised and trained personnel are available for employment in various security agencies like police forces, defence, private security. It now attracts many talented young men and women interested in 'understanding the world of security.'

After Doval took over as India's fifth National Security Adviser, he and the Prime Minister set about removing the cobwebs in the minds of security sector practitioners and the lethargy that had crept into the system.

In Doval, the Prime Minister had the advantage of a person who not only knew the inner workings of the security apparatus in the country, but also someone who commanded great respect amongst peers and juniors. The NSA's operational exploits are well-known and his high decorations include the Kirti Chakra, one of the highest military gallantry awards. Indeed, his achievements during active years in service accords him an unparalleled standing among the younger generation of officers.

Over the past three years, the Modi-Doval combine has put together a core team of security professionals across the board and created a seamless system where bickering and infighting of yore has been eliminated. Speaking to this author over three longish sessions—Doval rarely comes on record, both due to the sensitivity of his job and also because of years of being in the habit of operating in the shadows—the NSA remarked, 'For Prime Minister Modi, the only criterion is national interest when it comes to formulating national security policies, or taking difficult decisions. He is completely oblivious to political consequences when it comes to taking the right decisions on national security. This attribute gives the PM rare clarity of thought. He is never in doubt over a decision once it is taken. Most strikingly, he is an innovative genius. I have yet to come across an instance when he does not add a new dimension, or offer an innovative suggestion to any issue brought before him.'

Doval reveals that Modi's National Security approach is 'without fetters'. 'The advantage of such a doctrine is that he has no other focus except his deeply embedded patriotism and the awareness that for India to become a great power, a secure environment—both internal and external—is an absolute must,' the NSA remarked. More importantly, Doval says the Prime Minister looks at national security from a long-term perspective and 'does not get rattled with episodic ups and downs', referring to occasional setbacks in the fight against the Maoists and in J&K. His larger strategic objective is to make India secure and stable, said Doval.

As a result of this clarity, as Doval observes, in the last three years, India has managed to enhance its intelligence capabilities, strengthen its border management, and silently but resolutely enhance defence preparedness. 'There are very few people talking about any intelligence failure these days,' he points out. 'There has been enhancement in our real time response capability, speed and surprise in our operations, and a shift from improved coordination to inter-agency synergy,' he adds. According to the NSA, the Prime Minister's understanding of cyber security, maritime security, space research, and other such complex matters 'continues to surprise us all'.

Doval, who perhaps meets the Prime Minister more than anyone else, reveals, 'His comprehension and attention span is unbelievably high. His approach is essentially of a problem solver; he comes out with solutions that will often surprise you.' The NSA also reveals that the Modi approach to national security is also highly 'value based'. He strongly believes that as a responsible nation, with a high potential and promising future, we should not do or support anything that is not in consonance with India's core values, or that might be internationally unacceptable. The nation's commitment to democracy and rule of law must always be upheld. He wants 'India's security apparatus to be professional, seamlessly coordinated, well-equipped, and innovative.' Doval too believes in capability building, anticipating threats and leading from the front. As he observed, 'in security, it does matter what happens to you, but what matters more is how you respond.' There's no doubt that having spent long years of his life conducting operations on ground, Doval has developed a unique tactical and strategic sense. Elaborating further, he told me, 'Strategy without tactics is noise before the defeat, and tactics without strategy is the shortest route to committing suicide. Both are equally important and intertwined. For example, neutralising a terrorist commander is tactical, but degrading the capacity of a terrorist outfit is strategic.'

He also does not agree that a terrorist, even in a suicide mode, can strike any time. 'I believe terrorist incidents take place when three curves meet: the curve of intention, the curve of capability, and the curve of opportunity. We change their intentions and capabilities through strategic and tactical means, while denial of opportunity is mainly tactical, degrading the capacity of a terror group by proactive or preventive means is strategic. An effective counter-terrorist policy should therefore aim to ensure that the triangle is never formed and if it does, the area is minimised,' he stated.

The NSA appears to be satisfied with the increase in intelligence capabilities, but feels that there is still a long way to go. He said 'there is nothing so good that cannot be improved.' He was happy that whether it was Uri, Pathankot, Nagrota, or other terrorist strikes, 'we had good real time intelligence'. 'Yes, we have fallen short in some aspects, but setbacks in this fight are inevitable. The trick is to minimise the losses and keep the pressure on to degrade the enemy,' he remarked. He points to the fact that improved intelligence gathering capabilities has meant India has been free of any terrorist attack in areas outside J&K and some districts of Punjab bordering Pakistan. 'While we are not complacent about this, it must be pointed out that our agencies have managed to pre-empt and neutralise many terrorist modules both within and outside the country,' the NSA reveals without going into further details.

He admits that such an approach certainly necessitates planned and focused attention from the government, with an emphasis on capacity building rather than merely episodic response. These forms of conventional threats can be addressed through the strengthening of state police forces and it intelligence units. 'We are striving to bolster the capacities of the states through intelligence support, strategic guidelines, coordination mechanism, training, equipment and financial help. The states on their part need to streamline police administration, fill the existing vacant posts, implement police reforms as mandated by the Supreme Court, and ensure political interference in law enforcement abates,' the NSA concluded.

9

Testing Times, Post-Uri

I assure the nation that those behind this despicable attack
will not go unpunished.
— Prime Minister Narendra Modi
on 18 September 2016

For Col H and Col K (names withheld), the moment of reckoning
arrived on the afternoon of 18 September 2016.

Throughout that morning, the Commanding Officers (COs)
of two separate Para (Special Forces) battalions were like most of
their colleagues posted in Kashmir Valley, following the increasingly
grim news coming out of Uri, the garrison town not very far from
Srinagar.

*Defence Minister Manohar Parrikar with Gen Dalbir Singh and top
commanders in Srinagar, September 2016*

Well-trained and well-informed terrorists of the Lashkar-e-Toiba (LeT) had infiltrated across the Line of Control (LoC) and attacked an administrative camp in the 12 Brigade HQ located in Uri with deadly effect.

At least 19 soldiers of 6 Bihar battalion, camping in tents—days before they were to take their assigned positions along the LoC—were killed in the early morning attack. Majority of the soldiers died in their sleep, resting as they were in highly inflammable tents.

Although all the four terrorists were neutralised eventually, they had set off a chain of events that would culminate on the morning of 29 September.

But I am getting ahead of the story.

As the death toll kept rising by the hour—three, four, 10, 17 and ending on 19—the two SF COs knew they were going to have a busy time ahead.

In Udhampur, Northern Army Commander Lt Gen DS Hooda was distressed. He had been the GOC-in-C for over two years and witnessed his share of successes and setbacks as the head of India's most active Army command. Nevertheless, this was possibly the worst moment of his long and distinguished career, spent fighting insurgencies and terrorism in the north-east as well as Jammu & Kashmir. 'It was terrible. Very difficult to justify what happened. There were definitely lapses on our part,' Hooda says in retrospect.

But an Army Commander doesn't have the luxury of wallowing in his own state of mind. He has to set an example by leading from the front.

As he accompanied Army Chief Gen Dalbir Singh to Uri, Hooda knew the time had come to implement a plan, the seeds of which had vaguely taken shape in his mind some fifteen months ago. Even Gen Dalbir, aware of how the Prime Minister's mind worked, was thinking of something different.

Gen Dalbir, who had served all his life in combat zones—from north–east to Kashmir and in Sri Lanka—was a pragmatic leader. He planned well, refused to rush into a decision even when pressure was put on him to take immediate retaliatory action, and had interacted with Prime Minister Modi long enough since May 2014 to realise

Soldiers General: Army chief Gen Dalbir Singh in 2016

that Modi would not let the Uri attack go unpunished. So, the moment he returned to Delhi, Gen Dalbir told his DGMO to draw up plans to launch cross-border strikes since he had sensed that the current government will seek punitive action against Pakistan for the recent attacks.

Gen Dalbir was drawing on his experience during the cross-border raid in Myanmar more than a year previously when the PM had quietly authorised the strike against north-east militants holed up in the jungles of Manipur-Myanmar border after killing 18 Indian soldiers. Gen Dalbir had a hunch then that the Prime Minister may demand a Myanmar-like action if push came to shove in J&K.

Cut to mid-June in 2015.

In June 2015, it was under his watch as Army Chief that the soldiers of a Para SF unit of the Indian Army, based in the north-east, had carried out a precise attack on an NSCN (K) camp located inside Myanmar and eliminated at least 60 insurgents in the process.

While the cross-border raid inside Myanmar was making waves and dividing opinion (*see separate chapter*), discussions in TV studios in India centred around the possibility of similar raids against Paksitan. Minister of State of Information & Broadcasting, Rajyavardhan Rathore told TV anchors that the option of cross-border raids against Pakistan are a possibility. He also told

Indian Express in June 2015: 'This is a message for all countries, including Pakistan, and groups harbouring terror intent towards India. A terrorist is a terrorist and has no other identity. We will strike when we want to.'

Pakistan was quick to react to Rathore's remark. 'Pakistan is not like Myanmar,' Interior Minister Nisar Ali Khan said. 'Those having ill designs against Pakistan should listen carefully that our security forces are capable of matching response to any adventurism... Indian leaders should stop daydreaming.' Pakistan Army spokesman also issued a warning. A military conference in Rawalpindi, chaired by Army chief Raheel Sharif, took 'serious notice of recent Indian hostile rhetoric coupled with their covert and overt actions to destabilise Pakistan, and reiterated their resolve such designs... None should dare to cast an evil eye on Pakistan,' military spokesman Major General AS Bajwa tweeted.

Amidst all this public exchange, Indian Army HQ and Northern Command too were planning well ahead. Gen Dalbir said: 'I recall telling my Northern Army Commander to start thinking on the lines of the Myanmar strike.'

The success of Myanmar operations had planted the seed of thought about a surgical strike in Pakistan in everyone's mind. Once during his visit to the Northern Command, then Defence Minister Manohar Parrikar too had exhorted top commanders to be prepared for every eventuality. 'Although I didn't spell it out explicitly, I knew some day a grave provocation by Pakistan may require a Myanmar-like operation. So I told the Army Chief and his senior commanders to look at every possible response,' Parrikar recalls.

On his part, Lt Gen Hooda called the two COs (Col H and Col K) and told them that they needed to start looking at targets across the LoC, although frankly at that point in time (June 2015) neither Gen Dalbir, nor Lt Gen Hooda or the political leadership would have thought of such an eventuality arising. Till then, the thinking at the highest levels of India's political and military leadership was any major trans-LoC strike would be deemed escalatory.

Remember, in Kargil, the Vajpayee government had imposed the strict restriction of NOT crossing the LoC in spite of a grave provocation.

'I thought to myself, if tomorrow someone asks us to go, how can I, as Northern Army Commander say we are not prepared?' Hooda remembers thinking.

Gen Dalbir says: 'From my experience in planning and executing the Myanmar raids, I wanted my commanders to make sure that any cross-border raid should be carried out with minimum casualties. My instructions were, not one single soldier should be left behind in enemy territory even if we suffered any setback.'

Hence, in the immediate aftermath of the Myanmar operation, the two COs were told to seriously plan to hit targets inside PoK. Other senior officers in Northern Command's planning staff also held discussions a couple of times with the MO (Military Operations Directorate at the Army HQ). They identified targets, looking for more intelligence inputs on them, and consolidating a thought process in the presence of the Army Chief and the Northern Army Commander.

'Basically, we had started planning for a cross-border operation, something that had not been contemplated earlier...without this planning, both at Army HQ level and in Northern Command and a change in thought process, it would have been impossible to do what our boys eventually did. It is not something you do based on overnight planning,' Gen Dalbir said.

But were not cross-border raids carried out earlier too, I asked Gen Dalbir. 'Yes, they were,' he agreed 'but most actions taken in our younger days were, what we call, BAT (Border Action Team) raids on specific post(s) as retribution for something that the Pakistan Army troops would have carried out on our position(s),' he said. 'What we were now planning for was much larger with greater ramifications,' he explained.

After the Myanmar Operation, Gen Dalbir had already passed orders to get better equipment for the Special Forces... 'Immediately after Manipur, I had initiated a case for procurement of special equipment and weapons. Then we decided to equip at least two battalions of SF in the East and the North (Eastern and Northern Command) on a fast-track basis.'

This preparation and priming up of the Special Forces was necessary, since the two battalions, involved in a day-to-day engagement in Jammu and Kashmir for years, had somehow taken the focus away from their primary task of operating behind enemy lines and undertaking special operations in enemy territory.

So in the winter of 2015, the two SF battalions were told to concentrate fully on training for their conventional role (of infiltrating behind enemy lines and carrying out strategic strikes).

Although the COs were initially inclined to do both—carry out Counter-insurgency, Counter-terrorists (CI–CT) operations even while stepping up the battalions' training for conventional operations—Hooda ordered them to just do the latter in peak winter. Both Gen Dalbir and the then Northern Army Commander remember receiving flak from some Special Forces veterans for their move. But neither of them were budging.

For two months in the winter of 2015, the two battalions trained as whole units after years of operating in small, agile teams against terrorists in J&K. This training was to prove crucial in sharpening the set of skills needed for raids across the LoC.

In a way, it was like revisiting their basic tenets for the Special Forces men. And they loved it. Although no one could have anticipated that they would be called in to strike across the LoC, the very thought of crossing a line that was seen as taboo motivated the troops further. Indeed for over two decades no one at the highest political level had ever expressed willingness to sanction, or had demanded such an action inside PoK for the fear of escalation.

'The two to two-and-a-half months that these boys spent together helped them hone their skills in surveying targets, mount surveillance, practising infiltration and exfiltration, which in the final analysis helped them achieve what was asked of them,' a senior officer in MO Directorate, privy to the development now agrees, looking back at that decision. As a result of the reorientation, by the time the summer of 2016 arrived, the two battalions had added an extra edge to their repertory of formidable skills.

However, no one—not even the most imaginative scriptwriter in Bollywood—could have anticipated the events as they unfolded in September 2016.

URI ATTACK AND AFTER

Sunday, 18 September 2016 dawned with the worst news possible for the Indian Army and the nation.

A group of four heavily armed suicide attackers had trekked across the Haji Pir pass, infiltrated into the Uri sector and launched an assault on the administrative base of the 12 Brigade HQ located on the edge of the Uri Garrison. It was 0530 hours.

By 0900 hours, the terrorists were eliminated by the Army's quick reaction team.

But not before they had killed 19 Indian soldiers. It was the biggest hit that the Army had taken in any terror attack in 15 years. The last such big loss, old timers remember, was during an attack on the Kaluchak Army camp in 2002 when 22 soldiers were killed in a similar suicide attack.

The Army was shaken. And angry. For too long, the Army had been taking casualties in its own camps without hitting back in the same fashion.

Across the board, the *langar gup* (mess gossip) was full of frustration and rage. I remember speaking to some middle level officers posted in J&K in the immediate aftermath of the Uri incident. The anger was palpable. 'If this is not the last straw, what is,' many of them wondered aloud when the possibility of the Indian army's retaliation was discussed.

NSA Doval too remembers Prime Minister Modi telling him: 'This attack should not go without a response.' Gen Dalbir adds: 'During one of the meetings in the immediate aftermath of Uri, the Prime Minister said the retaliation should be immediate to send an unambiguous message.'

Parrikar, Doval and Gen Dalbir however knew they had to plan for several contingencies before attempting a Myanmar-style cross-border raid. For one, unlike on the Myanmar border, the Pakistani forces strung all along the LoC were on highest alert in the wake of the Uri attack. The terrorists would have also been told to lie low and shifted to camps located farther away from the LoC so that hitting those targets would have become harder.

Moreover, no matter how remote the possibility, India had to war game the likely escalation by Pakistan if retribution was ordered.

Defence Minister Parrikar, reviewing the preparedness of the forces, recalls how he had held a number of meetings within a week of the Uri attack and ordered fast track purchases of critical ammunition, spare parts and crucial equipment. 'It became apparent from the briefings I received from the Army Chief that we had to be prepared for a possibility of a short, swift skirmish, if not a conflict, once it had been decided to order a retaliatory strike,' Parrikar says.

Many deficiencies—which were in the process of being overcome in the normal course but would have taken at least another year—had to be made up in double quick time.

'In the week after the Uri attack, I remember chairing some 18–20 meetings taking stock of the urgent needs,' Parrikar said. 'When our government came to power in May 2014, we were shocked to find severe shortages that the three forces were facing. Certain types of ammunition were down to two days of supply as against the requirement of at least 20 days,' Parrikar said. He was only confirming what many defence analysts had noted. Lethargy and indecision under UPA's Defence Minister AK Antony had brought the situation to a sorry pass.

In fact Gen VK Singh, who was Army Chief between 2010 and 2012 before becoming a BJP MP and now a Minister of State in Ministry of External Affairs, had noted in a letter to then Prime Minister Manmohan Singh in 2012: 'The army's entire tank fleet is 'devoid of critical ammunition to defeat enemy tanks.' The then Army Chief also spoke about air defence being 97 per cent obsolete. He added that the infantry is crippled with 'deficiencies of crew served weapon' and lacks night fighting capabilities, elite Special Forces are woefully short of essential weapons and there are large-scale voids in critical surveillance as well as night fighting capabilities.

In the letter scooped by Saikat Datta in the *DNA* newspaper, Gen Singh pointed out that the present 'hollowness' in the system is a manifestation of the procedures and processing time for procurements as well as legal impediments by vendors. 'The general's plea is a direct indictment of the complex and slow defence procurement procedures,' Datta wrote.

Gen Dalbir, who became the Army Chief in July 2014 realised after taking stock with his Principal Staff Officers (PSOs) that the situation had not improved much even two years after what Gen VK Singh had written in his letter. So he pushed MoD for quicker procurement of key ammunition.

Against this backdrop, Parrikar had already initiated several contracts to make up for years of neglect. But now, in the wake of the Uri attack, when plans were being finalised to launch punitive strikes against Pakistan, he had to hasten the process.

Multiple conversations with those involved in the process reveals that India procured equipment, platforms, spares and ammunition worth anything between Rs 20,000 to 25,000 crores in the immediate aftermath of the Uri attack. Parrikar recalls he had to cut through red tape ruthlessly in order to get the deliveries on time. At the same time, he temporarily enhanced the financial powers of the Vice Chiefs (effectively the No. 2) of the Army, Navy, and Air Force substantially. They were told to stock up for a short and intense war even as the on-going plan to build reserves for a longer conflict continued apace. This was for the first time in recent years that the Vice Chiefs had been given enhanced financial powers.

In July 2017, the initial orders were formalised.

Media reports in January 2017, months after the Uri attack, spoke of ongoing purchases to make up for glaring deficiencies too. My friend Sudhi Ranjan Sen, writing for *HuffPost India* in January 2017 reported that India was continuing with 'fast-track' military purchases from Russia and Israel. 'In a move with tremendous strategic import, India has been on a secretive weapons shopping spree on an emergency footing, buying up anti-tank missiles, tank engines, rocket launchers and various kinds of ammunition, from

Israel and Russia. The purchases amount to more than $3 billion, persons close to the development said, asking not to be named. Deliveries have begun even as new orders are still being placed. From Russia, India has bought a few thousand anti-tank guided missiles, several T-90 tank engines and critical tank components. The Russia-made T-90 is the Indian Army's mainstay battle tank. The Russia list also includes multi-barrel rocket launchers that operate with the artillery against advancing columns and soft skinned targets, and large quantity of various kinds of ammunition,' Sen reported.

On ground however, neither Col H nor Col K were aware of or concerned about the high level confabulations. They were focused on the task they knew they had to do. This was a chance they knew they would never get again. This was the once-in-a-lifetime opportunity Special Forces wait for. 'The day Uri happened, we had, in our mind, decided where to hit, how to hit the other side since we had already planned for this eventuality in the previous six-eight months,' Col H said. 'We knew this incident called for a punitive response. There was no way this government would allow the Uri incident to go unpunished,' Col K added. 'Our boys were angry, not sad. They kept saying '*ek bada sabak sikhana padega Pakistan ko*' (we have to teach Pakistan a big lesson). We knew, the strike will have to be big enough to inflict major damage. A token raid would not have been sufficient,' both the COs recalled during our conversation. And sure enough, the call came from Udhampur by the evening of 19 September. The Army Commander wanted them at the Northern Command HQ forthwith.

The countdown to the surgical strikes had begun!

On 20 and 21 September, several briefings and discussions took place in the Command HQ's operations room. The focus was on specifics: targets, timing, methods. Only Lt Gen Hooda, the MGGS, the BGS and the two Commanding Officers were privy to the discussions.

As the two COs and the Northern Command MGGS and BGS got down to finalising the minutest of details, Lt Gen Hooda flew to Delhi at least thrice in that week between the Uri attack and the surgical strikes, to sit down with the DGMO and select officers of the Military Operations (MO) Directorate to fine-tune the plans.

Plate 1: *Doval with Modi: A trusted and effective relationship working to make India secure*

Plate 2: Tabook Camp, Garhi Habibullah, Mansehra, KPK (34.424521N, 73.405692E)

Plate 3: *India aircraft carrier INS Vikramaditya during Tropex 2019, somewhere in Arabian Sea*

Plate 4: *Two Indian Naval ships on the west coast after they transited from Tropex to actual deployment, February 2019*

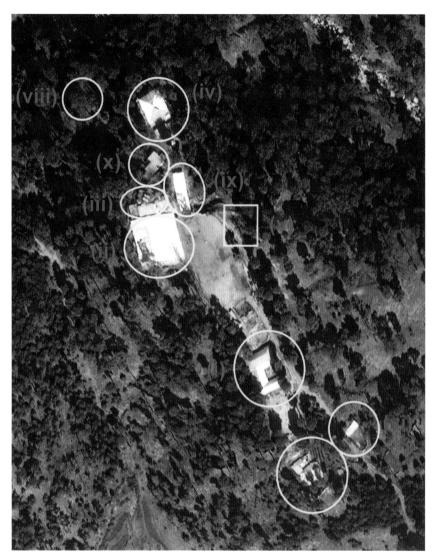

(i) Hall, Residence, Hostel

(ii) Main Hall

(iii) Guest House/Residence of Trainers

(iv) Big Hall/Hostel for Cadres

(v) Canteen Area

(vi) Residence of Yusuf Azhar and Abandoned School

(vii) Main Entrance

(viii) Swimming Pool

(ix) Jijama, Dispensary and Canteen

(x) Tailoring Faculty

Plate 5: *A clear satellite view of JeM's Balakot camp hit by IAF's Mirage jets on 26 February 2019*

Plate 6: US, UK and Israeli flags painted on the steps leading to the main training complex at Balakot so that trainees could 'crush' them as they entered

Plate 7: *Office cum Transit Camp, Shawai Nalla, Muzaffarabad, PoJK (34.3859N, 73.45712E) Part of the detailed dossier handed over to Pakistan in the wake of Pulwama attack, February 2019*

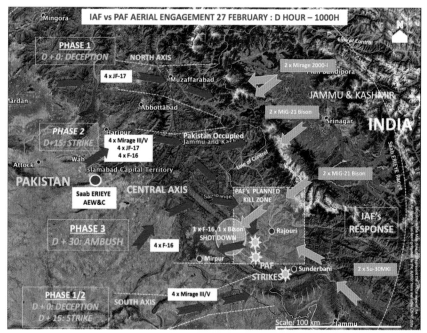

Plate 8: *A graphic explainer on how the air battle took place on 27 February 2019 (by Sameer Joshi)*

Plate 9: *IAF pilot Wing Cdr Abhinandan Varthaman (blindfolded) immediately after his capture*

Plate 10: *The ASAT missile taking off from the Balasore range in Odisha, March 2019*

THE PRESSURE BUILDS UP

The week of the Uri attack was also a testing time for the Prime Minister's leadership. Modi, adept at judging the public mood, was aware that people expected him to 'walk the talk' in acting tough against India's implacable enemy.

Public opinion in the country was inflamed. People were calling for an all-out war against Pakistan. Even saner voices were advocating at least some demonstrable retribution. Modi was aware of the public sentiment and the anger that was building up in popular perception. He vowed immediate retribution. '*I assure the nation that those behind this despicable attack will not go unpunished,*' he tweeted on the day of the Uri attack. Not many people took the statement at face value. After all, politicians and prime ministers in the past had pledged stern action against terrorists and their handlers many times, but had ultimately refrained from giving that final go ahead required to retaliate, urging restraint instead.

Almost everyone thought it to be the standard condemnation—*kadi ninda* (severe condemnation)—as some commentators have often categorised politicians' routine statements after each terrorist attack. However, the PM was clear in his mind that he cannot afford to be taken for granted like his predecessor, Dr Manmohan Singh, who often dithered and failed to launch any punitive action against Pakistan even after the outrageous attack on Mumbai in November 2008 that killed more than 170 people and made a mockery of India's security apparatus.

Modi had himself strongly criticised Dr Singh's inaction then. Now, the ball was in Prime Minister Modi's court.

The Opposition was up in arms. After a day or two of showing solidarity with the government and sympathy for those martyred, it was now mocking the government's inability to punish Pakistan. The Congress targeted Modi, holding him 'singularly responsible for the complete disarray' in the government's policy vis-à-vis Pakistan. Congress' chief spokesman Randeep Singh Surjewala had alleged that the Uri attack, which was planned and executed by Pakistan, was the result of the 'failure' of Modi government's political leadership. He had also alleged that the tragedy was the

India's security brains-trust: On the day of the Uri attack

result of a massive intelligence and operational failure inside the government.

Newspapers were critical too. *The Times of India* dug up old statements by the Prime Minister when he was the Chief Minister of Gujarat and the UPA was in power. It recalled a statement made by Narendra Modi at Rewari on 15 September 2013: 'The problem lies in Delhi, not at the borders... Only a competent, patriotic and people-oriented government at the centre can solve the problem.'

About a month before he made this statement, Modi had tweeted: 'India is going through a troubled situation. China intrudes our borders, Pakistan kills our soldiers time and again. But Centre doesn't act.'

Strategic affairs analysts were also unsparing. C Uday Bhaskar wrote: 'The Indian response to the Uri attack has followed a familiar pattern of anger against the adversary, the state-sponsored terrorist—and the 'deep state' represented by the Pakistan military. Home Minister Rajnath Singh has castigated Pakistan, called it a 'terrorist state' and imprudently cancelled his visit to the US and Russia. PM Modi has assured the nation that the perpetrators of this 'despicable attack' will be punished. The dominant question that has been deliberated upon with anger and anguish across the audio-visual medium and in social media over the last 24 hours is: 'When?'

Doval and Parrikar: Strategising after Uri attack

Amidst all the criticism, the Prime Minister continued to be unruffled.

Recall his aides: 'The PM went through with his daily routine and pre-scheduled appointments and programmes without any change, but made sure he had all possible options presented to him before giving the final go ahead (for a punitive strike against Pakistan).'

All options, economic, political, and diplomatic were considered. They ranged from downgrading diplomatic ties, revisiting the provisions of the Indus Water Treaty, mobilising international opinion by furnishing proof of Pakistan's complicity in terrorist attacks, and of course punish Pakistan militarily.

But he was not about to be rushed into any hasty decision.

The Prime Minister however made up his mind by 23 September, five days after the Uri attack. Later that evening, he and Doval, escorted by a Major General from the MO Directorate, walked the length of the South Block Corridor from the PMO to the Army HQ Ops room around 2100 hours, much long after the corridors had been emptied and offices had closed. Already present in the room were Defence Minister Parrikar, Army Chief Gen Dalbir Singh, DGMO, Lt Gen Ranbir Singh, and a couple of MO Directorate senior functionaries.

The PM sat through the briefing silently, listening with rapt attention. He was presented various options, shown targets that were planned to be hit inside PoK, and briefed on the possible retaliation/reaction by Pakistan.

Once the initial briefing was over, Modi had a couple of questions on other possible options like a precise air strike on terrorist camps, remembers a participant. Eventually, the Prime Minister agreed that a Special Forces raid across the frontier was the best possible course of action at that point, the participant added.

The PM's situational awareness and sharp memory was also were also in evidence that night. When the subject of international reaction came up, he reminded everyone that External Affairs Minister Sushma Swaraj was to deliver her speech at the UN General Assembly in the next one week or so. The PM therefore ordered that the operation be timed after her speech. However, beyond giving general directions about the need to be careful, Modi did not get into specifics.

'He left the planning and execution to us professionals,' Doval told me.

So the professionals got down to business. Parrikar, Gen Dalbir and Doval analysed the situation and sent out instructions to the Northern Command for an 'in-principle' go ahead for a trans-LoC strike. 'We told Udhampur (Northern Command HQ) to look for major terrorist camps. The idea was to destroy some of that infrastructure across the LoC in PoK,' Gen Dalbir remembers.

All decisions were however taken after long deliberations and thorough discussions. 'All of us knew that the Pakistani forces would be at their highest alert after the Uri attack, so we did not want to do anything rash,' the then Army Chief said.

India's external intelligence agency, the RA&W, and the Intelligence Bureau asked its operatives to assess the possible impact of a retaliatory strike inside PoK. 'We needed to be ready for any possible backlash,' a top intelligence operative recalls.

Gen Dalbir, cautious but pragmatic, also sought permission from Parrikar to redeploy some key formations just in case Pakistan decided to up the ante after the retaliation. 'As Army Chief, the onus was on me to make sure we did not fall short of firepower,' Gen Dalbir recalls thinking throughout the week following the Uri attack, planning far beyond the retaliatory strikes. 'I had already moved some additional forces to the Kashmir Valley to reinforce the existing security grid following large scale unrest, after we had eliminated Burhan Wani (the Kashmiri local commander),' Gen Dalbir revealed. 'Now I had to make sure that other areas too were ready for any possible backlash,' he told me.

So formations responsible for borders in Punjab and Rajasthan were put on alert. A review of shortages at the local level was carried out and orders passed to replenish inventory.

Meanwhile as debates—mostly acrimonious and bitter—continued to rage on television channels and in public discourse, the Indian security establishment was quietly preparing for a counter-strike on a scale that was always possible in theory, but had never been implemented in practice for fear of escalation.

As one week passed after the Uri attack, the debates tapered off; people seemed resigned to live with the bitter fact that the situation in J&K and on the LoC would continue to be volatile with the Indian army unable to take any deterrent steps.

Little did anyone know that India was about to unleash unprecedented and audacious cross-border strikes.

10

The Surgical Strikes in PoK

Once the political call was taken, the wheels began to move faster. In Udhampur, the Ops room was buzzing with activity. Now was the time to bring the two Corps Commanders of 15 and 16 Corps in the loop.

Accordingly, Lt Gens Satish Dua and RR Nimborhkar, heading the Srinagar-based Chinar and Nagrota-based White Knight Corps respectively, were also brought on board.

Col H and Col K meanwhile were back to their respective bases. They had much to do. Both had finalised the targets, but the men had to be selected for different tasks, although in their mind they had already earmarked some key personnel the previous winter when the entire units were training together.

As Col H remembers, 'Most of our reorientation took place in the mind; we were crossing a threshold that had been embedded in the mind: thus far and no further. Now we were being asked to do a job that had not been undertaken in decades.' Adds Col K: 'Our boys always had the skills, but they had applied the skills to a different set of circumstances, not the task we were about to undertake. However, due to our practice and reorientation, they were at the peak of their skills.' They were, like many Indian Army Officers before them posted along the LoC, aware of one-off, shallow raids launched by different infantry units into PoK. But all of them were individual punitive actions and not large-scale planned operations like the one that was being contemplated now.

The tasks were diverse. Teams had to be formed accordingly. Over the past quarter century, the Indian Army had created a strong network of intelligence operatives in the valley and within various tanzeems based in Pakistan-occupied Kashmir (PoK). Post the Uri attack and around the time when the surgical strike was being finalised, Northern Command tapped a couple of sources in Hizbul Mujahideen, located in the general area of Anantnag, to obtain more information about the layout of Pakistani camps (*see Plate 11*), and the possible routes that could be taken both to enter and exit PoK. These inputs were crucial to plan strategy and form teams for different tasks like mounting secret surveillance, raid the camps, and for guiding the troops back safely. They also had to do last minute rechecking of targets to make sure that the terrorists were still holed up there and launch pads were not emptied out after the Uri attack.

So what were the thoughts that were going through their minds as they prepared to launch the strikes, I asked the two Commanding Officers.

Looking back, with a quiet sense of pride in their eyes, both the officers recalled their state of mind: 'We knew we had to hit the adversary so hard that he would be humiliated. There was no time for half-measures, no place for token gestures,' recounted Col K. His colleague added: 'This is what we train for: That one chance to deliver a blow so lethal that the enemy will constantly think about it when planning any misadventure.'

Interestingly, both the Corps Commanders were clear that the operations had to be calibrated so that the backlash doesn't go out of hand. 'We had to hit them, humiliate them, but only to an extent that they kept looking over their shoulders, kept sweating, thinking what next, and not plan for a conventional escalation to an all-out war,' both Lt Gen Dua and Nimborkar recall having discussed during the planning stage.

Accordingly, the COs were told that the intent of the cross-border strikes was two-fold: inducing fear and extracting revenge. Simultaneously, total destruction of terrorist infrastructure directly opposite Uri was planned so that those who had launched the attack on 18 September would get the right message. 'The idea was to let them know that we know where you are based and where you launch your attacks from and more importantly, we know where to hit you. The message had to go up to Muzafarabad (the capital of PoK),' Col H said, reflecting upon the week in the run up to the actual operation.

The two Colonels were however critical of the media frenzy and pressure built by hyperbolic discussions on news channels that not only put pressure on the government, but also alerted the adversary. They knew that the essence of special operations lay in surprise, but no one in the media seemed to understand. 'There was endless rhetoric on TV Channels with some of our own army veterans theorising about what can be done, what is possible, giving ideas to the adversary. We in Special Forces abhor such public discussion,' the duo said. 'We prefer to be formless, an unknown entity that creates doubt in the minds of the adversary,' said Col K. As Sandeep Unnithan wrote about the surgical strikes in *India Today*, the Para-SF (short for Parachute Regiment-Special Forces) operatives know how to make themselves almost invisible in the area of their operations, 'They blended into the rugged topography because they had reduced their four S-es: shape, shine, silhouette, and smell. Their combat fatigues blended into the forest, and their faces were streaked with camouflage paint. Their skin was covered in a thin film of mud to suppress body odour. Their weapons had been blackened. They had lain in ambush for over 48 hours.

Both went about preparing meticulously, but at one point a flicker of doubt crossed Col H's mind as his team kept getting feedback of the situation on the chosen targets. 'We could see they were visibly beefing up their security. This, for a moment, made me think: is this going to affect my extrication plan? Will my boys get into a running fight? Later on, however, I felt that more the merrier (the number of people in the camps). We can inflict more damage,' Col H said, revealing conflicting thoughts in his mind in the run-up to the strike.

Week-long surveillance through HUMINT and satellite pictures revealed that the nature of deployment in the camps close to the LoC was being changed. Normally, Pakistani forces, especially in PoK and around terrorist camps, lounge around in Pathani suits and casual attire in border areas, but about a week after the Uri attack, spotters revealed a change in demeanour. More people were wearing uniforms now. There were signs that senior officers were about to visit these camps—a rare occurrence.

Back in the SF units, from 20 September onwards, preparations were in full swing. In that entire week in the run up to the actual strike, Hizbul Mujahideen operatives and other sources were providing the teams with important bits of intelligence about the targets. Images from ISRO satellites and pictures taken by Unmanned Aerial Vehicles were being used to corroborate the inputs provided by the human intelligence sources. The plan was finally taking shape. By 25 September, the teams were confident of going in at any time that the leadership decided. Coincidentally, the previous evening, the Prime Minister had already given the go-ahead, but the actual time and date were left to the people on ground. 'The Northern Army Commander told us on 26th that you are on a short notice,' Col K recalls.

For 72 hours—26 to 28 September—the two teams kept reviewing the plans, going over the routes, the terrain, and the return path, in their mind's eye. They were like musicians, rehearsing notes in their heads before a major performance. Except this was not a stage show. And there was going to be no audience.

The HM sources and SF surveillance teams, keeping a watch on the likely targets meanwhile reported major changes in some of the camps and in their vicinity (*see Plates 12 and 13*).

The HM operatives through their own knowledge of the area and also from their interaction with some Pakistani soldiers reported back that they could see a lot of movement in the camps. They said old sentries were changed and some specialised teams appeared to have arrived to beef up security. In short, the level of alertness had gone up. Says Col K, 'They (the Pakistanis) obviously had an inkling that something may happen, but given the large frontage of the LoC, they were not sure where (the attack could take place).' Adds Col H: 'It was a guessing game. Our scouts reported arrival of reinforcements. Behaviour on the targets had changed. It was not business as usual for them (the adversary) either. Now it was a matter of when and where.'

The wait was now getting shorter. It was finally over on 28 September.

That afternoon, Lt Gen Hooda signalled the launch of Operation X when he called both Col H and Col K. Separately, he wished them a simple 'good luck' and told them to go ahead and complete the assigned task.

Teams surged forward by late evening, poised on the edge of the LoC, ready to cross over later that night.

Back in Delhi, Gen Dalbir briefed NSA Doval about the mission plan and worked out a mechanism to update him as and when he received inputs from the ground.

'The die was cast now. The onus was on the Army that I was leading to deliver. But I was confident of our success,' Gen Dalbir recalls. Parrikar, meanwhile, was separately briefed about the roll-out of the action plan by the Army Chief.

OPERATION X

28–29 September 2016, J&K

From here onward, teams led by Col K and Col H were on their own. All of it depended on their skills, daring, ingenuity, and above all, determination to succeed in whether they would accomplish the task assigned to them.

There was no looking back now.

The operation, called Operation X in conversation but not officially named as such, was being monitored at Army HQ in Delhi, at the Northern Command HQ in Udhampur, and at Nagrota and Srinagar, the HQs of 16 and 15 Corps respectively.

As Prime Time television debates across different news channels were just about winding down, Col K's teams were making their way to the LoC. Col K, assigned to target camps south of the Pir Panjal range, led his teams across the LoC around midnight. In four hours, they were in close proximity of the objectives. Having bypassed some of the outposts close to the LoC on the Pakistani side, the teams were now truly behind enemy lines.

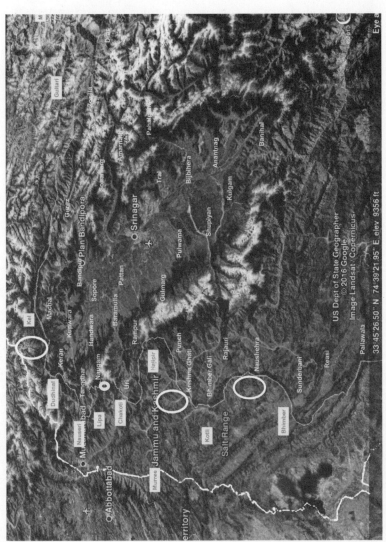

The LoC between India and Pakistan: Circles denote camps inside PoK that were hit in the surgical strikes

The camps—launch pads-cum-waiting areas for terrorists, co-located with Pakistani Army's forward establishments—that Col K's teams had chosen to target were in the Kanna area opposite the Nangi Tekri and Balnui battalions of the Indian Army. One of the camps in PoK, called Roshni crossing point, was located much deeper than others but Col K wanted to hit where it hurt, so even though there was a greater risk of retaliation, the SF teams eventually targeted it.

Some 300 km away, north of Pir Panjal, Col H and his team had also crossed the LoC. Their targets were in the general area of Kel and Lippa.

The most critical period of the operation had now commenced.

'We had observed the target closely and had mapped the behaviour pattern there. The best time to strike in the judgement of our reconnaissance team was around dawn or just an hour before that when the guard was at its lowest. But the Army Commander wanted us to wait, since the plan by the other team in the north was to hit the target at first light,' Col K revealed.

The difference of time over target between the two teams had an inherent risk. What if Pakistani formations south of Pir Panjal—once they were targeted—alerted others all along the LoC? What if the camps that Col H was to target was then fortified? What if the second team got ambushed even before they could strike?

All these thoughts crossed Lt Gen Hooda's mind, but eventually, he acceded to Col K's request. Col H was accordingly warned about the timing and the possible fallout of that decision.

As the teams moved in for the kill, close monitoring radar images indicated minimal activity in the camps with lax security.

Col K's teams spread out and got closer to the camp, they opened fire simultaneously, took out the sentries first and then rained accurate fire from their Cal Gustaf rocket launchers, M-4 Carbines, under barrel grenade launchers clipped on rifles and grenade launchers that spewed half a dozen grenades at one go. As the Special Forces Team unleashed its firepower on unsuspecting occupants of the Pakistani army-protected terrorist camp, all hell broke loose. The Special Forces troops, raring to get into action for a long time, used their precision weapons systems and their hand-to-hand combat skills when some of the occupants tried to resist the raid. Then they proceeded to completely destroy the camp and eliminate almost all occupants.

They of course had no intention to wait and do the headcount. Having accomplished their task, they quickly started making their way back. The team now decided to take a circuitous route to avoid any remote possibility of interdiction by the Pakistani forces. Thus, instead of taking the shorter, easier route, the teams went deeper into PoK and guided by advanced GPS system, as well as continuous feed from a UAV, made their way back to the LoC, avoiding possible Pakistani deployments.

Meanwhile, Col H's time over target was still two hours away.

Anxiety began to gnaw Lt Gen Hooda and his Corps Commander in the Kashmir Valley, Lt Gen Satish Dua. Col H's team was poised for a strike, but was not willing to be rushed into it until there was sufficient light for them to see the target clearly.

'Even before the operation started I had kept a two-line resignation letter in my pocket, lest anything went wrong. The buck needed to stop with me just in case something went wrong,' Lt Gen Hooda told me looking back at those anxious hours.

Thus, the seniors at the Command and Corps Headquarters had no choice but to wait anxiously.

As the clock ticked away, Col K's team meanwhile was safely back inside Indian territory, in the 16 Corps area of jurisdiction.

Lt Gen Nimbhorkar was pleased, but he too was now waiting to hear from across the Pir Panjal.

At dawn, Col H's men, primed and eager to pounce on the large administrative base and several launch pads deep inside PoK that they had in their sights on for past week, stealthily moved forward. As they neared the camp, it was clear from the casual movement of the sentries that no one had expected any attack at this time of the day. A few souls were up and about, perhaps answering nature's call early.

Wasting no time and showing no mercy, Col H and his men opened fire with their lethal weapons, aiming at living quarters and what looked like an ammunition depot. As the occupants, mostly Pakistani soldiers and many men in Pathan suits (mostly terrorists) tried to escape the firing, a lot of fell to the bullets. Barracks caught fire, there were at least three loud explosions as the Special Forces vented all their pent-up frustration on the hapless and utterly surprised Pakistanis, eliminating the token resistance put up by some occupants.

The raid over, Col K and team were now hurrying back. In such cases, extrication from behind enemy lines is more difficult than the attack itself. They had to cover at least four to five kilometres over a mountainous terrain in broad daylight. Will the Pakistanis bring the Air Force into play? Will helicopters chase them? The decision makers in Udhampur and Srinagar were thinking along these lines as they kept a close watch.

As the strike teams made their way back, one of the boys stepped on a landmine closer to the Indian side. His injury was not life threatening. In the meantime, two unmanned aerial vehicles (UAV), keeping a close watch on the progress of Col H's team, recorded huge explosions at the camp site. A particularly longish sequence showed many people running helter-skelter and falling to the ground.

Barring one minor injury, Operation X had gone off with clockwork precision. Complete surprise was achieved, resulting in the higher fatalities in the camps-cum-launch pads of the Pakistanis. It also validated many conceptual plans made over the years for trans-LoC operations.

So what was the death count? I asked the two COs.

Both were candid, admitting they didn't stop to count the dead. 'That was neither our remit nor the objective of the strike. We had been given a job to destroy selected targets to send a message. In light of which we performed to the best of our abilities. We can't give you exact figures. No one can, but what we saw with our eyes in those moments, tells us that we would have accounted for at least 70–75 fellows combined,' both Col K and H tell me. Later that day, radio chatter from across the LoC reportedly confirmed at least 80 fatalities in the camps that were hit by Indian Special Forces.

Looking back, Col H remarks that the Pakistanis were too dazed to react. One or two fellows who had the weapons within reach tried to retaliate but to no real effect. While the Indian government decided to make only one statement officially (by the then DGMO, Lt Gen Ranbir Singh), the Pakistanis chose to keep absolutely quiet.

Media reports on both sides of the border naturally varied in their style and content. One report in the *Indian Express*, quoting residents in PoK said: 'Eyewitnesses living across the Line of Control (LoC) have provided the *Indian Express* with graphic accounts of last week's Indian Army Special Forces strikes on jihadists' staging posts, describing how bodies of those killed in clashes before dawn on 29 September were loaded onto trucks for secret burials. The eyewitnesses also described brief but intense fire engagements that destroyed makeshift buildings housing jihadists before they left for the last stage of their journeys across the LoC.'

The *Dawn* newspaper, perhaps Pakistan's most authentic news source, was sceptical. In a news report headlined 'Was it really a surgical strike?' the paper quoted Lt Gen Bajwa, man in-charge of of ISPR (Inter-Services Public Relations), 'How is it possible that the target of a 'surgical strike' has no idea it took place?' he said. 'This was simply an episode of cross-LoC fire that they [India] have been doing. Small arms and mortars were used in the fire, similar to what has been used before...we gave a befitting response.' In India too, there were sceptical voices mainly because the government chose not to release either video footage (taken by the raiding teams or by the hovering UAVs) or photographs. The Prime Minister and his top security advisers decided to be ambiguous and secretive about the strikes. Even those with whom I spoke to, in order to piece together this account, were cautious in not giving out details that would jeopardise future operations of a similar kind. Denials by the Pakistani Army notwithstanding, in effect, the intended humiliation was strong.

For the first time, all bodies were taken away from the site to unknown destinations. Normally, if soldiers or terrorists are killed in any Indian firing, the victims are buried right next to the camp or in the nearest village.

After the surgical strike however, bodies were piled up in trucks by soldiers—and not by villagers as is normally the case—and transported out. The intent was clear: if the villagers came to know of the big losses suffered by the Pakistani Army and the tanzeems, the image of invincibility that had been carefully built over decades would be shattered. Over the next few days, Pakistanis were busy living in denial. Their patrolling became defensive and firing only speculative. More detachments started coming in to reinforce formations near the LoC.

Clearly, the tactical operation had achieved the strategic impact. Indeed, the effect of the cross-border strikes went beyond the security domain.

In fact, the global financial world, focused on India as an attractive investment destination was quite concerned over the possible fallout of the surgical strikes on the financial markets and India's economy. Within hours of the Indian DGMO going public about the Indian operations, I was part of many television discussions. In the middle of juggling appearances on the panel discussions, I remember receiving an unexpected call from Neelkanth Mishra, India Equity Strategist of Credit Suisse, a top global investment firm.

We didn't know each other from before but Mishra was on the line to ask if I could join a conference call with a few investors based in the US and Europe to give my assessment on the likely consequences of India's surgical strikes. I had never done this before but was reasonably confident about giving accurate assessment of the likely fallout. Within an hour, I was on the conference call, along with noted strategic affairs analyst Bharat Karnad. The nearly 70-min long conversation focused on the possibility of an all-out war and the likelihood of India having to increase its defence spending.

Mishra was good enough to send me a gist of the recorded conversation we had that day—29 September 2016. Here's the summary of what we said then:

- A further escalation is unlikely (i) India calls it an 'anti-terror' operation, and only attacked launch-pads, not any military camp; and (ii) Indian action fits the principle of 'proportionate response.'

- This may be a stabilising event and not a de-stabilising one because: (i) It sets a precedent and an action-reaction sequence that can discourage future provocations; (ii) It called Pakistan's 'nuclear bluff' (it never existed); (iii) and no public pressure/criticism of India by any of the big powers.

- Heightened preparedness on the LoC/border doesn't require additional troop mobilisation or significant spending for now and should stay within the budget.

Almost a year later, both Karnad and I have not been proved wrong, despite the fact that we were speaking with limited knowledge of the cross-LoC raids.

LESSONS LEARNED

Three crucial points stand out from the entire episode.

One, the fact that the simultaneous strikes were conducted for the first time on such a massive scale across a large frontage of nearly 250 km of the LoC—from Kel sector of Pakistan opposite Kupwara to Bhimber Sector opposite Naushera—was indeed a remarkable achievement.

Two, the planning and execution was done in complete secrecy, and no one, least of all the Pakistani Army, could anticipate such an operation.

Finally, the confidence shown by the decision-makers in the ability of the Indian Army leadership and its Special Forces is noteworthy. Once the political call was taken, it was left to the Army Chief to decide on the time and place of the strike. Gen Dalbir in turn let Northern Command handle the planning even while keeping a close watch on the larger picture. Before giving the final go ahead, Prime Minister Modi and his team had factored in the possibility of any escalation based on briefings by the military.

The fallout of the decision to strike across the LoC *and* own it at the highest level has had many consequences both in military and in strategic terms.

To begin with, the government's pro-active strategic initiative has given the military a signal that it need not perpetually be bound by a defensive or reactive approach in dealing with the proxy war waged by Pakistan in J&K.

By introducing an element of uncertainty in its response on the LoC and beyond, the military has now compelled the Pakistani establishment to dwell upon the nature of the escalatory dynamic that may inform its choices. When the surgical strikes were carried out in September 2016, India had factored in the possibility of Pakistan widening the conflict. That it did not do so—for a variety of reasons, from the then impending change of guard at the top in the Pakistani Army to the lack of preparedness of its military—is not a definitive conclusion that Pakistan will not try to retaliate in the future to a similar action across the LoC.

On the other hand, the Modi government's proactive stand on the military front—both against Pakistan and China—means that Pakistan will have to think twice before climbing the escalatory ladder. If, for instance, GHQ was to escalate the violence beyond the current level *after* a similar surgical strike in PoK, it runs the risk of freeing the Indian decision makers from their perceived hesitation to launch the cold start campaign that seeks to launch swift conventional military attacks into the Punjabi heartland of Pakistan. If that happens, will Pakistan be ready to face the consequences? Can it afford a wider conflict? That's a question that needs a detailed analysis elsewhere.

One aspect however is undeniable in the aftermath of the successful surgical strikes: India has opened up the space between a defensive response to the proxy war and an all-out conventional response below the nuclear threshold in the form of the surgical strikes.

Interestingly, despite most Pakistani writers and commentators going along with the Pakistani Army's denials, a senior Pakistani political analyst blamed Rawalpindi for continued hostility towards India. Within days of the surgical strikes, noted Pakistani political analyst Munir Saami confirmed that India carried out surgical strikes in PoK. In an interview to a Canadian news channel, Saami said that denial by Islamabad is meaningless in this context.

Saami said, 'If they (Pakistani establishment) admit to the surgical strikes carried out by India, it would be difficult for them to explain the situation to the people of Pakistan.'

'How will they tell the people that Indian army crossed the LoC? It's like a bone stuck in their throat. They want to take it out, but it's difficult for them to do so and that's why they are saying that the surgical strikes did not take place,' Saami told the news channel. According to Saami, India's patience had worn out on account of the continued terror attacks launched from across the border. He said, 'What happened (the surgical strikes) this time was due to the fact that India suffered in Mumbai, Pathankot and Uri.'

'We started this story (of cross-border terrorism) and now we want the world to support us. Unfortunately, the world is not supporting Pakistan,' Saami candidly said.

The surgical strikes also seemed to have garnered cautious support from the international community. The US government, while stressing the need for de-escalation of hostilities between India and Pakistan, reiterated its support for India's fight in combating terrorism. Chinese foreign ministry spokesperson, Geng Shuang, on the other hand said 'as shared neighbour and friend to both India and Pakistan, we are concerned about continuous confrontation and tensions between India and Pakistan.'

Russia too supported India, stating that it stood for 'decisive struggle against terrorism in all its manifestations.' In an interview given to an Indian news network, the then Russian Ambassador to India, Late Alexander Kadakin, said that 'the greatest human rights violations take place when terrorists attack military installations and attack peaceful civilians in India. We welcome the surgical strike. Every country has the right to defend itself.' A spokesperson for the British Foreign Office said, 'we are monitoring the situation closely following reports of strikes carried out by the Indian Army over the LoC in Kashmir. We call on both sides to exercise restraint and to open dialogue.'

Other neighbours in South Asia also backed India. The Bangladesh Prime Minister's adviser, Iqbal Chowdhury was forthright: 'India has got the legal, internationally accepted right to make a response to any attack on her sovereignty and her soil.'

Within the Indian military too, there is an acceptance that the Modi government is willing to employ force when necessary. Both the cross-border strikes (Myanmar and PoK) have demonstrated the willingness of the political executive leadership to unshackle the military when necessary. The proactive, specific and focused intelligence-driven operations against terrorists in J&K in 2017 are part of the fresh approach to tackle the Pakistan-backed proxy war. It must be noted that over 140 terrorists have been eliminated between January and August 2017.

It is however not necessary that India will exercise the option of another set of surgical strikes in case of another outrageous terrorist attack. There could be other methods to use as a retaliatory tool. A pro-active and bold leadership thus enables the military to think of different options rather than those which are predictable.

Clearly, the military leadership has war-gamed possible scenarios to give a realistic assessment to the NSA, and the Prime Minister, who should feel confident that the Indian military has the logistics, required lethal firepower, and requisite skills to meet any challenge.

The willpower of the nation was of course demonstrated earlier that year in Pathankot too.

11

Pathankot: Averting a Catastrophe

1500 hours, 1 January 2016, Subroto Park, New Delhi

Air Marshal Shirish B Deo had just finished a late but relaxed lunch at Trishul House, the official bungalow he was staying at in New Delhi's Subroto Park at that time.

As Chief of the Western Air Command, he was responsible for air operations across a vast area, stretching from the formidable heights of Ladakh in the north-west to the deserts of Rajasthan to the south–west of Delhi. Deo had spent over 35 years as an ace fighter pilot, survived two ejections, and was at the pinnacle of his distinguished career.

Little did the Western Air Command Chief know that he was about to embark on a journey that would pose a challenge which he could not have dreamt of facing as an air force officer.

1515 hours, 1 January 2016, Subroto Park

The secure phone in Trishul House rang persistently.

As Deo answered the call, he heard the familiar voice of his Air Chief Marshal Arup Raha on the other end. 'Shirish, there's a problem. I am coming from a meeting with the NSA. A definite intel suggests Pathankot is about to be attacked. Issue immediate instructions to be on the highest alert and increase patrolling. The Army and Punjab Police are also being informed of the specific information,' the Air Chief said.

The meeting that Air Chief Marshal Raha was speaking about had begun at 1340 hours in the office of the National Security

Adviser Ajit Doval. Doval's office had made hurried calls to the Army Chief Gen Dalbir Singh, ACM Raha, Rajinder Khanna, head of India's External Intelligence Agency, Research and Analyses Wing (R&AW), and Director of Intelligence Bureau (DIB) Dineshwar Sharma to assemble for the meeting.

After hour-long deliberations, a detailed plan of action was approved by the NSA and all concerned were asked to move without any loss of time. The strike he felt 'could now take place at any moment'. We should reach the target area before they do, the NSA told the assembled officers. 'One who outsmarts the terrorist in speed, surprise and skill will carry the day,' Doval remembers telling his top security managers.

For the previous three weeks, India's Intelligence agencies—the Intelligence Bureau, the National Technical Research Organisation (NTRO), and the Research and Analysis Wing (R&AW)—had tapped into terrorist chatter from across the border, tracked suspicious movements of terrorists, and received valuable Humint (Human intelligence) from Pakistan, to arrive at a definite conclusion that a group of terrorists had been assigned to attack a major Indian military installation in Punjab, or in the Jammu region.

Information about recovery of Punjab Police officer Salwinder Singh's commandeered vehicle at Tajpur, about 4 km from Pathankot air base the previous day, also flowed in to Delhi. The SP had meanwhile informed the Punjab Police that there were four armed occupants in the vehicle when he was let off (*see box*).

As the world woke up to a New Year, a fresh challenge was being mounted on the border.

The lead was consolidated further by 12 noon as Indian intelligence agents intercepted three calls to Pakistan in quick succession from the vicinity of Tajpur-Pathankot (*see Appendix II*). It was now clear that a group of terrorists were on the loose in the area even though the target their handlers had given them was not clear. Urgent preventive action was clearly needed.

As a senior intelligence officer recalls, 'Pathankot was not a tip off. It was an assessment that had been arrived at after Indian agencies had analysed a series of intelligence inputs. India had zeroed in on a terrorist handler based in Sialkot. In fact, on 31st December, our NSA actually conveyed this definite information to Pakistan's NSA (Lt Gen Nasser Khan Janjua). We had lot of specific information that was passed on to the Pakistani NSA. We even sent him the fellow's telephone number and coordinates based in Sialkot and asked him to take immediate action. Gen Janjua assured us he would take immediate action and not allow the attack to go through. But nothing happened (*see Plate 14*).'

Doval, with a lifetime of experience spent in the shadowy and secretive world of intelligence, instantly recognised that they had a serious problem at hand. The area around Pathankot-Mamun had several high value military installations, but none more tempting than the Pathankot air base. 'We may be on a very short fuse and unless we respond faster than the terrorists, we might be in for a serious disaster', he told the Army and the Air Chief, the DIB and Secretary who had assembled in his office on 1 January.

'In theory, a frontline strategic air base like Pathankot has always been vulnerable to terrorist attacks, but now the possibility was real,' the NSA added.

Any damage to the fighter aircraft and other high value assets based in Pathankot would have been a major setback for the Indian establishment and a massive publicity for the terrorists. No one, not even the NSA however knew for certain whether only Pathankot

Juicy target: The Pathankot Air base

Embarking on a crucial mission: Members of NSG's 51 SAG on board the IL-76

was the target. He and his advisers assumed that any of the military establishments could come under attack.

'I knew there was no time to lose. The priority was to prevent the attack,' the NSA recalled in our recent conversation.

Without a moment's hesitation, he decided to take the lead and get cracking, since there was no time to go through bureaucratic rituals. The defence and security top brass—all of them probably skipped their lunch—assembled in the NSA's chamber in the South Block.

'We discussed and decided only the actions that were to be taken. Eight columns of the Army were moved first by Western Command. Para Commandos from Nahan were asked to reach Pathankot forthwith,' Gen Dalbir Singh recalls. By 1630 hours the Western Air Command chief too was on his way to Pathankot with Garuds (IAF's own commandos) followed by the National Security Guards (NSG).

The decision to send the NSG was in fact a masterstroke.

During the meeting in his office, Doval had sought suggestions on how best to tackle the situation. Air Chief Arup Raha and Army Chief Dalbir Singh had both agreed that besides mobilising Army columns and Garuds, it would be prudent to send the NSG just in case terrorists tried to get into any built-up area or living quarters in any of the military establishments. With over 10,000 non-combatants—families and civilian employees—living on the air base, the possibility of a hostage situation could not be ruled out either.

For such a situation, the NSG would be best suited, Doval reasoned.

So as the meeting broke up, Doval told the NSG to get its crack 51 Special Action Group (SAG) commandos ready for immediate deployment.

1545 hours, 1 January 2016, WAC HQ, Subroto Park, New Delhi

Meanwhile, back at the Western Air Command, Deo's mind was already racing ahead of his thoughts. What if the terrorists were already inside the base? Having served there as a young officer, Deo knew that the base was one of the biggest in Asia with its 2000 acre area and 25 km perimeter wall. Guarding every inch of the area had always been a tough task; searching for someone determined to hide was going to be tougher. Especially, considering that the compound had many wooded and grassy patches.

As C-in-C, he was also aware of the important part played by the Pathankot base in guarding India's airspace close to the Pakistan border. Squadrons based here had played a crucial role in the IAF's spectacular show during the 1965 and 1971 wars. As the frontline air base, it was home to important fighter squadrons, missile, and radar assets. Damage to any of these strategic assets would be disastrous, he conjectured, as he planned his departure.

As soon as the call with the Chief ended, Deo summoned his Staff Officer, Squadron Leader Yashu Bhardwaj and gave him multiple instructions: 'Get the Embraer ready; tell ops room I am headed to Pathankot; get me AOC Pathankot (Air Com J S Dhamoon) on the line; get SASO to meet me at Palam...'

In less than 30 minutes, Deo's Embraer (the 14-seater transport aircraft used by senior officers of the three forces and important ministers) was ready for take-off from Palam. The Western Air Command Chief had decided to rush to Pathankot, one of the IAF's most important frontline air bases.

Bhardwaj remembers rushing back home—a stone's throw away from Trishul House—stuffing a couple of sets of uniforms and getting into the light green overalls all air warriors have to wear when flying in the service aircraft. Luckily, Delhi's Palam airport was just a 10-minute drive away from the Western Air Command HQ.

As the Commander-in-Chief's car reached the Palam Technical area, acting SASO (Senior Air Staff Officer) Air Vice Marshal DS Rawat walked up to Deo. Rawat, then Air Defence Commander in the Command was standing in for Air Marshal B Suresh who was on leave. At that moment, he was effectively the number 2 in the command. Deo and Rawat conferred for two to three minutes. Meanwhile, Deo got through to Dhamoon. 'I told him to not to take any chances,' Deo remembers vividly. 'Search every area and make sure everyone is on his toes,' the Air Marshal told the station commander at Pathankot.

1630 hours, 1 January, Palam Airport

The Air Officer Commanding-in-Chief, Western Air Command, along with his SO was airborne en route to Pathankot.

For Sqn Leader Bhardwaj, this was a totally new experience. 'I have travelled with Deo Sir on a number of sudden trips, but this was something else. As soon as we were air borne, I learnt Sir had asked for a stopover at Adampur (another IAF base in Punjab). We landed there in 15–20 minutes. Six Garuds, in battle gear clambered on board and we were off again,' Bhardwaj recalls.

In fact for Bhardwaj too, it was the first glimpse of a Garud in full battle gear. 'A young, fit Sikh airman in the Garud uniform was in fact sitting on the seat next to me,' Bhardwaj remembers. The young Sikh was Gursewak Singh, the man who made the first contact with the terrorists before being fatally hit later that night.

'I thought it's better to take a small team of Garuds to Pathankot, just in case,' Deo remembers. At that point they were available at Adampur, hence the stopover.

1740 hours, 1 January 2016 Pathankot Airbase

Air Commodore Dhamoon, Air Officer Commanding of the base received his boss, Air Marshal Deo and acknowledged the arrival of the Garuds. As Deo donned a bulletproof jacket and picked up an AK-47, he and Dhamoon got into the AOC's car and drove away for an inspection of the base and to take stock of its peripheral security (*see Plate 15*).

As already mentioned, spread over 2000 acres with several patches of thick shrubs and trees, Pathankot is not an easy area to secure. More importantly, besides fighter planes, it is also the base for India's attack helicopters. Furthermore, that week, Pathankot was also hosting a group of foreign military officers undergoing training on the base. By all accounts, Pathankot was quite vulnerable to a terrorist attack.

As Dhamoon drove his boss around, Deo was informed that the IAF had requisitioned troops from nearby cantonments, but they were yet to arrive since the army was also securing its own bases.

Deo and Dhamoon reached the technical or the core area (where the aircraft are parked). The C-in-C realised he needed more boots on the ground to guard the ammunition depot and the huge residential area. Another request was sent to the Army to rush troops to guard valuable assets. Simultaneously, a systematic search was launched by the Air Force personnel across the mammoth base.

By evening, Western Command, on instructions of Army Chief Gen Dalbir Singh, had deployed Army columns around Pathankot and over 20 odd military installations in the area, assisting the local police in patrolling and establishing nakas/barriers and beefing up general area security. The Army Chief had told Lt Gen KJ Singh, then the Western Army Commander, of the meeting with NSA and the intelligence that was shared. 'I remember telling KJ since the intel is generic, let us secure all bases. They could come for any one of our cantonments. Make sure each one of them is well-secured.'

Even before the Army Chief had called the Western Army Commander, Lt Gen KJ remembers getting the first tip off about a bunch of terrorists on the loose around 1630 hours on 1 January from the DG of Punjab Police. The DGP had come to the conclusion that the terrorists who had let off Senior SP Salwinder Singh and his friend the previous night even as they commandeered his vehicle, were lurking around in the vicinity of Mamun-Pathankot. The tip off was followed by a short conversation with Army Chief Gen Dalbir Singh who called after the meeting in the NSA's office to tell his Western Army Commander about the decisions at the conference in Delhi.

'The DGP wanted the Army to mount a search for the terrorists immediately,' Lt Gen KJ told me, recalling that New Year's day. 'My question to him was, where do we search? Army can be deployed in a specific area but we can't be searching all over the place like the police, I remember telling the DGP,' Lt Gen KJ revealed.

The DG promised to come back with more details, but the Western Army Commander was not about to take chances given that one of the largest Army cantonments—Mamun—was in the area that was thought to be on the terrorists' radar. 'A quick vulnerability analysis in my mind told me that many of my smaller units in the vicinity would be easy picking. So I quickly ordered Infantry QRTs (Quick Reaction Teams) to guard the vulnerable establishments which had little or no perimeter protection.' Next, the Western Army Commander moved a team of Special Forces soldiers from Samba to Mamun and replaced the Samba team with a back-up contingent from Nahan to Samba.

Soldiers at the Mamun-based Division were also kept on high alert in case they were needed at multiple locations. 'At that stage, no one knew the location of the group of terrorists. All that we knew (because of the intercept) was that the armed terrorists had got into some base.' Lt Gen KJ says, looking back at that eventful evening.

A coordination mechanism with Punjab Police was established immediately as the search for the terrorist group was further intensified.

The police had been in fact on the lookout for a group of terrorists since 31 December after Gurdaspur SP Salwinder Singh had claimed that his car was waylaid by four gun-toting terrorists (*see NIA chargesheet Appendix II*). However, the police search was not thorough enough as subsequent events were to prove.

1700 hours, 1 January 2016, 7 Race Course Road

In New Delhi meanwhile, even as Deo was on his way to Pathankot, NSA Doval drove to the Prime Minister's residence to brief him on the emerging threat.

'I told the PM what had transpired so far and the measures that had been taken. I also remember telling him that our assessment may be completely off the mark, but we were not going to take any chances,' Doval tells me while remembering the incidents of that crucial day. I asked the NSA what the Prime Minister's reaction was. Was he disappointed that soon after his attempt to reach out to Pakistan (the PM had made an unscheduled stopover at Lahore just a week prior, to meet his counterpart Nawaz Sharif), the Pakistanis had chosen to launch another terrorist attack? 'Well, he was quite cool and composed. He knew a serious problem was at hand and his resolve to meet the threat squarely was quite visible. He gave specific directions and wanted us to ensure that our vital air assets and personnel were protected. The Prime Minister also wanted us to redouble our efforts to locate and neutralise the terrorists. Though he wanted us to clear the area of the terrorists at the earliest, the Prime Minister did not betray any anxiety. I thought it was his implicit faith and confidence in the ability of our forces. I do not remember him mentioning anything about his Lahore visit. He was focussed on nothing but the problem at hand,' the NSA told me

But why wasn't the Cabinet Committee on Security (CCS)— the highest decision-making body on security matters in the country—convened, I asked the NSA.

The NSA's answer reveals his practical side. 'Assuming that CCS was called, what would have been the question in front of the CCS to decide? Whether to take immediate counter measures and neutralise the attack? Could it have said anything else except to issue instructions to counter the threat and neutralise it? The process would have only delayed the whole process by several hours and if terrorists had fired one bullet, it would have been impossible to land an aircraft (at Pathankot). The NSG, Garuds, and army commandos would have potentially reached there hours after the terrorists had taken position. So the whole criticism is misdirected. There was no option but to take the decision right then and there. In an emergency, on-the-spot decisions need to be taken. The country has trained and positioned us to take the responsibility. If we do not take that responsibility when the country's vital security interests are endangered, what is the justification for us to be there,' he wondered.

Doval, who led the negotiating team in the infamous Kandahar hijack episode in December 1999, had clearly learnt his lessons. That time the Crisis Management Committee and the CCS took an inordinately long time to arrive at a decision. By the time it was convened, the plane had already taken off from Amritsar when it could easily have been neutralised in Amritsar.

Delay and dithering in decision-making at the highest level in Delhi and the bumbling security establishment on the ground had forced India to release Masood Azhar and others in exchange for passengers on the Indian Airlines plane. Doval still simmers with anger on the shameful handling of the hijack crisis because affected families, instead of showing patience and faith in their security agencies, virtually forced the Government to wilt under the pressure of the public mood. Many people in official positions insisted on following protocol when the need was to take urgent action. Doval was mortified to witness the release of Masood, the dreaded terrorist. The same Masood would then go on to form the Jaish-e-Mohammad, whose operatives were now about to launch an attack on a military installation in Pathankot.

Clearly, Doval was not about to repeat the mistakes of 1999, convention be damned.

2100 hours, 1 January 2016, Pathankot

Back at the base, Air Marshal Deo, having finished the tour and inspected the measures taken by the AOC, came to the officers' mess to stay put. He had ordered that Mi-35 helicopters and Remotely Piloted Vehicles (RPA) be launched in the evening to enhance surveillance and detection in the dark. A C-130 flight was due to arrive later that night to further increase surveillance across the vast air base. The RPAs and C-130 were both equipped with night vision capability.

Deo also knew that an NSG team was on its way to Pathankot on the dedicated IL-76 plane that is always on standby at Palam for them. The NSG's counter-terrorism task force I (CTTF-I) or 51 Special Action Group (SAG) contingent consisted of 140 specially selected and trained soldiers on deputation from the Army.

The NSG squad was capable of tackling both terror and hijack situations. The operational commander of the 51 SAG was Brig Gautam Ganguly. Originally a Grenadier Regiment soldier, Ganguly had come on deputation to the NSG to head the 51 SAG that looks after counter-terror operations. Maj Gen Dushyant Singh, the IG (Operations), who had relinquished command of an

The NSG's CTTF-I Lands at Pathankot

Infantry division in Jammu (and hence was intricately familiar with the general area and topography of the area around Pathankot), also accompanied the NSG squad to Pathankot.

The decision to send the NSG to Pathankot was to save the day.

By the time the NSG team alighted with all their special equipment, it was past 2200 hours on 1 January 2016.

They were supposed to have driven out of the Pathankot base and stayed at an accommodation arranged for them at the nearby Mamun Army cantonment. 'Somehow, to me it didn't seem right to leave Pathankot since I knew the base had valuable air assets and did not have enough protection,' Brig Ganguly recalls thinking that night.

On that pure hunch—call it gut feeling, describe it as instinct honed by years of experience—the NSG squad stayed back on the base and was assigned to secure the technical area where the aircrafts are parked.

That one hunch was to prove decisive in the next few hours. The Garuds were also primed and ready!

As the night progressed, everyone, from the sentries on duty to the Garuds, and from army soldiers to the NSG men, were on high alert.

The unstated strategy was to let terrorists show their hand IF they were inside the base.

0330 hours, 2 January 2016, Pathankot Air Base

The silence of the night was suddenly shattered by a burst of fire, most probably from an AK rifle. In the VIP suit of the Officers' Mess, Sqn Leader Bhardwaj was woken up by a knock on his door. A Wing Commander was standing at the door. 'The AOC has sent me to alert you and the C-in-C. Suspicious movement has been spotted inside the base. There is already some firing taking place. I am here to provide protection to the VIP suite,' Wing Commander Sarin told Bhardwaj. Sarin further added that one Garud had been killed as were two DSC guards.

One terrorist was also supposed to have been eliminated in the first contact. However, details were still hazy. Even as they were conversing, Air Marshal Deo called Bhardwaj on the phone. 'Where are you, Deo Sir asked me. I told him I was in the room. He said stay put, don't go out. We are under attack.' Even as they were speaking, Deo came to Bhardwaj's room.

'Take this weapon,' the AOC-in-C handed a pistol to his SO. So Bhardwaj took hold of the pistol while Deo himself was carrying an AK-47 and had put on a bullet proof jacket. They quickly switched off the lights and waited in the dark. The DSC guard outside was also told to be on alert. Wing Commander Sarin meanwhile went to the terrace to take guard even as Deo and Bhardwaj kept a watch from their positions. 'The only thought in my mind at that time was to make sure my boss was safe,' Bhardwaj, who was without a bullet-proof jacket, remembers distinctly. 'If he remained safe, everything else could be handled,' the SO thought to himself as he peered out into the dark, trying to make sense of what was happening out there.

Deo himself was all charged up. 'If it comes to the crunch, I will surely take down a couple of them,' he remembers thinking as he clutched the AK in his hand. The night however passed without any incident in the VIP suite.

Later, at first light, Deo was briefed about the first contact with the terrorists and what had transpired.

Evidently, images received from the RPA had indicated suspicious movement at about 0215 hours (*see photo*). The location of the terrorists was close to the western boundary wall near the small arms range. The Garuds were rushed there to check on the suspicious movement. As the Garuds started sanitising the area, slowly and methodically, first blocking the route to the family quarters, they came under sudden and heavy fire near the MES yard. Grenades were also hurled by the terrorists. The Garuds fired back.

The clinching evidence; image captured by IAF's asset showing terrorists location

The first contact with terrorists had been made.

In the ensuing fire fight, a heavy burst had hit Corporal Gursewak Singh, the Garud who had sat next to Bhardwaj on the plane. As he fell, three terrorists ran towards the DSC living billet.

As the Garuds chased the terrorists, they entered the DSC living quarters, firing indiscriminately. Five DSC men—all unarmed— died in the firing. But one of them, Sepoy Jagdish Chand jumped on a terrorist, wrestled with him and shot him dead with his own gun.

His action was reminiscent of a similar brave act by Constable Tukaram Ombale in the Mumbai attack of November 2008. Ignoring personal safety, Ombale had wrestled down Ajmal Amir Kasab. Without Kasab getting caught alive, it would have been difficult to prove that the 26/11 attacks was a Pakistani conspiracy. However, like Ombale, Jagdish Chand was shot down by another terrorist.

All this happened in a matter of minutes.

The three remaining terrorists ran away towards the open ground full of tall, thick elephant grass not very far from the DSC billet. As the Garuds, NSG men and DSC personnel got down to evacuating the injured, Ganguly started redeploying the available manpower.

Five unarmed DSC men and Corporal Gursewak had laid down their lives. One terrorist was killed.

Three were still at large. There was no time to mourn the dead. The threat to the air base, the families, and the air assets was real.

Pathankot was in lockdown as the sun rose on 2nd January.

0700 hours 2 January 2016, Pathankot Air Base

Deo decided to drive to the Air Traffic Control tower. Air Commodore Dhamoon and Maj Gen Dushyant Singh too had reached the ATC, now serving as the unofficial war room.

As they took stock of the situation, it was clear the terrorists were well armed and determined to cause maximum damage.

The priority therefore was to neutralise them without taking any more casualties or allowing any harm to critical air assets.

Deo decided to make sure the tarmac and the technical area was completely sealed although flying operations were allowed to continue.

On the ground meanwhile, the NSG, the Army troops and Garuds resumed their slow, deliberate search in the grassy area. Mi-35 attack helicopters were once again pressed into service. The helicopters made some 12 low passes, but the thick grass made it impossible to take accurate aim at the terrorists.

By 0900 hours it was clear that the three terrorists were holed up in the wooded area and firing intermittently whenever they thought the security forces were getting close.

In the meantime, the media had gathered in strength just outside the base, TV studios were trying to give a ball by ball commentary except that they did not know what was actually happening inside!

By noon, as the cordon started tightening, and more exchange of fire took place, terrorists were slowly running out of ammunition. By afternoon, NSG sharpshooters had picked one of the terrorists in the crosshairs of his sniper rifle. One of the three terrorists fell, hit by a precise shot. The remaining two terrorists held on, but by evening, the NSG commandos had neutralised both of them.

Bodies of three neutralised terrorists

Back in the ATC tower, Sqn Leader Bhardwaj was fielding multiple calls, answering a bank of phones and mobiles. Calls were coming from Raksha Mantri Parrikar, the Western Air Command control room, and the Air Chief. 'After the first hour, I became the de facto telephone operator, taking numerous calls and passing information both ways,' Bhardwaj remembers.

By evening, Brig Ganguly and rest of the ground forces had given the all clear signal, having eliminated the remaining three terrorists hiding in the tall grass.

The terrorists had been confined to a 250 m by 250 m area after the initial contact and were prevented from inflicting any further damage to the critical air assets or from taking any hostages.

As night fell on 2 January, a quiet sense of accomplishment was palpable.

From the Defence Minister to the Home Minister and from the NSG Chief to the Chief of Air Staff, everyone shared a word of congratulations on the successful completion of the operations.

Unlike in other such similar attacks on airfields and air bases in the recent past, it was ensured that no harm had come to the aircraft or the ammunition dump. Civilians too had been fully protected. The terrorists were in fact boxed into a small area and not allowed to run amok as they had done in similar attacks in Pakistan, Afghanistan and Sri Lanka.

Although six lives had been lost, the combined effort of all the forces and the timely intelligence that was generated had ensured a successful termination of operations.

Or so everyone thought.

0800 hours, 3 January 2016, Pathankot Air Base

The day after.

The task of sanitising the area and the search for any explosives left behind by the terrorists remained. The bomb disposal squad—an integral part of the 51 SAG—was led by Lt Col EK Niranjan, a Sapper officer. As he and his men started combing the grassy patch of land where the three terrorists were gunned down the previous evening, Deo and his staff arrived at the scene and after commending the excellent work done by the troops the previous day, he proceeded towards the administrative offices of the base.

Within minutes, the calm of the morning was shattered. Lt Col Niranjan and his men pulled out two of the three bodies from the thick grass and laid them out in an open space. The body of the third terrorist was proving difficult to be retrieved; it was repeatedly getting stuck in a ditch. So Niranjan and another soldier went closer to pull it out. Once they succeeded in getting the body to the open space, both were standing over it when Niranjan decided to check the terrorist's pockets. As soon as he opened his chest pocket, a huge blast blew up Niranjan and injured his buddy. The terrorist had kept a hand grenade primed by taking out its safety pin in the top pocket which had then exploded the moment Niranjan had touched his top pocket.

The NSG squad was devastated. Niranjan was rushed to the hospital on the base, but he succumbed to his injuries. This was a crushing blow. But even before the NSG squad could mourn Niranjan's death, sudden gun shots rang out from the two-storied airman's billet located right behind the open area where the terrorists' bodies were laid out.

Retrieving the bodies of killed terrorists

Lt Col EK Niranjan (right) moments before his unfortunate death

The airmen's billet, later burnt down

This was a shock. No one knew where the fire was coming from and who was firing. Everyone had thought all the terrorists had been neutralised.

Later some suspicion arrose whether there could still be more terrorists left. All precautions were taken and necessary search operations were carried out. They, however, turned out to be a false alarm.

The firing once again put all the forces back into action.

The 51 SAG men as well as the Army troops guarding the assets were back in alert mode.

The airmen's billet had been emptied the previous evening and the sound of firing stumped everyone. Were there more terrorists hiding?

The NSG men began their search once again. The periphery was sanitised once again. Cameras that could see beyond the wall—available with the NSG—were deployed to detect who, if any, was hiding inside the building. The cameras however failed to establish conclusively if any one was indeed holed up. The NSG, with its experience of the 2008 Mumbai attack, wanted to move slowly and deliberately.

It therefore took the entire day, probing every room with speculative fire, searching for any clue that could determine if there were more terrorists hiding.

Upon realising that no progress was being made, the NSG and Air Force decided to burn down the building and smoke-out—if they were sitting inside—terrorists. By evening, the building was gutted and as NSG men entered the shell of the barracks, stench inside the burnt down barracks was unbearable as Brig Ganguly remembers (*see Plates 16 and 17*).

Forensic experts were called in to figure out if indeed there were any human remains in the burnt down building. As it turned out, in absence of any bones or teeth, it couldn't be established if there had been more than two terrorists. The NIA therefore stuck to its finding even in the charge sheet that four terrorists had entered India and were finally eliminated.

By evening, a combination of heavy fire and incendiary material had completely gutted the building, bringing to an end the saga that had begun on the afternoon of 1 January with the meeting in the NSA's office.

As forensic and NIA (National Investigation Agency) teams arrived on the scene, it was clear, India's security managers led by the redoubtable Ajit Doval had averted an audacious attack planned and executed by the JeM with full support of the ISI.

Looking back, nearly a year and a half after the Pathankot operations, it is agreed by the experts that all the criticism heaped on those who had handled the response, was based on misinformation, incorrect assumptions, and in some cases, deliberate mischief.

One of the main points of criticism was: How could terrorists enter the Pathankot base when the NSA and his intelligence team claimed they had advance intelligence?

TIMELY DECISION SAVED THE DAY

The fact is: due to the fluid tactical situation—the exact location of the terrorists was unknown, and it was uncertain whether they had already entered the air base. Therefore, it was decided that it would be prudent to first secure vital assets and the families living on base. Over 10,000 civilians and dependents of air force personnel stay inside the air base. Due to this factor and the criticality of time, it would have been counter-productive to first secure the long 25 km

Then Defence Minister Manohar Parrikar with the Millitary top brass and NSG officers at Pathankot

outer perimeter of the air base. The main focus was on protecting aircraft, radars, anti-aircraft batteries, and ammunition/POL dumps, etc.

The second priority was to protect vital installations and assets in and around Pathankot. The army alone has over 25 big and small installations—including Asia's largest cantonment at Mamun—in the vicinity. All of them needed to be secured.

A chorus of criticism blamed Doval for apparent micro-management of the operation, but as the preceding paragraphs reveal, the on-ground operations were carried out under the directions of the military commanders present on the scene. Of course, he was monitoring the situation, but as all the operational commanders would testify, Doval was not breathing down their necks as many would have us believe.

As I wrote in a column for the *Outlook* in the wake of the Pathankot operations: 'Contrary to reports, after the initial planning done in his room on January 1 with the Army and Air Force Chiefs, the overall coordination was left to the Commander-in-Chief of the Western Air Command. While I feel the anti-terror operation was clinically executed, the government failed to win the perception battle because it failed to communicate the correct and essential information about the anti-terror operation in time. Absence of quick factual information led to much uninformed reporting, creating an impression that Doval had side-lined the Army, rushed in the NSG, and controlled the operation from Delhi.'

Even as the Prime Minister visited the Pathankot airbase (*see Plate 18*) days after the mopping up operations were over and he was briefed in detail, one question that took precedence in citizens' minds at the end of it was: Can Pathankot be counted as a successful counter-terrorist operation?

Yes, for the following reasons:

- The security apparatus was able to collect and collate operational intelligence that was accurate and actionable.
- Less than an hour was taken to assess the intelligence inputs, prepare an action plan, and operationalise counter-terror forces.
- Actual mobilisation and deployment of forces and action on decisions taken in record time that included quick mobilisation by the Army, movement of Air Marshal SB Deo, AOC-in-C Western Air Command to Pathankot with Garud Commandos, deployment of Army troops in and around Pathankot under the supervision of Lt Gen KJ Singh, Western Army Commander movement of NSG, movement of bomb disposal squads, and casspirs armour/ mine protection vehicles.
- No collateral damage was caused and none of the 10,000 personnel, including 3,000 in adjacent family quarters, suffered casualties despite heavy firing and explosions.
- The security forces suffered only one casualty in actual combat, the Garud Commando, Corporal Gursewak Singh.
- Finally, not one aircraft was damaged or destroyed, which was the main purpose of the audacious attack that had perhaps been planned months in advance.

LESSONS LEARNT, SOME QUESTION UNANSWERED

Every operation—even if successful—has many takeaways. But before listing out the lessons learnt, it is instructive to compare similar attacks that have occurred in India's neighbourhood in the past decade.

SRI LANKA OPS

- On 25 March 2007, a 25-member LTTE Black Tiger team including three females waited in a coconut estate, at northern end of Anuradhapura airbase, where the runway extension work was in progress.
- The Black tigers wore crumpled camouflage uniforms, had hair cut short, spoke Sinhala and wore explosive laden 'suicide' belts around their waist.
- They had an assortment of weapons, including Chinese built T-56 assault rifles, Russian made AK-47 kalashnikovs, Czech Automatic pistols, Light Anti-tank weapons, RPG with launchers, LMGs, Chinese made hand grenades, 1EDs. They had walkie-talkies, satellite phones, mobiles phones, medical kits, chocolates and a flag of LTTE.
- At around 0300 hours, the guerillas crawled towards the chain link perimeter fence. They cut a large hole and crept in one by one, four of the Black tigers remained outside.
- Then 21 of them divided into two groups. A few feet away from the outer fence, within the base there is a similar protective

Destruction at PNS Mehran

fence made of concertina wire running parallel to the first net. In between these two nets is a smaller electrically charged net. The electrified net was apparently not connected to the electricity supply.

- The two groups entered the inner perimeter of the AF base from two different directions towards north of the base.

- The SLAF soldiers near the three perimeter bunkers were 'most probably asleep' as they did not provide any resistance to moving LTTE cadres.

- The first team comprising 14 cadres tasked to neutralise the bunkers reached the helicopter hangar area, while the others waited to enter into the fixed wing hangers and destroy them.

- The two teams then started indiscriminate firing to neutralise the bunkers and damage the fixed and rotary wing aircraft.

- The time was almost 0320 hours. The entire airbase now knew that they were under attack. The entire base was put on red alert. The communication lines between Anuradhapura and Colombo were busy.

- The intruders took control of Anti Aircraft gun and neutralised communication, radar and Anti-aircraft gun positions.

- The guerillas informed their handlers at Vanni that they were in control of the base.

- Around 0410 hours the radar systems at Vavuniya and Badarnaike International Airport in Katunayake captured movement of two unidentified flying objects.

- The two aircraft reached Anuradhapura, dropped three bombs and returned towards Killinochchi. A Bell 212 was launched to intercept and destroy the two LTTE aircraft which crashed 15 km short of Anuradhapura probably due to hit by ground troops.

- Heavy confrontation continued.

- Six LTTE cadres had captured two bunkers and fired at troops while others destroyed aircrafts one by one.

- A 40 member elite team of Sri Lankan Special Forces was air inducted in two waves from Vavuniya. They were successful in locating and completely annihilating the Black Tiger unit within a few hours.

Aircraft destroyed by LTTE

- The LTTE members however blew up three helicopters, two fixed-wing aircraft—one of them a trainer—and three unmanned drones.

ATTACK ON PAKISTANI AIR BASE

- On 22 May 2011, several armed terrorists attacked PNS Mehran, one of the most densely populated naval bases located in Karachi. According to Pakistan's then Interior Minister Rehman Malik, four to six armed militants used ladders to climb the naval base, triggering a fierce gun battle and a series of explosions. One of the attackers was believed to have blown himself up, while bodies of three others were found. Moreover, two attackers had managed to escape. According to Malik, the militants, of Tehrik-i-Taliban Pakistan (TTP), invaded the base from three different points adjacent to Karachi's residential areas. The attack and operation lasted 17 hours. Ten security personnel were killed in the attack. Two US-manufactured P-3C Orion surveillance planes, were also destroyed during the attack.
- Just over a year later, on 16 August 2012, eight heavily armed personnel launched an attack on Pakistan Air Force's (PAF) Minhas Airbase located in Kamra (Attock) in Punjab. Again, the TTP claimed the responsibility for the attack and damaged one of the US-supplied Saab 2000 Eriye plane and damaged two others.

ATTACK OF US AIR BASE IN AFGHANISTAN

- In 2012 again, US forces in Afghanistan, with all their high-tech equipment and attention to detail and high grade perimeter security could not prevent an attack on US Air Force Camp Bastion and the destruction of six US Harrier jets. The 14 September attack killed a US Marine Corps Officer and one soldier, and wounded 16 others besides significant damage to other aircraft, vehicles and infrastructure. Fourteen Taliban attackers were eliminated. The review of security however revealed that the arrangements for manning of the guard towers around the perimeter of Camp Bastion were not adequate to detect or stop the attack.

US aircraft destroyed at Camp Bastion, Afghanistan

By comparison, in Pathankot, all air and missile assets were protected, all families and civilians were kept out of harm's way and attackers were eliminated in reasonable time.

There are some unanswered questions though. For instance:

1. One question regarding the role of Punjab Police officer, SP Salwinder Singh who was ostensibly waylaid by the

PATHANKOT: AVERTING A CATASTROPHE 163

terrorists, is troublesome. There is no clarity on what the SP was doing at night in a village near the border point where the four terrorists had crossed over into India. He had no jurisdiction in the area, so what he was doing there has never been fully explained. Moreover, after Salwinder Singh was let off by the terrorists (why was he allowed to go?), how long did it take him to inform his superiors is not clear. If he had informed immediately and had the Punjab Police alerted every post and barricade about the suspicious movement of the four terrorists, they could easily have been intercepted before they entered the Pathankot base.

2. Why did the terrorists wait for nearly 24 hours before launching the attack despite the fact that they had already landed in the area? Was there some larger plan that failed to take off? Had the four Pakistanis not waited and launched an attack on the morning of 1 January, the consequences might have been disastrous since the IAF base did not have enough defenders.

In the final analysis, a combination of luck and capability (of intercepting suspicious communication) and the quick decision to deploy forces at various bases saved the day. Had the NSA not decided to move quickly to get all the top security managers on board and press into action a cordinated plan in little over an hour, the outcome of the attack on Pathankot air base would have resulted in mayhem of unprecedented proportions.

Pathankot was not the first example of proactive approach. Swift decision-making of the Modi government was first evident in June 2015 when it ordered quick retaliation against north-east militants based in Myanmar.

ABDUCTION OF SALWINDER SINGH AND OTHERS

Pathankot District Police had registered case vide FIR No. 01/2016 dated 01.01.2016, at Police Station Narot Jaimal Singh, u/s 364, 365, 367, 368, 397, 398, 419, 171 IPC and 25 Arms Act, on the complaint of the victim, Salwinder Singh, SP, that he and his two other fellow passengers, were abducted along with his vehicle, Mahindra XUV 500, from Kolian Morh at about 2300 hours on 31 December 2015 night by unknown persons while they were returning from village Talur.

The accused persons were wearing army uniform and carrying AK-47 rifles and backpacks. They forcibly got inside the vehicle and took control of it. They dumped the complainant and one of the fellow passengers in a forest area. Later the terrorists tried to kill one of the passengers, by slitting his throat and abandoned him and the vehicle at village Akalgarh.

Investigation into the present case, vide RC 03/2016/NIA/ DLI, revealed that this act was also committed by the same group of terrorists while they were proceeding to execute the terror attack at the Air Force Station, Pathankot.

Investigation further disclosed that on 31 December 2015 night, after abandoning the damaged Innova vehicle of Ikagar Singh at a service station at Kolian Morh, district Pathankot, the terrorists hid in the nearby sugarcane fields and waited for a vehicle to come. The terrorists then hijacked a Mahindra XUV vehicle bearing Regn. No. PB02 BW 0313 of Salwinder Singh, S.P., from Kolian Morh, district Pathankot and moved towards the Air Force Station, Pathankot. The terrorists pushed the three occupants inside the vehicle and took control of the vehicle. One of the victims was pushed to the rear seat while the other two, were pushed in the leg space between the front and the middle seats. One terrorist was in the driver's seat, the other in the co-driver's seat, while the third one sat in the middle seat and the fourth one occupied the rear seat.

The terrorists, further, snatched the mobile phones of the victims, and used the mobile phone number to communicate with their handler, Kashif Jan and senior leaders/operatives of the JeM in Pakistan on four Pakistan numbers.

The phone number was the same which was contacted using the phone of Ikagar Singh.

After some time, the terrorists tied, blindfolded and dumped Salwinder Singh and his cook Madan Gopal, at an abandoned place in a forest area near village, Gulpur Simli, district Pathankot, on way to the Air Force Station, Pathankot. However, the terrorists took the third victim, i.e. Rajesh Verma, along with them. The dumped victims managed to untie themselves and rushed to the nearby village, Gulpur Simli, on foot for help. Salwinder Singh then called up Gurdaspur Police Control Room at 0252 hours and also informed SSP, Gurdaspur, about the incident at 0321 hours.

The terrorists, on learning from Rajesh Verma that Salwinder Singh was a police officer informed their handler who directed them to go back and look for him. Since Salwinder Singh and Madan Gopal had already left the spot, the terrorists resumed their journey to the Air Force Station.

(Extracted from *NIA chargesheet*)

12

Striking Hard in Myanmar

Date: **5 June 2015**, a day after a group of north-east militants had ambushed and killed 18 soldiers of an Infantry battalion of the Indian army in Chandel district of Manipur, bordering Myanmar.

Location: Operations (Ops) Room, 57 Divisional HQ, Leimakong, in Imphal, Manipur.

Army Chief Gen Dalbir Singh had flown in from Delhi. Lt Gen MMS Rai, then the Eastern Army Commander, and Lt Gen Bipin Rawat, the General Officer Commanding (GoC) of 3 Corps at that time (he later succeeded Gen Dalbir Singh as Chief), and a couple of representatives from the Intelligence Bureau and the Research and Analysis Wing (R&AW), India's external intelligence gathering agency, were part of the conference.

The conference was to decide on when and where to strike against the group of militants who had carried out the ambush on the Army convoy. The top brass apart, there were two others—the Commanding Officer of 21 Para (SF) unit and his second in command—sitting around the table. They would be the ones to finally execute the plan that was being formulated at that point.

In fact, Gen Rawat remembers having ordered an immediate retaliatory action by dispatching a team of 21 Para (SF)—permanently based in the north-east—in hot pursuit of the group that had killed the Army soldiers. He was, however, told to hold on because the Centre wanted a bigger, demonstrable action. In a way therefore, the Special Forces were already primed and raring to go.

The previous day's ambush had been one of the worst in the north-east for several years. A group of militants had killed 18 soldiers of a Dogra regiment battalion. The militant faction was led

The Myanmar raid heroes: 21 Para (SF) troops (file photo)

by a middle level insurgent leader of the National Socialist Council of Nagaland (NSCN-K), one of four factions of Naga militants then active in the north-east. The NSCN(K), led by SS Khaplang, a Burmese Naga, had walked out of a ceasefire with the Government of India some months before this ambush took place. It had teamed up with a couple of other militant groups in Manipur like the KYKL and PLA.

As the news of the ruthless attack on the Army convoy came in, Home Minister Rajnath Singh convened a meeting in Delhi attended by Defence Minister Manohar Parrikar, NSA Doval and Army Chief Gen Dalbir Singh. He had ordered strongest retaliation possible. The NSA had also briefed Prime Minister Modi. Modi had tweeted: 'Today's mindless violence in Manipur is very distressing. I bow to each and every soldier who has sacrificed his life for the nation.'

Parrikar, barely seven months into his high profile job as defence minister of the country, was visibly disturbed. 'I was beside myself with rage. How could anyone get away with killing our soldiers? I asked myself,' he recalled. 'As we went in for the meeting at Rajnathji's office, I told the Army Chief this must not go unpunished,' added Parrikar.

At the meeting, the Home Minister too demanded a quick retaliation, but the professionals in the room—Doval and

Gen Dalbir—counselled patience. The NSA assured effective action, however, at a time and place that would be carefully chosen. Gen Dalbir said he would personally go to Imphal, take stock of the situation, discuss with the local formation commander (the GOC 3 Corps), and then order a strike.

The then Army Chief knew the area well since he had been the GOC 3 Corps in a not too distant past and had used the Special Forces for small, pin-pointed raids against militant camps along the India–Myanmar border. However, in this instance, the retaliation had to be larger in scale and more effective. Thus, the Army Chief was not willing to be rushed into a hasty reaction.

He also knew that a team of 21 Para (SF) were waiting in Delhi to take a special flight to South Sudan since they had been selected to go on the UN deployment. Without a moment's hesitation, the Army Chief ordered them to get back to base in the north-east. 'The UN deployment could wait I reckoned. Their first task is to conduct special operations. To the credit of the team, no one complained. On the contrary, they saw this as a chance to prove themselves on home ground,' Gen Dalbir recalls. He himself was supposed to fly to London to participate in week-long celebrations to mark the 200th anniversary of the Gorkha regiment in the British Army. 'The moment I heard of the ambush, I asked my staff to tell the organisers of my inability to attend. The MEA and even the RM (Raksha Mantri or Defence Minister) said don't cancel. Postpone it. So eventually we put that visit on hold,' Gen Dalbir added.

Less than 12 hours after that high level meeting at the Home Minister's office, the Army Chief was now conferring with his Eastern Army Commander and the GoC 3 Corps at the Leimakong Cantonment. As the members of the conference deliberated upon the options, it became clear that the Special Forces will have to hit two camps across the border in Myanmar. One of them was a large camp, with a capacity to harbour over two hundred cadres, while the other was normally used to shelter between 50 to 60 militants of different groups. The bigger camp had already been under surveillance for some time. As Gen Rawat recalled, 'In our contingency planning at 3 Corps, we already had all the required coordinates and details of the bigger camp. The only issue was: it was inside Myanmar. A call needed to be taken if we were prepared to cross into another country's territory and attack the camp.'

That decision took some time since several factors had to be considered. Myanmar, after all, is a friendly country. Was it feasible to keep the Myanmar government and its Army in the loop? Would Myanmar agree to such an operation? These questions needed quick answers. Finally, after several rounds of consultations amongst all the stakeholders (Ministry of External Affairs, the Army, and the NSA), it was decided that the large camp would be the target of a hit. It was left to the NSA and the MEA to handle the communication with Myanmar. Newspaper reports later suggested that the Myanmar government had been brought on board at the highest level before Indian Special Forces crossed into Myanmar territory.

Back at the crucial meeting in the Operations Room of 57 Division, the participants were engaged in firming up a plan.

Remembers the Special Forces officer who eventually led the main raid: 'During discussions, we were told that the government wanted to send a message "that if you hit us here, we can hit wherever we want."'

Since time was short, the planning had to be done quickly. Initially, the Army HQ proposal was to hit the actual perpetrators of the 4 June attack. Their camp was among the two to three targets that had been selected. But intelligence on that particular camp was sketchy. The bigger camp, where all the groups housed their cadres together and trained them, had been under surveillance for quite some time. So Gen Dalbir, in consultation with the Eastern Army Commander, the Corps Commander, and the SF team leader, decided to hit the bigger camp. Apart from the bigger camp, a smaller 'transit' camp was also to be raided. The second camp was across Noklak in Nagaland.

The targets decided, the next question to be answered was how soon could the operation be launched? The SF officers said they needed at least forty-eight hours to prepare. The top brass agreed.

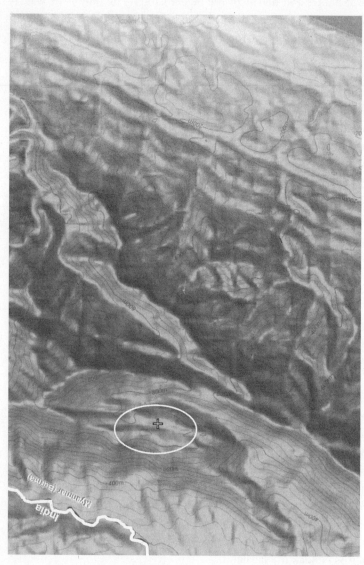

The tough target: The militant camp (circled) was located on a ridge 10 km inside Myanmar

In the meantime, the South Sudan-bound team had made its way back to Imphal on an IAF C-130 Hercules transport plane by 5 June evening. As one of them joked, 'instead of going abroad by air, we are going to go into another country (Myanmar) on foot!'

Another challenge was to keep the planning and execution of the raid confidential. Therefore, communication on open lines was completely banned. The Corps Commander (Gen Rawat) had decided to co-ordinate with the SF teams himself, or through his senior Staff Officers, in order to minimise information outflow. All other officers—the sector commanders and so on—were kept out of the loop to ensure the security of information. Everyone was told not to ask questions about the movement of SF troops. The preparations were underway from 6 June. The countdown had begun.

Armed and ready, one SF team travelled to Ukhrul town, considered the de facto headquarters of another militant faction NSCN I-M, which has been in ceasefire mode with the Government of India since August 1997. Going past the town, the vehicles carrying the Special Forces boys, most of them drawn from different parts of the north-east, reached Phaiko, the last village before the international border began with Myanmar. As the team entered the Assam Rifles camp located nearby, a couple of Kuki jawans (Kuki is one among the numerous tribes in the north-east) changed into civilian clothes and went into the village to pick up any information they could get. The villagers had not seen any movement from the militants. The villagers were neither suspicious nor hostile to the Special Forces jawans since they were used to these teams operating along the border.

Next morning, 8 June, the 50-strong Special Forces team began its journey on foot towards the international border, about 20 km away. As they trekked through the thick jungle amidst intense humidity, the team, led by an officer who also belonged to the region, suddenly came across a group of Myanmarese hunters looking for game. They had about eight hunter dogs with them too. The hunters were as surprised as the Special Forces troops when they had come face to face.

Now the Special Forces team had obviously not factored in this complication. As the jawans rounded them up and asked questions about militant camps further deep inside the Myanmar territory, the team leader had to come up with a plan to deal with them.

Leaving the hunters on the loose was not an option, so the young officer simply decided to carry them along. 'They were better off being with us rather than on their own,' he remembers thinking. That of course meant some of the already limited manpower being diverted to guard them. 'I had no other option since killing them was out of the question,' the team leader recalls. In hindsight, the hunters' knowledge of the terrain, and some information about the camps and the behaviour of militants in the area that they possessed actually helped the Special Forces to fine tune the final plan.

By late afternoon on 8 June, the team was about five kilometres away from the big militant camp. The hunters now refused to go any further since they feared for their lives. As scouts of the Special Forces (the operatives who stage forward, ahead of others, to survey the area) went nearer, they spotted the assortment of small and big huts and sheds on a ridge at a distance. The scouts came back and reported to the team leader that their task was going to be tough since the only way to reach the location undetected was to climb the sheer cliff and then attack before retracing the same route back.

As night fell, the team leader had to take a call on how best to get nearer to the camp and accordingly determine the most opportune time to launch the assault. The troops decided to rest after what had been a gruelling, almost day long march through an insect and mosquito infested forest. The officer, on the other hand, conferred with his JCOs and started dividing manpower for the task ahead. 'The basic drills are of course common but each assignment is new and unique. We had to take into account the fact that we were already on foreign soil and that our team was most likely outnumbered in strength since our intelligence had suggested that there were at least 150 militants in that camp and we were just 50 in number,' recounted the team leader.

So the officer decided to go with the original idea of hitting two or three main buildings to inflict maximum casualties and make a quick return without bothering to count the dead. He divided the team into two parts. One section carried heavy calibre weapons, while the other half carried light weapons.

By midnight of 8 June, the entire team, sans two soldiers left behind to guard the captive hunters, had staged forward and lodged itself at the base of the steep cliff (at a 70 degree incline) that rose some 600 metres straight up. The Special Forces soldiers heard firing and a group of militants approaching the edge of the cliff. The soldiers, their faces darkened by black paint, dressed in camouflage, lay absolutely still; the big challenge for them was not to panic and open fire first.

'Will we be detected well before we can get to the target?' many of them thought. The officer however, was dead sure that the militants did not have definitive information about any Special Forces movement, but were on a routine patrol and generally taking precautionary steps to protect the camp. And sure enough around 2 AM, the militants seemed to relax as they started singing songs. Gradually, the voices faded. The patrol had presumably returned to the camp. The soldiers down below also sat down to conserve their energy. Now they had to wait for the first light before climbing the cliff and rushing towards the target.

At dawn, the first group of Special Forces soldiers slowly started climbing up the steep ridge. Others followed in a well-practised drill. Stealthily, they moved forward, spreading themselves in a semi–circle and rushing towards the target.

As luck would have it, as the soldiers neared the camp, they realised the lookout sentries at the entrance compound had left their posts for their morning ablutions! The SF troops reached the compound fence without being challenged. Each soldier took up the pre-decided position and let loose a heavy barrage of fire from their automatic weapons and rocket launchers, and lobbed hand grenades. For the first fifteen minutes, the occupants of the camp—most were either asleep or just about waking up—could not fathom what had happened. 'There was no retaliation in the first fifteen minutes. That is when we killed most of them and caused huge damage to their thatched houses and barracks,' the officer recalled.

Soon the others, living in the second and third tiers of the large camp, regrouped and started retaliating with whatever weapons they could lay their hands on from behind well-fortified positions. 'That's when I decided to fall back. Since the surprise element had been lost by then, it had become difficult for us to stay on,' said the team leader. It was time to begin the return journey. The soldiers regrouped and then retraced their way back in a well-rehearsed manoeuvre. 'Our instructions were clear: Don't stop to count the dead. Inflict as many casualties as you can and return. No proof, no photos are needed,the Corps Commander had told us,' recounted the team leader.

The trek back wasn't easy. As the sun rose, it became unbearably hot and humid in the tropical forest. More than the heat, it was the possibility of the militants or soldiers of the Burmese Army giving them a chase which loomed large in their mind. So the Special Forces team, despite the exhaustion, walked back briskly. They did not stop until they had crossed over into Indian territory around noon. The hunters were still under captivity. They were released with a stern warning not to speak of the episode under any condition. The team leader commented, 'We were sure they would not utter a word since their life would have been in danger if they revealed their ordeal.'

'The moment we were inside India, I called our Corps Commander (Gen Rawat), who was monitoring the progress of our raid in the Ops Room at Leimakong. He just said, well done, and asked us to come back on the helicopters that had been kept ready to transport us back to the headquarters,' said the team leader.

The moment the helicopters took off, Lt Gen Rawat called the Army Commander and the Army Chief to give them the good news. Gen Dalbir immediately informed the Defence Minister and the NSA, who in turn conveyed the news to the Prime Minister. By 1600 hours, news had filtered out that India had carried out a Special Forces raid inside Myanmar in retaliation of the killing of 18 Indian Army soldiers just a week prior.

So how deep did you go, I asked the Special Forces team leader. 'Oh easily eight to ten kilometres,' he replied. And how many militants would have been killed in the raid, I probed further. 'As I said, we did not stop to count the casualties, but our estimate is we would have easily eliminated at least 65 to 70 of them which was later confirmed by cross-border sources living in the vicinity of the camp,' the team leader revealed.

Meanwhile, the second team which had targeted the smaller camp opposite Noklak also reached the area around dawn. However, the militants had vacated it fearing retaliation from the Indian army following the 4 June ambush. Thus, that team had to return empty-handed.

No sooner had the young officer and his team reached the Cantonment on the outskirts of Imphal, than he got a call from the Defence Minister who congratulated him on a job well done.

Meanwhile, back in Delhi, the MoD and the MEA in consultation with the PMO decided to make a public announcement of the news of the precise strike.

The DGMO read out a brief statement to announce the successful raid just in time for prime time news bulletins to take up the issue for discussion.

At Leimakong, Gen Rawat was waiting. As soon as the force commander came back, Defence Minister Parrikar called and congratulated the officer personally.

Gen Suhag, who had postponed his trip to the UK, meanwhile received a call from the PMO to go ahead with his UK visit. 'I telephoned my wife to tell her that we have to leave later that night. She was not happy. "How can I be ready at such short notice?" she asked, but we eventually took the late night flight to reach in time to participate in the celebrations of the 200th anniversary of the Gorkha regiment. Although we missed the dinner hosted by the Queen at the Buckingham palace,' Gen Suhag recalls with amusement.

Later that week, select few soldiers from the team which had conducted the successful strike, were flown into Delhi and taken to the PMO to meet Prime Minister Modi. The Prime Minister lauded their courage and praised them for a task well done. In the subsequent weeks, the designated team went ahead for their UN deployment in South Sudan.

A fortnight later, NSA Doval and foreign secretary Jaishankar visited Myanmar and met with the top political and military leadership to further co-ordinate security cooperation between the two countries. Both reached out to the Myanmarese and ironed out any wrinkles that may have emerged following the Indian Special Forces raid in the Myanmarese territory on 9 June that year.

Myanmar-based *Mizzima News* reported, 'The Indian delegation has also shared with Myanmar specific details on approximately 25 anti-India insurgent camps in its territory along the 1,643 km border with India.

The Indian strike on militant camps earlier this month seems to have had the desired effect on insurgent groups. 'We have confirmed reports that insurgents have moved out of camps, particularly from Taga and across the Manipur border, as they fear more reprisals from the Indian side,' said a senior official.

Although the main purpose of the visit was to seek cooperation from Myanmar on anti-India groups not being allowed to set up camps east of the Chindwin river, the high-powered delegation met Myanmar's top political leadership, including President Thein Sein and Myanmar's military commander Senior General Min Aung Hlaing, to assuage any hard feelings in Nay Pyi Daw over the 9 June operations.

Both sides have decided to initiate better coordination on operations along the border. It is understood that Nay Pyi Daw was peeved with Indian media outlets reporting that the strike was carried out deep inside Myanmar territory.'

Whatever the fallout of the operation, three standout aspects of the operation have been more or less forgotten. One, the swift response by the top political leadership in giving a go-ahead for a counter-offensive. And three, the India–Myanmar military cooperation that allowed the forces to cross over and raid militant camps inside that country.

Prime Minister Modi, Home Minister Rajnath Singh, Defence Minister Parrikar and NSA Doval were quick to seek action against the perpetrators of the 4 June ambush. Once the political backing was forthcoming, the Army chose its best force trained for counter-insurgency and jungle warfare, the 21 Para (Special Forces), based in Jorhat and directly reporting to the Eastern Command. Nicknamed Waghnakh (Tiger's Claw)—the unit was originally 21 Maratha Light Infantry battalion before being fully converted into a Para (SF) battalion—after Chatrapati Shivaji's famous act of killing Afzal Khan by using the waghnakh, the 21 Para (SF) were tasked to hit the two camps located not very far from the border.

As details begun to emerge, Myanmar acknowledged India's operation: Zaw Htay, director of the office of Myanmar President Thein Sein, confirmed to *The Wall Street Journal* a day after the raid that Indian troops had entered his country. He said that there was 'coordination and cooperation' between the Indian troops and Myanmar's armed forces based in the area of the raids, but added that no Myanmar soldiers were directly involved. 'We will never allow or support insurgents, whether [they are] against Myanmar or against our neighbouring countries,' Mr Zaw Htay added.

Now came the most crucial phase: the battle of perception. The government needed to send multiple messages to different constituencies without compromising on operational and tactical details.

At one level, it had to signal the change in mindset at the highest level in responding to provocative acts such as the ambush on the Army that killed 18 soldiers on 4 June. On the other hand, India's adversaries needed to know that there is a cost to pay if the country's interests are harmed.

The DGMO read out a statement, 'The Indian Army engaged two separate groups of insurgents along the Indo–Myanmar border at two locations, along the Nagaland and Manipur borders. Significant casualties have been inflicted on them. As a consequence, threats to our civilian population and security forces were averted.' No other details were shared. Neither was any footage or photographs. But it was enough to send a signal to north-east insurgents that they were no longer safe even outside the boundaries of India.

However, the Army statement by itself would not have satiated the huge media demand for more information. So the junior information and broadcasting minister, Rajyavardhan Rathore—note that it was neither defence minister Manohar Parrikar nor home minister Rajnath Singh—a former Army Colonel, was instructed to give interviews to television channels. The intention was to send a larger political message: India will not waste time in ordering retribution, if provoked.

At that time, no one, including me, could even imagine that the Myanmar raids would serve as a template for similar strikes inside PoK. One man—then Defence Minister Manohar Parrikar—was however perceptive enough to understand that Prime Minister Modi would not hesitate to seek a similar action on the western Front in a crunch situation. 'I was very restless on the night when our Special Forces team went into Myanmar. I was anxious until the boys came back,' Parrikar told me. The next day however, looking back at the entire week—from the time when the new of the deaths of 18 soldiers came in until the good news of the successful surgical strikes on the militants camp was conveyed to him—Parrikar realised the Prime Minister may demand similar action in PoK. 'I realised the Special Forces needed to be used selectively and effectively and asked for a report on their equipment status, shortages and requirements,' said Parrikar. Subsequent events have proved his hunch right.

The Myanmar raid set the ball rolling for pro-active policy in India's bid to strengthen both its internal and external security.

13

Internal Security:
Challenges Remain

Although foreign policy successes have been in the limelight when it comes to counting the Modi government's successes so far, the considerable improvements in the internal security situation has gone mostly unnoticed. Except the episodic ups and downs in J&K, the rest of India has remained free of big terrorist attacks and large-scale riots that periodically shake India. In J&K, Pakistan has continued to wage a proxy war and create unrest, especially after the coalition government of the local Peoples' Democratic Party (PDP) and the BJP came to power in the state.

In the Maoist affected areas, mostly spread over 10 states in central India, episodic setbacks apart, the government's long-term, two-pronged strategy appears to be succeeding with lower violence levels, higher arrests, and elimination of the cadres of the CPI (Maoists) in the past three years. The tide had started turning in favour of the government forces in 2014, but picked up pace in 2015 and 2016 (*see table*), according to figures available on the Ministry of Home Affairs (MHA) website.

The Maoists have been steadily pushed into a corner as government forces make incremental gains in different states. With their backs to the wall, the Maoists have mounted desperate attacks on the security forces in Bastar, long regarded as the stronghold of the CPI (Maoist). In April 2017 for instance, Maoists killed 25 CRPF jawans in an ambush in Chhattisgarh. Occasional setbacks notwithstanding, the campaign against LWE or Left Wing Extremism (officialese for Maoist-led insurgency) has been

Comparative Important Parameters of Maoist Violence during 2010 to 2017 (up to 15 August 2017)

S. No.	Parameters	2010	2011	2012	2013	2014	2015	2016	2017 (upto 15.08.2017)
A.	No. of incidents	2213	1760	1415	1136	1091	1089	1048	554
B.	Civilians killed	720	469	301	282	222	171	213	113
	(Out of which 'Police Informers' killed)	323	218	134	113	91	95	123	63
C.	No. of Security Forces killed	285	142	114	115	88	59	65	69
D.	No. of SFs injured	NA	177	189	170	183	159	145	107
E.	No. of encounters with police	272	223	216	218	221	247	328	147
F.	No. of attacks on police (including landmines)	230	131	135	143	155	118	111	55
G.	No. of cadre killed (during encounters as well as attacks on police)	172	99	74	100	63	89	222	76
H.	No. of cadre arrested	2916	2030	1901	1397	1696	1668	1840	1116
I.	No. of cadre surrendered	266	394	445	282	676	570	1442	489
J.	Total no. of arms snatched	256	67	55	89	58	18	3	34
K.	Total no. of arms recovered	642	636	591	628	548	724	800	374
L.	Arms training camps held	94	84	53	27	34	18	20	12
M.	No of Jan Adalats held	75	97	62	63	54	41	21	12

Source: Ministry of Home Affairs, GoI.

Plate 11: *Satellite images of two of the camps hit by Indian Special Forces in PoK Dhuhada (top) and Khaled*

Plate 12: *Stealthy Silhouette: A Para Commando in action in one of the surgical strikes*

Plate 13: *Keeping a hawk's eye: The surveillance team in September 2016*

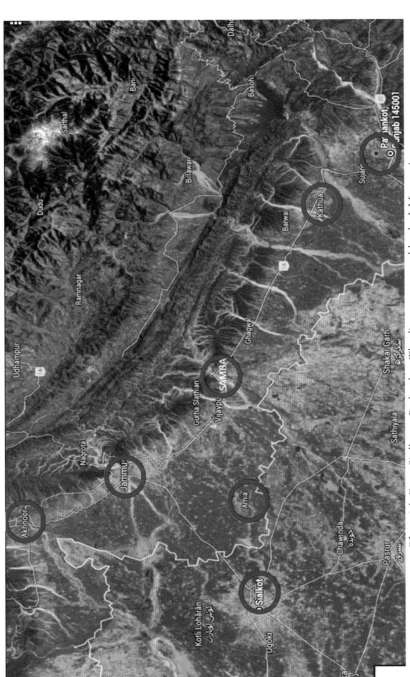

Plate 14: *From Sialkot to Pathankot: The distance traversed by the JeM terrorists*

Plate 15: *The layout of Pathankot Air base; Note the area where terrorists entered*

Plate 16: *The gutted building*

Plate 17: *NSG in action in Pathankot (above and below)*

Plate 18: *PM Modi, NSA Doval, Air Chief Arup Raha and*
Army Chief Dalbir being briefed at Pathankot

Plate 19: The location of the 73-day faceoff between Indian and Chinese soldiers at the tri-junction of India-China and Bhutan

Plate 20: *Catching Xi by surprise: Prime Minister Modi breaks the ice at Hamburg in July 2017*

Plate 21: *Indian Army and Chinese PLA troops' face-off at Dolam, August 2017*

Plate 22: *Prime Minister Modi with the first couple of China at Xiamen in September 2017*

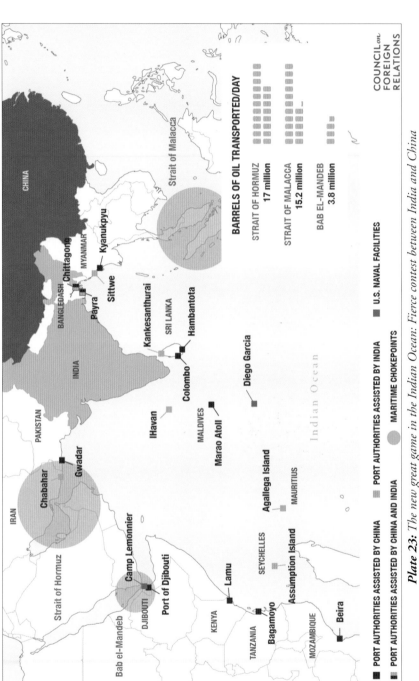

Plate 23: *The new great game in the Indian Ocean: Fierce contest between India and China*

successful in regaining control of areas earlier under the total sway
of the Maoists. With over 100,000 Central Armed Police Forces
(CAPFs)—CRPF, SSB, CISF, BSF and ITBP—deployed in ten
states affected by LWE, the Centre is lending a strong hand to
state governments in combating Maoist insurgency. However, the
fight has to be led by state governments, not just on the security
front, but also in implementing socio-economic policies meant for
the people's welfare. The Ministry of Home Affairs under Rajnath
Singh has combined the hard power of the security forces with the

CRPF jawans in action in Chhattisgarh

soft tools of development, fine-tuning an approach that had begun in 2012–13. The results are gradually becoming visible.

Reviewing the campaign, India's Home Minister Rajnath Singh told a meeting of the Chief Ministers of the affected states in May 2017: 'Unified Coordination and Command is needed on the LWE front. Along with strategic command, unified command is also required at the operations level. LWE cadres are constantly trying to inflict losses on security forces to boost the morale of their cadres. Today, we need to consider whether to react only after the occurrence of any incident or we should be more proactive,' he said. 'We need to use UAVs, PTZ cameras, GPS tracking, thermal imaging, radar and satellite images. There is need to chalk out a specific action plan for each theatre with short term, medium term and long term strategies clearly defined,' he said. Mr Singh also underlined need for choking the financial resources of the LWE cadres and groups.

The Home Minister, effectively No. 2 in the Modi government, told the assembled Chief Ministers and officials that he wanted the anti-Maoist strategies to revolve around short, medium, and long term policies at different levels. 'There is need to find a solution for this problem and the strategy is available.' He encapsulated the strategy in the word 'SAMADHAN' which means:

1. S – Smart Leadership
2. A – Aggressive Strategy

Home Minister Rajnath Singh at a review meeting on LWE

3. M – Motivation and Training
4. A – Actionable Intelligence
5. D – Dashboard Based KPIs (Key Performance Indicators) and KRAs (Key Result Areas)
6. H – Harnessing Technology
7. A – Action plan for each Theatre
8. N – No access to Financing

For years, successive governments have identified lack of roads in remote and distant underdeveloped areas of LWE-affected states. So by 31 July 2017, under Road Requirement Plan-I (RRP-I), the construction of 4,447 km roads was completed out of the 5,422 km road that had been envisaged in the Plan. Building on the success of these plans, the MHA informed a Parliamentary Committee that a new plan, Road Connectivity Project for LWE affected areas (RRP-II), has been approved which envisages the construction of 5,412 km of roads and 126 bridges in 44 districts of LWE affected States at an estimated cost of Rs 11,725 crores. Roads apart, the government has been pressing state governments to open up job avenues for the local tribal population. One of the ways to create jobs in backward areas is to raise special police battalions exclusively manned by locals. According to the Home Minister, 743 Scheduled Tribes candidates from four most affected

Home Minister Rajnath Singh with NSA Ajit Doval at an internal security review meeting

LWE districts of Chhattisgarh—Bijapur, Dantewada, Narayanpur and Sukma—have been recruited in 'Bastariya Battallion' in order to enhance local representation in Security Forces. More Kendriya Vidyalayas and Skill Development Centres have also been opened in LWE affected districts in the past three years. Over 1,800 new branch post offices, 405 bank branches and 818 ATMs have also opened in 35 most LWE affected districts in the last two years, the Home Minister told the parliament.

As the security forces establish dominance over increasing areas of erstwhile LWE strongholds, efforts towards civil consolidation have also increased. MHA officials say the implementation of the scheme for Fortified Police Stations for construction/strengthening of 400 Police Stations in ten LWE affected States is now near completion, with over 350 police stations modernised and fortified.

The Maoists are certainly on the run in their erstwhile strongholds, but the Centre and State governments will have to continue with their efforts to achieve lasting peace and security, and gain full control over Maoist insurgency, which former Prime Minister Manmohan Singh once described as the country's 'greatest security threat'.

The other big internal security challenge in India is the ever present danger of radicalisation, especially among Muslim youths. Since 2012, the fatal attraction of Daesh the world over (also known as the Islamic State of Iraq and Syria or ISIS) has travelled to India. Several youth in the cities and small towns in India have been lured by the seductive ideology which ISIS propagates. Online radicalisation has been on the rise.

There have been extensive warnings in the media about this new phenomenon since 2014, but in reality, it has not manifested to the extent feared by observers, thanks to preventive arrests and constant vigil of the law enforcement and intelligence agencies. The Daesh threat, while ever present, tapered off in India in 2017. Only 132 Daesh operatives from India are known to have had some affiliation to the outfit. This is relatively a small number compared to the inroads made by ISIS in Europe, West Asia, other parts of South Asia, and even Australia. Many of the ISIS operatives have turned out to be former members of some terrorist and radical outfits such as Indian Mujahideen and Students Islamic Movement of India (SIMI). Over 70 per cent of these have either been arrested or intercepted before they could travel to Syria or Iraq, which is a testimony in itself to the vigilance of the Indian agencies. Significantly, many of the ISIS Indian members were radicalised while living and working in Gulf countries for a prolonged period of time. These are minuscule numbers given that India is home to 175 million Muslims.

However, the threat of ISIS will not disappear in a hurry since many Muslim youths will continue to nurse real and imagined grievances against the Indian state. The law enforcers have done a commendable job so far to keep the threat under check, but they will have to be on guard to ensure that the danger of ISIS spreading its wings in India under some other garb is minimised, as correctly assessed by Dhruva Jaishankar and *Sara Perlangeli of Brookings India. In a newspaper article, the Brookings India scholars observe*, 'As ISIS is defeated as a state—a self-proclaimed Caliphate with defined territory and a military—it could very well morph into a global network, akin to al-Qaida. This presents a new kind of challenge for India and the world. Without unnecessarily exaggerating the threat, details available in public about IS recruitment and propaganda can be a valuable way of anticipating its future challenge to India's national security.'

Significantly, the Government informed the Rajya Sabha (Upper House of India's Parliament) on 9 March 2016 that Central and State agencies had arrested 46 Pakistani ISI agents between 2013 and 2016. Furthermore, according to partial data compiled by *satp.org*, at least 159 ISI modules have been neutralised across the country between 2004 and 24 April 2016, indicating Pakistan's sustained efforts at subversion and destabilisation. Therefore, the proxies trained, equipped, nurtured, and harboured by Pakistan continue to be the main source of danger from Islamist terrorism.

It's worth remembering that the only two major terrorist attacks outside J&K—the Pathankot attack in January 2016 and the strike on the Dinanagar police station adjacent to Gurdaspur in

July 2015—were executed by Pakistan-backed, Kashmir-oriented groups in Punjab.

Both these attacks exposed worrying vulnerabilities in the Punjab police force. As detailed in another chapter in this book, only pro-active measures at the highest levels saved the day in Pathankot, but the overall coordination mechanism between different central and state police forces continues to be a cause of worry.

J&K: LONG-TERM CHALLENGE

The situation in J&K, in a way India's festering wound for decades, has witnessed extreme swings between 2014 and 2017. As Modi took charge of the government in the summer of 2014, his invitation to the then Pakistan Prime Minister Nawaz Sharif for his oath-taking ceremony was seen as the new Prime Minister's desire to extend a hand of friendship to Pakistan. It was as if Modi wanted to start with a clean slate with Pakistan. Hope was in the air in the first couple of months of the Modi government's ascension to power.

Within a couple of months however, the illusions of any normal relationship with Pakistan were shattered when the Pakistani Army broke the informal understanding on the Line of Control (LoC) and made repeated ceasefire violations in July 2014. The 'deep establishment' in Rawalpindi was clearly not comfortable with any likely normalisation in its fraught relationship with India.

New Delhi, in the meantime, had taken an 'in-principle' decision to break a decade-old convention of allowing a bunch of separatist leaders from Jammu and Kashmir, collectively known as the Hurriyat leadership, to be part of India–Pakistan dialogue process. This was informally conveyed to Pakistan. However, in clear defiance of that request, the Pakistan High Commission in Delhi invited the Hurriyat leadership for talks on the eve of the scheduled Foreign Secretary Level talks between the two countries. New Delhi decided to draw the red line. It cancelled the Foreign Secretary level talks without any hesitation, leaving Pakistan stunned and the Hurriyat leadership searching for relevance. The

Modi government had made it clear that it wanted the dialogue with Pakistan to be strictly bilateral.

The relationship nose-dived from thereon. A backlash from Pakistan was inevitable. In the latter half of 2014, the LoC and the International Border between the two sides heated up with frequent ceasefire violations from the Pakistani side, resulting in the displacement of civilian population along the border. India retaliated in kind and with ferocious fire assault not witnessed in years on the International Border. In 2014, official data indicates that there were 430 ceasefire violations along the International Border, the bulk of it after India had cancelled the foreign secretary level talks. By comparison, in 2013, the IB had witnessed only 148 ceasefire violations.

It was clear that the Pakistani Army, which controls and calibrates the Kashmir policy with India rather than the civilian government, was unhappy with Modi's ascent to power. The clergy in Pakistan, along with the Army, have for long regarded the Bharatiya Janata Party (BJP) as inimical to its interests and therefore the 'Mulla-Military' complex was unlikely to sanction any peace effort attempted by the civilian government in Pakistan.

For a year after the cancellation of the Foreign Secretary level talks, the freeze in relations continued until Modi and Sharif met on the side-lines of the Shanghai Cooperation Organisation (SCO) at Ufa in Russia in July 2015, much to the surprise of hardliners on both sides. The much-publicised meeting between the two Prime Ministers appeared to signal a breakthrough. A joint statement included five points: (i) a meeting would be held in New Delhi between the two National Security Advisers (NSA) to discuss all the issues linked to terrorism; (ii) an early meeting of the Directors General of the Border Security Force and the Pakistan Rangers followed by that of the Directors General Military Operations (DGMO); (iii) the decision to release fishermen in each other's custody, along with their boats, within a period of 15 days; (iv) a mechanism for facilitating religious tourism; (v) and both sides agreeing to discuss ways and means to expedite the Mumbai case trial, including additional information like providing voice samples.

The declaration created a mini storm in Pakistan since there had been no explicit mention of Kashmir, yet terrorism had been very much on the table. Hawks in Pakistan were up in arms over what they called a deliberate oversight. Some of them went to the extent of describing the joint statement as being drafted in South Block (India's seat of power). Seeds of failure were thus embedded in the joint statement itself.

However, hardliners in India were unable to fathom the exact reason why India agreed to break the ice. For Pakistan, the compulsion to reach out stemmed from its desire to ensure Prime Minister Modi's presence at the SAARC summit, slated to have been held later that year in the country. For Modi, the reason was more substantial. Having assumed power on the back of a decisive mandate, he wanted to utilise the strong base he had created domestically to secure peace with Pakistan so that his government could concentrate on ensuring rapid economic development.

As anticipated, within a month of the Ufa declaration, the resumption of dialogue was stalled. India objected to Pakistan's insistence on arranging a meeting between its then NSA Sartaz Aziz

Prime Minister Modi and Nawaz Sharif: Trying to break the deadlock at Paris in June 2015

and the Kashmiri separatists before Aziz could meet Doval in Delhi. The talks collapsed as Aziz chose not to travel to New Delhi. *The Mint* newspaper reported: 'Technically, it was Pakistan's "expansion" of the agenda for the talks—well beyond what had been agreed upon at Ufa—that killed the talks. Islamabad wanted its NSA to meet leaders of the secessionist All-Parties Hurriyat Conference before meeting NSA Ajit Doval. In addition, it wanted to discuss Jammu and Kashmir at the meeting. Both were unacceptable to India and in spite of repeated entreaties not to do so, Pakistan persisted and that spelled the end of the talks.'

The process went into deep freeze until Modi and Sharif met once again at the United Nations Climate Change Conference. Building on a brief encounter in Paris and coming to some kind of personal understanding, Modi surprised people in South Asia by making an impromptu stopover at Lahore on his way back from Kabul on 25 December 2015—Nawaz Sharif's birthday—trying to break the mould.

However, the Prime Minister had clearly underestimated the Pakistani Army's resolve not to let any peace building succeed between India and Pakistan. Within a week of the surprise detour by Modi, terrorists of Jaish-e-Mohammad (JeM) attacked the Pathankot air force base on 1–2 January 2016 to blow away any chances of rapprochement between the two sides.

The Indo-Pak bonhomie was moving too well and too fast for the liking of the ISI/military establishment. Post-Pathankot too, there were several incidents in the first six months of 2016 which convinced the Modi government that the hostile elements within the Pakistani establishment were determined to create conditions that would eventually derail the process of political engagement. The process was paused, but not totally called off post-Pathankot.

On 8 July 2016, Burhan Wani was eliminated. The elimination of the young Hizbul Mujahideen leader from Tral, who had captured the imagination of disgruntled young minds in Kashmir, witnessed the beginning of a new phase in Kashmir's counter-insurgency operations. His burial procession attracted huge crowds, leading to law and order problems. During the first week itself, agitators started confronting the security forces with intense stone pelting, leading to police firing and deaths and injuries, including the blinding of scores of young people. Each morning, groups of young agitators started coming out, some spontaneously, most under duress, in pre-designated areas determined by a few Pakistani and local activists acting under instructions from their handlers across the borders. For six months, it seemed as if it was a free for all in Kashmir valley.

Significantly, no one disputed whether Burhan Wani was a terrorist, or questioned the genuineness of the encounter, both were indisputable facts. What was being described by the media as an 'uprising' was instigated and micro-managed from the Pakistani side, largely confined to the five rural districts in south Kashmir.

In the entire phase that spanned over nearly three months, according to the CRPF, over 90 civilian agitators were killed and nearly 12,000 injured in approximately 200 violent incidents. The forces however maintained major restraint, reflected in the fact that over 2580 CRPF jawans were injured in these incidents, 122 of them seriously.

It was a testing time for security forces, especially the Indian army, leading the counter-insurgency operations in Kashmir for over two decades. Trained to kill, the Army was being called to show restraint in the face of massive crowds. The situation deteriorated

CRPF jawans facing the ire of Kashmiri agitators

to such an extent that Army Chief Gen Bipin Rawat—who had taken over in a surprise choice by the government on 1 January 2017—had to issue a tough statement warning trouble makers in Kashmir to desist from obstructing operations by his troops or else face the consequences.

There was one section—and I don't want to call them intellectuals—which pays lip service to the army but in reality stands against everything that the army seeks to protect and defend. This group variously dubbed the Army Chief's remark as an 'intemperate statement', 'belligerent stand', and 'declaration of war against Kashmiri youth.' This group of people have sought to create an impression that the Army Chief had ordered his troops to kill and maim indiscriminately. This was nothing but deliberate distortion of an emphatic assertion by a professional entrusted with the security of the country.

However, Gen Rawat's unambiguous stand acted as a much needed confidence booster for the troops—young officers and soldiers at the cutting edge—who were often left wondering if they were doing the right and necessary thing in combating the terrorists, many times paying with their lives.

In the wake of the elimination of Burhan Wani, and the subsequent turmoil in the Kashmir valley, abetted in no small measure by the Pakistani deep state through the support of the selfish and self-centred separatist leaders, politics had dominated the discourse on J&K. It was conveniently forgotten that irrespective of his origin (as a Kashmiri youth), Burhan Wani was after all a terrorist whose days were numbered once he had taken up arms against the Indian state. His killing in an encounter with the security forces should have been treated as just that—neutralisation of a terrorist. Instead, a narrative was

Maj Leetul Gogoi

sought to be built, blaming the security forces for doing their job and doing it professionally.

Months of unrest following Burhan Wani's death often hampered the movement of security forces, disrupted their logistics chain and disturbed a well laid out security grid. The Army can take the setbacks in its stride and learn lessons from them. However, what demoralises the soldiers are the barely concealed barbs from ill-informed critics who do not have the faintest idea about the difficulties and constraints under which the troops have been operating in the unending war in J&K for over a quarter century now. No Army in the world has maintained the relentless tempo of operations as the Indian Army has done since 1990.

It is to the credit of Indian Army leadership over the years that troops have retained the highest degree of motivation despite mounting odds.

However, the unwarranted criticism about strategy and tactics, and the contempt that some of our prominent opinion-makers had held against the Army had begun to affect the soldiers on the ground. A slight hesitation had begun to creep into their approach in counter-insurgency and counter-terrorists operations. Fortunately, the Army Chief's statement and his open support to an officer, Maj Leetul Gogoi who had used his presence of mind in saving several civilian officers by tying a protestor in front of his jeep would have removed any lingering doubts the soldiers may have had about the necessity of their job and boosted the morale no end.

On another level, the warning by the Army Chief to those hindering operations and the support extended to him by the political leadership over his stand sent the right message to those fishing in Kashmir's troubled waters. In 2017 alone, motivated and re-energised security forces, including the Jammu and Kashmir Police, have eliminated more terrorists than in the previous years. By end of August, the number of terrorists killed in pin-pointed operations was over 140. The security forces have reclaimed their dominance after six months of consistent and accurate intelligence-based operations, justifying New Delhi's approach towards J&K:

Peace first, political outreach later. Even though many critics of the government had taken it to task for its 'take no prisoners' policy which had been in operation in the second half of 2016.

The relentless counter-insurgency operations were coupled with a much needed crackdown on the Hurriyat leadership and their proxies who were fuelling terror by using the *hawala* route and *benami* properties, to receive funds from their Pakistani backers and other dubious sources. The National Investigations Agency (NIA) initiated investigations against the Hurriyat members. In what is clearly a departure from past practice of shielding and mollycoddling the Hurriyat leadership, the NIA's raids on the Hurriyat leadership caught the terrorist-enablers by surprise. The arrested Hurriyat foot soldiers (six from Srinagar, one from Delhi) are admittedly not the big fish, but it's a start. Moreover, the crackdown is a signal to the top Hurriyat leadership to not take the Centre for granted. The NIA cases have demonstrated the will of the Centre and now must be followed up vigorously.

Noted commentator Minhaz Merchant wrote: 'It took a major policy change by the Centre to end soft-pedalling the Hurriyat. Since the crackdown on separatists by the National Investigation Agency (NIA), several Hurriyat leaders are in jail. The NIA estimates that the family of the head of the Hurriyat's hardline faction, Syed Ali Shah Geelani, owns 14 properties in Kashmir and Delhi valued at over Rs 150 crore. These include a prime seven-acre land in Sopore, Baramulla.'

The Geelani family has done well for itself out of the terror financing through *hawala* and *benami* transactions from Pakistan. The properties owned by the Geelanis include an educational institution, residences and agricultural land in Kashmir and flats in Delhi.

Going beyond the immediate however, the Centre and the State governments will have to build on the tactical gains made in 2017 and look at the larger picture to ensure a better future for the people of the entire state of Jammu and Kashmir (that includes Jammu and Ladakh), and not get bogged down with the concerns of a handful of leaders, politicians, businessmen, and their supporters in the Kashmir valley alone.

There have been suggestions that the Centre must reach out to the youth of Kashmir. Perhaps the time has come to do just that and ignore the usual suspects, but before that the youth must begin to understand the difference between mindless protests and legitimate demands. Kashmiri parents must also begin to ask the question: Why allow the young to be used as a smoke screen for political objectives?

That said the state government must start delivering on basic governance issues. By August 2017, insurgency and violence were brought under reasonable control in the Kashmir Valley, prompting Prime Minister Modi to reach out to the ordinary Kashmiris even while he vowed to continue to crack down on the trouble makers. In his Independence Day address from the Red Fort on 15 August 2017, Modi said: '*Na gaali se, na goli se, parivartan hoga gale lagaane se... samasya suljhegi har Kashmiri ko gale lagane se*' (Kashmir problem cannot be resolved by either bullets or by abuses; it can only be resolved by embracing Kashmiris), referring to the on-going violence in the Kashmir valley. Only a handful of separatists, he said, were resorting to 'various tactics' to create problems in the state. But the government is committed to making Kashmir a paradise once again, said the Prime Minister. Making it clear that there will be no softness towards terrorism, he added that India's security is a top priority for the government, and the surgical strike had underscored this belief.

In light of the relative success in managing the internal security situation, MHA officials and security professionals stress on the need to have sustained efforts to bring the situation under complete control. 'There are too many intangibles and gaps right now in our approach to internal security. Our basic policing needs total overhaul and less political interference from politicians,' a serving security practitioner commented, not willing to come on record because of his sensitive appointment. He is right. For years, police reforms have been put on the backburner. Consensus continues to elude political parties on how to implement the reforms and because of the country's federal structure, the Centre has a limited role in ensuring law and order.

As *satp.org* comments: 'Indeed, while the immediate challenge of terrorism and insurgency has receded across the country and across the ideological spectrum, the conflict potential in India remains high, and is often exacerbated by state policy and partisan politics. Crucially, first responders, the State Police Forces, as well as most Central SFs and the intelligence apparatus, remain ill-equipped, poorly-trained and under-strength. Despite enormous emphasis, particularly after the Mumbai 26/11 attacks in 2008, technological capabilities of Police, Intelligence and specialised CT Forces remain poor. Critical projects such as the Crime and Criminal Tracking Network and Systems (CCTNS), National Intelligence Grid (NATGRID) and GPS-based surveillance of sea vessels, among others, have been fitfully funded, and implemented, as a result of which the cumulative impact of limited capacity augmentation on capabilities to secure the nation has, at best, been marginal. Furthermore, a rising demographic burden, resource crises, growing unemployment, and adherence to a growth model that has limited potential to address the aspirations of the overwhelming mass of people, continuously exacerbates tensions, leaving the country ripe for the picking for new or resurgent movements of violence.'

Modi's National Security team must pay heed to the signs that are evident even as it can take satisfaction in having kept the situation under tight control across the country, which allows Prime Minister Modi to meet the bigger challenge from India's biggest adversary, China.

14

Standing Up to China

28 August 2017: It was the usual busy Monday morning in Delhi. Newspapers were full of speculation over a sentence that a local court in Haryana was supposed to declare against cult leader Ram Rahim. The Prime Minister's clear condemnation of the tendency of people taking the law into their hands dominated the front pages of the newspapers. Hence, the tense, ongoing stand-off between Indian and Chinese troops at a remote border point on a desolate plateau, variously called Dolam, Doklam, or Donglang, situated on the tri-junction of Sikkim, Bhutan and Tibet, was far from most people's mind. (Dolam is the name used by the Indian Army and people in Bhutan, although Doklam is being officially used even by India's external affairs ministry; the Chinese call the place Donglang). The stand-off had started in late May and was easily one of the longest face-offs in recent memory (*see Plate 19*).

Most China watchers in India, including me, were aware that the week starting that Monday was crucial since Prime Minister Modi was supposed to travel to China for the upcoming summit of BRICS countries, hosted by the city of Xiamen. Having returned from a weeklong trip to China the previous weekend, I had a fair idea that hectic back-room diplomatic negotiations were on between Indian and Chinese officials in order to resolve the stand-off ahead of the BRICS summit. However, no details were available on the progress, if any, concerning the negotiations. On the face of it, China's extreme position seemed to create an impression that the People's Liberation Army (PLA) was spoiling for a fight. Furthermore, the belligerent tone adopted by official Chinese media on the issue—'India should not forget 1962', 'Time for a second lesson for forgetful India'—which were some of the headlines in *The Global Times*, an aggressive tabloid which often acts as a hound dog for the Chinese establishment contributed towards that impression. Xinhua, the official Chinese news agency in fact produced a comical video titled 'Seven Sins of India', trying to mock India, but ended up earning derision from all those who saw it. India, on the other hand, had maintained a restrained stand, issuing just one official statement that had been followed up by a speech in Parliament by External Affairs Minister Sushma Swaraj. She offered a way out to Beijing which would restore the status quo as it had existed before the standoff began.

Against this backdrop, no one expected a two-paragraph statement around noon that Monday from the Spokesperson of the MEA, Raveesh Kumar, announcing that New Delhi and Beijing had mutually resolved the standoff. The bland statement, made public through a tweet, said: 'In recent weeks, India and China have maintained diplomatic communication in respect of the incident at Doklam. During these communications, we were able to express our views and convey our concerns and interests. On this basis, expeditious disengagement of border personnel at the face-off site at Doklam has been agreed to and is on-going.' All hell broke loose as foreign policy reporters and analysts scrambled to make sense of the rather unexpected development. All eyes were now on what China's Ministry of Foreign Affairs would say.

China, continuing to adopt the stance that it was India that had acted illegally, stated at a Press conference in Beijing: 'At about 1430 hours of 28 August, the Indian side withdrew all its border personnel and equipment that were illegally on the Chinese territory to the Indian side. The Chinese personnel onsite have verified this situation. China will continue fulfilling its sovereign rights to safeguard territorial sovereignty in compliance with the stipulations of the border-related historical treaty. The Chinese government attaches importance to developing good neighborly and friendly relations with India. We hope that India could earnestly honor the border-related historical treaty as well as the basic principles of international law and work with China to preserve peace and stability in the border area and promote the sound development of bilateral relations on the basis of mutual respect for each other's territorial sovereignty.'

Pressed further if the withdrawal was mutual or unilateral by India, the Spokesperson said: 'I have made myself very clear. In light of the changes on the ground, China will accordingly make necessary adjustments and deployment. I also stressed that the Chinese border troops will continue fulfilling the sovereignty rights to safeguard territorial sovereignty in compliance with the stipulations of the border-related historical treaty.'

If the remarks seemed confusing and contradictory, they were actually meant to be so. By remaining vague in its statements, the Chinese were able to sell the resolution as a 'victory' for Beijing to their domestic audience. India, on the other hand, had achieved what it wanted: stopping the construction of a road that China had sought to resume in the first week of June. China did not want to openly admit to it, hence the roundabout wording of its official statement. This part of the statement, 'In light of the changes on the ground, China will accordingly make necessary adjustments and deployment,' stopped short of saying it in clear terms, but was sufficient for diplomats to understand that China had agreed to India's main demand.

In reality, the resolution was mutually accomplished after sustained and often bruising negotiations in Beijing (sources say there were at least 38 meetings between the two sides during the crisis). Led by India's Ambassador in Beijing, Vijay Gokhale, a China specialist and known to be a quiet but effective diplomat who is unruffled in tense situations, the Indian team was given clear instructions by Prime Minister Modi and his two principal aides— NSA Doval and Foreign Secretary S Jaishankar—on India's redlines. The team was told that India will remain 'resolute on ground and reasonable in diplomacy'. In other words, India was willing to discuss mutual disengagement or withdrawal, but it would not step back just because the Chinese were making threatening noises!

India's strategy of quiet diplomacy and refusal to join issues publicly had paid off. Once the initial disengagement was

NSA Doval with Chinese President

announced, it was left to Modi and Xi to work towards dissipating the acrimony that had crept into the relationship over the Dolam issue and start afresh when they met bilaterally for over an hour on 4 September 2017. The meeting, initially scheduled only for 30 minutes, went on for much longer, indicating that the two strong men had much to talk about in the wake of the border crisis.

So how and why did the standoff begin (*see box*)? And how was it resolved? According to those in the know, the stage for a prolonged diplomatic engagement was set by Prime Minister Modi at Hamburg when he walked up unannounced to President Xi in the lounge for G-20 leaders (*see Plate 20*). According to Indian diplomats witness to the impromptu meeting, the Chinese team was taken aback, if not stunned, by Modi's initiative to meet Xi informally. 'In that brief meeting, Modi suggested to Xi that the two Special Representatives (SRs) appointed by India and China— NSA Ajit Doval and State Councillor Yang Jiechi—should lead the effort to resolve the standoff at Dolam,' reported a person who had been familiar with the circumstances under which the off-the-cuff meeting and the conversation thereafter had taken place. 'Our strategic ties are far bigger than small tactical issues like Dolam,' Modi reportedly told Xi. A surprised Xi apparently thought over

Modi and Xi showed leadership in resolving a serious standoff

the proposal for half a minute and agreed—even if reluctantly—to let the two SRs lead the effort to find common ground. Later, at an informal gathering of BRICS leaders, Modi and Xi had a discussion on a range of issues, about which the Spokesperson of India's MEA tweeted. This was on 7 July 2017, almost a month after troops from either side were in an eyeball-to-eyeball posture at Doklam (*see Plate 21*).

As the tense face-off continued amidst a flood of analysis, advice and speculation from both the Indian and Chinese media, a fortnight after the Hamburg initiative, Doval travelled to Beijing for a round of pre-scheduled meetings of NSAs from the BRICS countries. He met Yang on 27 July and even President Xi the next day. The exchange between Yang and Doval was testy according to *The Times of India*, but officially not much is known about what transpired between Doval and Xi. The Chinese continued to maintain their standard stance. Foreign Ministry spokesperson Lu Kang stressed that in China's view, 'meaningful dialogue' on the stand-off at Doklam was not possible until India withdrew. 'China and India have a smooth diplomatic channel,' he said.

'The crux now is that Indian border troops illegally stayed on China's territory. Once again we urge India to pull back to the Indian side of the boundary. I want to stress that this is precondition for any meaningful talks between the two sides,' he said. Despite the aggressive public stance, the Chinese were not averse to discussions.

STANDING UP TO CHINA 201

Diplomatic sources say dozens of meetings were conducted in Beijing between the Indian side, led by Ambassador Vijay Gokhale, and his Chinese counterparts. Senior journalist Bharat Bhushan had put out a blow by blow account of the last mile negotiations. There is another theory behind the Doklam standoff which claims that PLA generals wanted to assert themselves before the crucial 19th party Congress, scheduled for October 2017, in order to jockey for positions in the Central Military Commission (CMC). That is yet to be proven but there is certainly much turmoil within the Chinese Communist Party (CCP) following President Xi's widespread crackdown on corruption within the PLA. Noted geo-strategist Brahma Chellaney is of the opinion that the PLA had acted on its own in Dolam. Writing in *Japan Times*, he remarks: 'In seeking to use road construction to change the status quo in a disputed Himalayan territory, the PLA, in a strategic miscalculation, anticipated Bhutan's diplomatic protest but not India's rapid military intervention. With the attempted land grab also threatening Indian security, New Delhi was quick to turn Bhutan's call for help into India's own fight...As part of his effort to reassert party control over the military and carry out defence reforms, Xi has used his anti-corruption campaign to ensnare a number of top PLA officers. He has also cut the size of the ground force and established a new command-and-control structure.

But just as a dog's tail cannot be straightened, asserting full civilian control over a politically ascendant PLA is proving unachievable. After all, the party is ideologically bankrupt and morally adrift, and depends on the PLA to ensure domestic order and sustain its own political monopoly. The regime's legitimacy increasingly relies on an appeal to nationalism. But the PLA, with its soaring budgets and expanding role to safeguard China's overseas interests, sees itself as the ultimate arbiter of nationalism.

To make matters worse, Xi has made many enemies at home in his ruthless effort to concentrate power in himself, including through corruption purges. It is not known whether the PLA's upper echelon respects him to the extent to be fully guided by his instructions.'

The PLA and the government appeared to be on the same page during the Dolam standoff, with the Chinese foreign and defence ministries and other state organs keeping up a barrage of threats and vitriol against India. But no sooner had Xi fired the chief of the Joint Staff Department, Gen Fang Fenghui, than a deal with India was clinched. This suggested that the topmost general was reluctant to end the stand-off.

Whatever the reason, there were multiple miscalculations on China's part which led to Beijing painting itself in a corner over one of the longest standoffs in a series of such crises since the 1980s. While the Sumdorung Chu episode in the mid-1980s took nearly eight years to be finally resolved, recent face-offs—2013, 2014 and the current one in 2017—have ended relatively faster for two reasons. Firstly, India's comprehensive national power has improved (relatively speaking), making it difficult for China to bully it over a prolonged period of time, even though unarguably even China's economic and military capabilities have increased manifold. Secondly, the rise of multi-polarity has made it tougher for bigger powers to bully smaller neighbours.

But let us look at the Chinese miscalculations. One, Beijing did not expect India to cross the line and come to Bhutan's aid when it became apparent that the PLA was trying to alter the status quo. Two, China took Bhutan for granted and thought Thimphu would succumb to its pressure tactics but it did not. Three, Beijing unleashed a three-pronged psychological warfare by deploying its shrill media, analysts and official spokespersons in trying to unsettle India. But the Indian government adopted a mature, calm, and assured approach refusing to take the Chinese bait, further infuriating Beijing. Despite Chinese provocations, India kept the diplomatic engagement going, stressing time and again that it was not spoiling for a fight but if push came to shove, it would not hesitate to meet force with force. As mentioned earlier, it took sustained spells of negotiations between diplomats from both sides, paving the way for a win-win solution. Both sides refused to issue a joint statement, keeping the terms of disengagement vague so that both could claim 'victory' back home. It also helped that China was to host the BRICS summit in Xiamen (*see Plate 22*). Having invested vigorously in the BRICS platform, China could not afford India's absence at the summit, even if the chances of that happening seemed remote. To be fair, New Delhi had not indicated that it was even thinking along those lines. In the end, China could claim to its citizens that it had forced Indian troops out of its territory. In return, it had agreed to stop road construction, without saying it in so many words. Thus, a face saver India has been magnanimous in granting a make-believe victory to China, having proved a point that New Delhi can longer be bullied.

So what are the long term implications of the Dolam episode? To begin with, other smaller nations in China's neighbourhood will study the sequence of events and learn lessons from it in their future dealings with Beijing. Secondly, India will have to keep its guard up all along the contested border with China because the Chinese do not forget or forgive easily. Possibility of another incursion, a probing manoeuvre in areas where Indian defences are vulnerable cannot be ruled out in the medium term. Thirdly, India may have had the military advantage in Dolam, but the Prime Minister and his national security adviser must make sure critical deficiencies are overcome expeditiously to allow the military to take on any future challenges from China.

Since 2014, Prime Minister Modi of course has had a more challenging time in managing New Delhi's engagement with China, clearly the stronger and more expansionist power than India's permanent headache—Pakistan.

It must be remembered that Xi Jinping had become the President of the People's Republic of China two years before Narendra Modi stormed to power in the summer of 2014. As a quintessential second generation, privileged insider in the Chinese Communist Party, President Xi spent the first two years consolidating his hold over the government and the party—getting rid of potential rivals like Bo Xilai and cracking down on corruption in both the People's Liberation Army and in the top echelons of the government. By the time Modi had taken over as India's Prime Minister, Xi was firmly in the saddle and China's influence in the Indian Ocean and the subcontinent was rapidly growing, posing a real challenge for India in its traditional sphere of influence.

By 2014, the gap between India and China—both on the economic and defence fronts—had also widened to alarming levels. Moreover, during the decade-long UPA regime, the difficult negotiations on the boundary issue had become more and more intractable. Instead of resolving the issue through the mechanism of Special Representatives, New Delhi and Beijing were back to managing the recurring crises on the border. Globally, new power equations were emerging, following an increasingly assertive China under Xi and a more accommodative United States during former President Barack Obama's second term in office.

Thus, Modi inherited a complex legacy in 2014, but he began on a positive note with Beijing, hoping to use his insights in dealing with the Chinese as Chief Minister of Gujarat. In order to work towards better India–China relations, Modi was going to bank on the personal goodwill that he had generated among Chinese businessmen during his at least five trips to China, the most number of visits that he had undertaken to a foreign country during his 12-year tenure as Chief Minister. China too was prompt to recognise the beginning of a new phase in Indian politics.

A Chinese expert was quoted as saying in June 2014: 'Modi will have a major impact on China–India relations,' said Wang Dehua, President of the Special Commission for South-Asian Studies, Shanghai Association for International Studies, and Vice President of Shanghai Institute for International Strategic Studies. 'For China, it will be good news—because he will put the focus on economic relations,' Wang was as quoted as saying by Johnathan Ward of the Jamestown Foundation. Added Ward: 'Modi's economic stewardship of Gujarat, which grew rapidly during his tenure, was widely cited in Chinese coverage of the Indian election, and the concept of Gujarat as India's "Guangdong" province—referring to the southern province in which economic reforms were tested under Deng Xiaoping—has been circulated alongside the idea that Modi's India will chose the "Chinese Model" for growth. Comparisons with China are frequent in India, and the Modi election has revealed a deep thirst for India to act upon what many see as its untapped economic potential.'

In keeping with that spirit, China did not lose much time in reaching out to Modi.

In fact in May 2014, the Chinese Premier, Li Keqiang, became the first foreign head of government to call up Modi. During the 25-minute long telephonic conversation, Li conveyed the Chinese government's desire to establish a robust partnership with the new government to Modi. The Indian Prime Minister too was quick on reciprocation. The Prime Minister underlined his government's resolve to utilise the full potential of 'our strategic and cooperative partnership with China' and his keenness to 'work closely with the Chinese leadership to deal with any outstanding issues in bilateral relations by proceeding from the strategic perspective of our developmental goals and long-term benefits to our people.'

The warm beginning kept getting better by the month. In June 2014, China's foreign minister Wang Yi visited New Delhi to hold talks with his Indian counterpart Sushma Swaraj as well as with Prime Minister Modi. 'China stands by your side throughout your efforts of reform and development,' said Wang. Later in the same month, India's Vice-President, Hamid Ansari, travelled to Beijing for a five-day visit. In July 2014, India's then Army Chief, Gen Bikram Singh, in his last month as head of the world's third largest standing land forces, went to Beijing for a three-day visit to different military institutes and held talks with the top brass of the PLA.

In end-July 2014, Modi met Xi for the first time during the BRICS summit in Brazil. The meeting went on for over 80 minutes. 'When India and China meet,' remarked Xi, 'the world watches us.' Thus, it was clear that Beijing accorded high priority to its relationship with India.

So far, so good.

However, in August 2014, Modi demonstrated that he was not going to take the Chinese at face value. He not only chose to visit Japan (at the invitation of his long-standing friend Prime Minister Shinzo Abe) for his first bilateral visit outside the subcontinent, but also flagged China's hegemonic quest in Asia.

Modi and Xi in Ahmedabad in September 2014

In one of his speeches in Japan, Modi made a pointed remark aimed at Beijing, without mentioning China. 'The world is divided into camps. One camp believes in expansionist policies, while the other believes in development. We have to decide whether the world should get caught in the grip of expansionist policies, or whether we should lead it on the path of development and create opportunities that take it to greater heights.' China did not officially react to Modi's remark, but one of its more aggressive newspapers, *Global Times*, played down the Modi–Abe friendship, opining 'It is not necessary for us to read too much into Modi's Japan visit.'

It was against this backdrop that President Xi's visit to India was taking place in September 2014, expectedly a grand affair.

A Chinese diplomat based in Mumbai had even made a grandiose announcement about the possibility of Chinese investment worth nearly 100 billion dollars coming into India.

New Delhi too was keen to highlight the visit as an example of India's rising status; Xi's visit was coming close on the heels of the Prime Minister's successful sojourn to Japan. After hosting Xi in India, Modi was slated to visit the US for what was going to be his maiden trip as the Indian Prime Minister to a country that had denied him a visa for over a decade.

Modi, keen to inject a bit of informality in what is normally a very stiff interaction between Indian and Chinese leaders invited Xi to Ahmedabad—capital of his home state—before starting the official part of his visit in New Delhi.

As Xi and his wife landed in the Gujarat capital, they were feted like royalty. Modi took them to Mahatma Gandhi's Sabarmati Ashram and then organised a cultural evening on the banks of the River Sabarmati. Their personal chemistry looked good—they were smiling and exchanging notes—sitting on an intricately-carved wooden swing along the Sabarmati riverfront.

Xi's smiling visage however hid the cunning mind at work. Even as Xi and Modi were exchanging pleasantries in Ahmedabad, 1000 Chinese PLA troops were pushing their way into Indian territory at a remote outpost called Chumar (Chumur in local parlance) in Southern Ladakh.

Chumar is the southern-most portion of Ladakh's boundary with Tibet. The Gya peak, which forms the boundary between the western sector and middle sector of the India–China border, is located approximately 35 km to the south-west of Chumar village. Pare Chu River enters into Tibet from this area and further along joins the Spiti River in Kaurik area of Himachal Pradesh. The terrain in this area is characterised by high altitudes, rugged mountains with average heights ranging from 16,000 feet to 18,000 feet.

The confrontation had been building up for a week before Xi was slated to travel to India, but peaked exactly on the day of his arrival.

A mere coincidence?

Not really, say those who have dealt with the Chinese along the Line of Actual Control (LAC) in Ladakh. Nothing that China or the PLA does is without authorisation at the highest levels. However, to understand what was happening on that day in September of 2014, one has to rewind a little—to the summer of 2013 to be precise—and understand the context.

Face off with PLA in general area Chumar in September 2014

The Chinese had been itching for a showdown at Chumar since April–May 2013, after a tense faceoff at Depsang plains, nearly 300 km north of Chumar.

The standoff in the Depsang plains, near an outpost called Dault Beg Oldie (DBO) in 2013, had lasted three weeks. The Chinese had intruded nearly 20 km into Indian Territory and pitched tents to stay put. Salman Khurshid, then India's External Affairs Minister had in fact tried to make light of the serious intrusion as 'acne on the face', inviting a lot of derision from many in the Indian media and the polity.

Speaking at a trade association conference, Khurshid had said: 'Doomsday predictions are absolutely absurd. It's absurd not so much for China as it's absurd for us.' Further adding, 'We shouldn't destroy years of investment, years of contribution that we have made to this relationship because somewhere some little thing goes wrong. One little spot is acne, which cannot force you to say that this is not a beautiful face... that acne can be addressed by simply applying an ointment,' implying that the incident should not be considered as a surrender or admission of defeat.

'Ointment is part of the process of growing up, just as acne is part of the process of growing up. And the relation between India and China is a relationship which is growing up. We started off as children who fought over something they needed, demanded or believed were theirs. They have grown up into two beautiful adults who can talk about these things and find a solution,' said Khurshid.

Media reports at that time commented that the Chinese had their way and decided to withdraw after having made their point. There were other reports—unconfirmed—suggesting that the Chinese prevailed upon India in Chumar where they got the Indian Army to halt the construction of an observation, but as a quid pro quo for vacating Daulat Beg Oldie. Moreover, Beijing wanted its new Premier Li Keqiang's scheduled visit to India to go on unhindered.

However, India's National Security Adviser during the Depsang episode, Shiv Shankar Menon says that compared to earlier standoffs, it was resolved relatively early. In his book, *Choices, Inside the making of India's foreign policy*, Menon writes: 'Unlike the Sumdorongchu incident, when the Chinese set up a post on the Indian side of the LAC in 1986, in 2013, India discovered the new Chinese presence on its side of the line immediately, took countermeasures and moved force within days, and insisted that the status quo be restored before it would discuss any of the matters the Chinese tried to raise. In 1986, this resulted in a seven-year standoff, which was only partially defused on the ground. On the other hand, in Depsang in 2013, India succeeded in getting the Chinese to vacate the area within three weeks.'

Menon was right. The then Northern Army Commander, Lt Gen KT Parnaik had also told me in an interview for NDTV at that time, that India did not compromise on its position in either Chumar or Depsang. 'I just want to tell you that our response at Depsang was patient but firm. We ensured our concerned areas were secure. We engaged in dialogue with PLA as per the established norms. Understanding each other's point of view does take time, we don't speak their language and vice versa. The entire incident was put through border personnel meetings and dialogue and ultimately both sides agreed to retreat to 15 April status quo and the de-escalation which took place; it happened without us making any compromise on the issue. We lost nothing, did not dismantle any of our defences. We broke none of our structures,'

Lt Gen Parnaik had said in his last interview before retiring that year.

Taking advantage of the crisis in Depasang plains that summer, Lt Gen Parnaik had in fact deployed an additional brigade in Sub-Sector North (SSN)—DBO is located in this area—to send a firm signal to the Chinese. Earlier on, because of terrain and logistics constraints, the presence of the Indian Army in that remote, desolate area was thin. Previously, only the Indo–Tibetan Border Police (ITBP) was deployed in penny packets in the area, tempting the Chinese to take advantage of the vast gaps along the LAC. Since 2013 however, one full brigade now looks after the SSN. Consequently, requisite support infrastructure including all-weather road connectivity has been developed in the area.

As an aside, I must mention that Lt Gen Parnaik, a fine soldier with a no-nonsense approach to problem solving, was asked for an explanation by the MoD and the Army HQ for talking on record to me about the Depsang incident, days before he was to retire. This was because some politicians and a section of the military leadership at the top were still hesitant to show teeth to the Chinese, despite the spunk shown by bold, on-ground commanders and the deft diplomacy of China specialists like Menon and his team.

While Menon and Gen Parnaik were correct in their appreciation of the handling of the situation in April-May 2013, it was also a fact that the PLA had started creating fresh trouble in Chumar post the Depsang episode. Before that, Chumar used to be one of the more peaceful areas along the LAC. However, from the summer of 2013, the moment the Chinese realised that the Indians could be pressured to concede positions at vulnerable points, trouble erupted.

Meanwhile, Lt Gen Parnaik retired and was replaced as Northern Army Commander by Lt Gen DS Hooda.

In May 2014, the Modi government assumed office in Delhi.

On the surface, diplomatically and politically the Chinese were showing a friendly face, but in the wake of the April–May 2013 incident, the Chinese realised that their infrastructure in the general area of Chumar was less than ideal and they needed a permanent road up to Chepzi and then further up to Chumar. It is against this context that the bigger crisis in August–September 2014 must be viewed.

NOW BACK TO AUGUST–SEPTEMBER 2014

By August 2014, the PLA had stepped up its presence in Chumar considerably. However, they were not coming across the LAC and were generally confined to their own side.

Then, on 7 September, devastating floods hit Srinagar, the capital of Jammu and Kashmir, and the rest of the state was lashed by heavy rains, keeping a bulk of the Army in the Kashmir Valley and the Staff in the Northern Command HQ busy in flood relief and rescue operations.

In less than a week, the Chinese decided to up the ante in Ladakh. As Lt Gen Hooda observed, 'No one has linked the events, but if you look back, the Chinese would have known that the road to Ladakh was in a precarious condition because of the incessant rains. They knew we were preoccupied with the floods, and rushing in reinforcements in case of any border standoff in Ladakh would have been impossible. So they spotted an opportunity in Chumar, which was in any case bothering them.'

And sure enough, by the second week of September 2014, the Indian army and ITBP—co-located at the southernmost tip of the Eastern Ladakh border—started noticing visible increase in PLA patrolling in the area.

Speaking to me, the then brigade commander (still a serving officer, so I am not naming him) entrusted with the defence of Chumar recalled: 'Initially the PLA patrols used come up to the IB. Then, subsequently they started to trespass up to three km into Indian territory. So our boys (troops) started preventing the transgressions. We formed Quick Reaction Teams (QRTs) and deployed them close to the border to react swiftly.'

Initially, the assessment of the local Commanding Officer was that the Chinese would try and trespass for a week or so and then go back to the existing status quo, like they usually do along the LAC. But after constant intrusions and face-offs for three to four days, the brigade commander realised that his troops needed to stay as close to the border as possible to respond instantly to any further Chinese attempts to trespass. Therefore, after consultation with the top brass of Northern Command, the brigade commander decided to construct an ORL (OR—Other Ranks—Living shelter), jargon for a temporary shelter. It should be noted here that even in the summer months (May to end-September), night temperatures at Chumar (located at about 16000 feet), can go down to near-zero, topped by chilly winds that strike like a whiplash. It is therefore unadvisable for the troops to stay out in the open. Thus, India started building the shelter, located well within Indian territory (approximately 7.5 km from the LAC) and beyond all of the various Chinese claim lines.

On 9 September, while in the process of construction, two PLA helicopters flew three km inside the Indian territory, perhaps to observe more closely what the new construction was all about or just to send a signal. The Indian forces duly noted the violation of air space and protested.

The next day, 10 September—at about 0330 hours—soldiers deployed near the border (a point called 30 R) noticed some movement on the Chinese side. Alerted by his troops, the CO

Indian and Chinese troops facing each other at Chumar

rushed with a strong Quick Reaction Team (QRT). He spotted about a dozen bulldozers and heavy construction machinery being brought closer to the border.

As the sun rose that morning, the Indian side counted the presence of some 300 PLA soldiers and a sizeable construction team that had also started preliminary work on the track. Indian troops, already present in the area, prevented the Chinese from either moving further or continuing to work on the track. Throughout 10 and 11 September, Indian troops kept a watch on the Chinese, who after the initial road cutting activity, were now camped in the area as if waiting for the Indians to make the next move or for further instructions from their own side. The Indian and the Chinese troops had been face to face for over 24 hours by then.

The standoff had begun.

It soon spread to seven areas, along a 10 km frontage starting from the general area of 30 R and moving along Point 5109 through Point 5212.

On 14 September, the Indian Brigade Commander also decided to camp at Chumar. Secure Army phone lines buzzed between him and the Northern Command via the 14 Corps HQ in Leh, even as the Brigadier decided to summon another battalion as back-up.

The ITBP too beefed up its presence to prepare for any eventuality.

As Northern Command alerted Army HQ, consultations with MEA and NSA Ajit Doval also began in earnest, since the PLA seemed to be itching for a showdown.

India, upon the directions of the Prime Minister, decided to stay firm on the ground, and if necessary, pump in more troops in the area, even as New Delhi prepared to welcome the Chinese President.

Lt Gen Hooda remembers: 'That summer I had ordered our reserve division-39—to send one brigade to go on an exercise in Ladakh, their area of operation when deployed. The troops were exercising in Eastern Ladakh when the standoff began, so we ordered them to stage forward to Chumar.'

Soon, by 14 September, India had a full brigade strength (3000 soldiers) lined up to counter the Chinese intrusion.

President Xi Jinping was about to begin his maiden India visit three days later. Initially, as good hosts, India tried to reason with the Chinese commander and asked him to withdraw. However, he was in no mood to relent, forcing the Indian troops to stick to their positions. The status quo persisted even as President Xi and his wife arrived in Ahmedabad on 17 September.

Almost as if on cue, 1,000 more Chinese PLA troops arrived in Chumar that afternoon. Indian observers also noticed massing of more troops near Chepzi, on the Chinese side.

In Ahmedabad, the public functions to honour the Chinese first couple were going on as planned. In Delhi, the NSA was being regularly briefed by Army Chief Gen Dalbir Singh about the developing situation.

As it became clear that the Chinese were determined to embarrass the hosts, the Prime Minister quietly authorised the NSA to start deployment of more troops upon the advice of the Army HQ and Northern Command. India was about to take a stand that Beijing was not used to.

That evening, additional troops were inducted into Chumar. Overnight, two more brigades (6,000 troops) were airlifted into the area in a massive show of strength from the Indian side. By the time President Xi ended his India visit, PLA's 1,500-odd troops were faced with the presence of a 9,000-strong Indian Army deployment. This was a clear departure from the past when the first instinct had been to talk rather than act. Here, the order was reversed. Force was met with larger counter-force.

A substantial number of Indian Force and Army Aviation helicopters were pressed into service to ferry troops to Chumar from other locations in Ladakh in order to save time. Recalls Air Marshal SB Deo, the DG Air Operations at Air HQ in Delhi at that time: 'Our pilots and air crew worked round the clock in that period transporting soldiers and maintaining the supply lines to sustain them in that 10-day period.'

Meanwhile, in Ahmedabad, Modi raised the issue with President Xi and told him that he expected China to behave as a responsible nation and not take steps that would create mistrust, referring to the Chumar incident. Apparently, the Prime Minister made a very strong pitch with President Xi. He told him upfront that as neighbours with a long and contested border, China should realise that this kind of incident detracts from confidence building. It was conveyed to the Chinese side that India would see the intrusion at Chumar coinciding with President Xi's visit as an act of 'deliberate provocation'. What exactly President Xi had said in response to PM Modi's straight talk is not public knowledge, but those who dealt with the matter both militarily and diplomatically remember the Chinese interlocutors searching for an hounourable exit from the standoff since the Chinese side had not expected a rapid Indian build-up at the border point.

Journalist Uday Mahurkar, who has known Modi for three decades, writes in his book, *Marching with a Billion*: 'Modi is a hardened politician with strategic view on geopolitics. Jinping got a dose of Modi's medicine inside the very tent where he was being hosted on the banks of the Sabarmati River in Ahmedabad. Modi reportedly told him, looking deep into his eyes: "This was not

Indian and Chinese military officers at a border meeting in Ladakh

expected of your country. Can you tell me when the troops are withdrawing?"'

Although Mahurkar writes that the Chinese troops withdrew in the next few days, the reality is that it took another week to resolve the issue. It took two flag meetings at Chushul (the designated border meeting point), one at the Brigade Commanders level and one more at the Major General level, to come to a resolution.

An incident during the standoff in which a young PLA officer slipped from a peak and rolled down into the Indian side also helped diffuse the tension on ground. Whereas firefights and brutal hand-to-hand combat marks the face-to-face deployment of India–Pakistan troops along the LoC, soldiers positioned along the Line of Actual Control (LAC) with China are mostly unarmed and can often be seen jostling with each other in order to prevent advance into the other's territory. The PLA officer however was not involved in any jostling. He lost his foothold while trying to bypass a group of Indian soldiers up a steep slope and slipped down a ledge in a precarious manner. On crashing down, he lay motionless. Indian troops then launched a rescue mission to bring the PLA officer back to safety and resuscitated him. The doctors did a thorough medical check-up before he was revived. Then Indian soldiers offered him warm coffee and biscuits.

The leader of the Indian delegation, a Brigadier himself ensured that the PLA officer—who was more shaken than injured—was safely returned to the Chinese side after a final health check-up at the 30R point. This kind Indian gesture went a long way in improving the on-ground communication. 'In a way,' an officer pointed out, 'we gained moral ascendancy by our action.'

Moreover, both sides had to invoke the provisions of another forum—the Working Mechanism for Consultation and Coordination on India–China Border Affairs—and a meeting each in New Delhi and Beijing to achieve a resolution. Established in 2012, the Working Mechanism is headed by a Joint Secretary level official from the Ministry of External Affairs and a Director General level official from the Ministry of Foreign Affairs of the People's Republic of China and comprises diplomatic and military officials of the two sides.

Eventually, the standoff was resolved a week after President Xi left India, but not before India had made its point by standing firm and disallowing Chinese bullying tactics to prevail over India.

From then onward, there have been several instances of Indian troops refusing to accept Chinese aggression. Senior Army officials recall at least two more prominent incidents—one at a location called PP (patrol point) 15 near DBO in 2015, and the other at Yangtse in Arunachal Pradesh—when the Chinese found the Indian response qualitatively different from previous occasions. Gen Dalbir Singh, whose tenure bears witness to most of these standoffs, recalls: 'The instructions from us at Army HQs—based on political directives—were clear: There will be no succumbing to Chinese pressure tactics on ground. I had told my Army Commanders to carry out aggressive patrolling in our own areas and upgrade surveillance across the LAC.' Adds Lt Gen Hooda, 'Once in Ladakh, the Chinese started constructing a permanent structure which came to the notice of the patrols a few days later. Without a moment's hesitation, I told the Corps Commander (of 14 Corps) to send a strong patrol, seize the construction equipment, and demolish whatever had been raised thus far. The QRT moved overnight and carried out the task. The Chinese were angry and perturbed by our action, and had no choice but to comply.'

The essential difference, most commanders in the field agree, is the change in New Delhi's attitude. 'The Modi government appears to have decided that the only way to counter aggressive Chinese moves on the border is to stand firm and not give into their tactics of creeping nibbling of territory,' a China specialist in the Indian military observed. 'Not for a moment am I saying that we have become as strong as the PLA, or we are spoiling for a fight, but when we stand firm, they also get a message,' he added.

In 2016–17, China's belligerence peaked after India refused to join the Belt and Road Initiative (BRI) Forum in Beijing, refusing to kowtow to China's effort towards creating a China-centric world. New Delhi also exposed China's blatant anti-India stand by seeking membership of the Nuclear Suppliers Group (NSG). Knowing fully well that China, a key member of the NSG, will oppose India's quest to enter the NSG, New Delhi made an all-out bid, lobbying hard with other member states, with PM Modi personally leading the effort. Most agreed that India's case was strong. Only Beijing vehemently opposed India's bid for NSG membership. This was the reality of a vastly different China. In 2008, Beijing had gone along with the United States' request to make a one-time exception for New Delhi, which had enabled India to engage in nuclear trade. The waiver had been necessary to operationalise the US–India civil nuclear cooperation agreement. President George W Bush had taken a personal interest in backing the requisite exemption.

In 2016, however, the geo-political equation was completely altered. The United States was not as powerful as before, or rather China had become more assertive under President Xi. President Xi was not afraid of demonstrating and exercising Beijing's raised economic and military clout. Hence, he opposed India's entry into the NSG, stating that there cannot be an exception to the rule for just one country. Since the NSG operates on the principle of consensus, India's all-out bid was thwarted by China in November 2016. In a statement on 15 November, four days after the NSG meet, China's Foreign Ministry announced that 'any formula (for membership) worked out should be non-discriminatory and applicable to all non-NPT states; without prejudice to the core value of the NSG.'

Beijing's opposition to India's membership stemmed from its plan to prop up Pakistan—its all-weather friend and ally—which in turn loves to be China's 'Cat's paw,' in South Asia. So in a clever move, China asked Pakistan to apply for the membership of the NSG the moment India did. Beijing was insistent that if exception had to be made for the membership of the elite grouping, the yardstick should be uniform. While most members were supportive of India's bid—given its clean record on nuclear non-proliferation— they were wary of admitting Pakistan which is known to be among the leading nuclear proliferators. The process was stalled. The silver lining is that in the bargain, China's blatant opposition to India was exposed.

Another development that New Delhi had been keeping a close watch on was Pakistan's increasing dependence on China for survival. Over the years, Pakistan has been importing more Chinese weapons than ever before, as at present, China can be considered to be its only dependable ally in global affairs. This comes in the wake of both the United States and Saudi Arabia having distanced themselves from Islamabad because of its open support for the Taliban and other terrorist groups like the Lashkar-e-Toiba, arguably one of the deadliest terror outfits in the world.

The China–Pakistan friendship—described sometimes as 'deeper than Indian Ocean and higher than the Himalayas,'—has been cemented further since 2015 because of the China–Pakistan Economic Corridor (CPEC) that Beijing had proposed to build, in order to gain access to the two Pakistani ports, Gwadar and Karachi. China now proposes to invest up to 60 billion dollars initially, starting with a figure of 46 billion dollars, in order to 'build a network of roads, railways, energy pipelines and other infrastructure projects that will run from the city of Kashgar in China's western Xinjiang province through each of Pakistan's major cities before terminating at the Arabian Sea ports of Gwadar, near Iran, and Karachi, to the east.'

However, neither China nor Pakistan expected India's strong opposition to the CPEC. The Modi government took exception to the CPEC passing through Gilgit–Baltistan, officially part of Pakistan-occupied Kashmir (PoK), which India claims as its own. New Delhi has maintained that the CPEC passing through G-B violated India's sovereignty and territorial integrity.

Points out China scholar Jeff Smith, of the Council for Foreign Relations, a Washington DC-based think tank and author of *Cold Peace*, a book on India–China relations: 'Prime Minister Modi has approached China with a greater sense of confidence and purpose than his recent predecessors. He's mostly done so indirectly, allowing his actions to speak louder than his words. He's maintained at least the veneer of diplomatic comity and has refrained from publicly criticising China (with the exception of two early speeches delivered in Arunachal Pradesh and Japan).

Instead, he and his team have privately conveyed their concerns to China and acted with greater confidence in their approach to issues traditionally sensitive to Beijing. It was evident early on in the invitation to Lobsang Sangay, the Prime Minister of the Tibetan Government in Exile, to attend Modi's inauguration.

It's evident in the Modi government's rather public concerns about endorsing Xi Jinping's signature One Belt One Road (OBOR) initiative, despite India being featured as a way point on various OBOR maps published in China. External Affairs Minister Sushma Swaraj reportedly told President Xi Jinping that Modi found the China–Pakistan Economic Corridor (CPEC) "unacceptable", given its course through Indian-claimed Kashmir. Beyond that Foreign Secretary Jaishankar has repeatedly lamented the fact that India has not been adequately consulted on OBOR or CPEC. He and Prime Minister Modi himself at this year's (2017) Raisina Dialogue, have implicitly criticised OBOR by stressing that regional connectivity initiatives must be inclusive in nature and driven by commercial—not strategic—interests.'

This stand has deeply displeased Beijing. China's irritation was further aggravated once India decided to boycott its showpiece event in May 2017—the Belt and Road Initiative (BRI), also known as the OBOR project—citing concerns over 'good governance, rule of law and transparency.' In fact, India and Bhutan were the only two countries in South Asia to have abstained from the BRI.

So how will India cope with China's rising antipathy?

A senior official had a clear take on India–China relations. He said, 'With China, we are increasing our bilateral trade, which shows that we don't consider it as enemy country. However, we do consider that some of China's activities militate against our strategic interests. We express our concerns about that through political and diplomatic channels, be it on the issue of CPEC, the border, or about Gwadar and so on.'

India will of course continue to assert itself.

In a way, China is trying to gauge how long New Delhi can sustain the firm stand and how serious it is about this approach.

Earlier, Beijing might have felt that India always makes noises and then climbs down or dilutes the stand. The Chinese might have assumed that since India is used to Chinese aggression, its intrusions and attempts to reclaim land, New Delhi even under the Modi government will continue to accept the situation in the future. That has been proved to be a miscalculation on China's part.

'They are still trying to gauge whether PM Modi really means business or if it is just a temporary phenomenon. Although one must say we have not been able to drive home the point to them so far, we are getting there. We would neither like to understate nor overstate the problem. We would like to be reasonable, legitimate, and friendly as well as firm. We will do nothing to convey any wrong impression,' is how a former diplomat who has dealt with China describes India's approach.

Agrees Jayadeva Ranade, who as a senior RA&W functionary has watched and dealt with China for four decades: 'India–China relations are presently in a difficult phase, with each testing the other. Exhibiting decisiveness in foreign policy as well as his strong nationalist credentials, Prime Minister Modi initiated a phase of hectic diplomacy that sought to re-energise some important relationships and highlight India's space for manoeuvre. In the process he has outlined the geographic perimeter of India's neighbourhood of strategic interest, thereby also implicitly identifying areas where India and China's national and strategic interests collide.'

Harsh Pant, a scholar at King's College, London observes, 'The Modi government has energised the Indian foreign policy bureaucracy, which had become moribund in the last few years, and succeeded in giving it a sense of direction. Ideationally, it has taken India out of a reactive non-aligned foreign policy posture. And operationally, it has been able to carve out a robust China policy, the most important challenge facing India today. It has challenged the conventional wisdom that nothing much changes in the foreign policy of a nation with the change in government.' Pant adds, 'Modi's biggest success is a quiet burial of the idea of non-alignment and standing up to China. Together, these moves restore Indian credibility in the international system, especially in the Indo–Pacific, which is in a state of unprecedented flux.'

Clearly, Modi's biggest challenge in the coming years will be the uncertainty of geo-politics and the fast-moving diplomatic changes taking place in the Asia–Pacific because of China's unprecedented rise. So far, he and his team have displayed rare resolve and reasonableness in dealing with a more aggressive and assertive Beijing. The test lies in sustaining the policy even as India builds its own military-diplomatic and political strength in coming years.

Simultaneously, the Modi government is crafting a multi-polar foreign policy, building an alliance of democracies in East and South-East Asia even as it re-engages with the Middle East.

TIMELINE OF DOLAM STANDOFF

Background and Overview

Location

Dolam Plateau is situated south of the Chumbi Valley in the Tibetan Autonomous Region. The area of contention between Bhutan and China is due to a differing perception of the tri-junction between India, China, and Bhutan. While India and Bhutan consider Batang La as the tri-junction and the boundary between Bhutan and China running along Merugla-Sinchela ridge line, China considers Mt Gymochen as the tri-junction and the boundary running along Jampheri Ridge.

Strategic Importance

From the Indian security point of view, control of Jampheri ridge is very critical as the Siliguri Corridor, also known as 'Chicken's Neck', lies within 30 km of this area and vulnerable to threats. In addition, any ingress by the Chinese in this region is construed as a threat to Indian defences.

Previous Claims

Due to its claim over the region, Chinese patrols have been visiting this area for at least two decades. According to the records with the Indian army and the Ministry of External Affairs (MEA), from 1981 to 1991, Chinese patrols visited the area only once a year. In 1999, China commenced construction of the road from Yatung to Dolam Plateau via Sinchela. The road to the present location was completed by 2003. Once the road was constructed, the frequency of visits by the Chinese patrols increased to a range of nine to eleven per year.

The Trouble

In 2017, trouble erupted at Dolam plateau in late May. The dispute can be divided into three distinct phases based on the status of activities on both sides: (a) a 'quiet' stand-off from end of May 2017 to 25 June; (b) a build-up of forces on both sides, complemented by the shrill propaganda of a bellicose Chinese media from 26 June to 14 August; (c) and a subsequent 'thaw' leading to the disengagement during the period of 15–28 August.

The Chinese strategy of 'three warfares'—media, psychological, and legal warfare—was displayed in large measure throughout the 72 day stand-off period.

Activities: 21 May to 16 June

- **21 May:** Local Chinese Commander informs Indian counterpart, 'we are going to undertake some 'infrastructure activities in the area.' The Indian officer, aware of the earlier instances of the Chinese constructing some shelters and improving existing bunkers, noted the input but did not feel alarmed.

- **24 May:** The first patrol of the summer of 2017 by the PLA, came up to the parking area, interacted with Royal Bhutan Army (RBA) personnel even as Indian Army troops watched the encounter from their post at Doka La (*see Plate 12*). The encounter ended soon as the PLA and RBA soldiers went back to their respective posts.

- **5 June:** Another PLA patrol came to Parking area. RBA troops again came to the area. But this time, the encounter was not peaceful. The PLA troops started jostling with the RBA soldiers and forcibly 'escorted' them to the Bhutanese posts after threatening them. What exactly happened was not immediately apparent.

The Indians later learnt from their Bhutanese counterparts that the PLA soldiers warned the RBA troops not to interfere in the work that they were about to undertake in the area.

The Indian officer, duly reported the matter up the chain. The Indian Army brass decided to play it by the ear and deal with the situation as it would evolve and increased the vigil on ground.

Nothing happened for about 10 days thereafter.

Activities on 16–18 June 2017

- **16 June:** At 0730 hours, one light vehicle and nine heavy vehicles, including plant equipment, reached the parking area (200 metres opposite Doka La, a pass). An interaction between Indian troops and PLA personnel took place at Contact Point with effect from 0750–1010 hours. From 1251–1331 hours, a patrol of eight Royal Bhutan Army (RBA) personnel, which had come from Chela Post on the Jampheri Ridge on Dolam Plateau, interacted with PLA patrol at Parking Area.

     The PLA patrol accompanied RBA patrol along the alignment of an under-construction track. At 1350 hours, Indian troops passed a message through a loud hailer on Doka La to stop the construction. However, the construction party did not pay heed. A temporary PLA road construction camp was established in general area of Parking Area.

- **17 June:** In the morning, the JCBs commenced road construction work. The Indian troops interacted twice with the PLA patrol. Indian troops repeatedly asked the Chinese side to stop the construction activity, but to no avail.

- **18 June:** In the morning, JCBs commenced work again, south of Parking Area. The local Indian officers present on location carried out four interactions with the PLA. The Chinese were asked to stop the construction activity. As the matter was reported up the military hierarchy, orders were issued by Delhi to stop the road construction of PLA.

Immediately a 'human chain' was formed by Indian troops along the watershed at 0752 hours to effectively block PLA troops.

In response, by mid day, a human chain was formed by 150 PLA troops opposite Indian troops, which was again effectively overwhelmed by an increased strength of Indian troops.

The Standoff in True Sense Began Now

20 June: The highest Military Commander (Major General) Level Flag Meeting was held at Nathu La, wherein both sides stated their stance.

Chinese Strategy

During this phase, there was a mutual anxiety on future courses of action. However, on ground PLA loud hailer messages conveyed the threats referring to a repeat of 1962.

Build-up Phase Between 25 June to 14 August

Major Highlights

Major highlights of events between 25 June to 14 August are as follows:

(a) *Increased Chinese Belligerence:* The Chinese were the first to report the event in the Media on 26 June (Prime Minister Modi was to meet President Donald Trump in Washington DC). This was also a precursor to an increase of overall tempo of Chinese activities in and around Chumbi Valley and across the entire Sikkim front.

(b) *Temporary Infrastructure in Dolam Plateau:* This period saw a steady increase in temporary infrastructure construction in the Dolam Plateau. This included erection of pre-fabricated structures as well as new road alignments.

(c) *Temporary Defence Infrastructure Across Sikkim:* Sustained efforts were made by the PLA for construction of temporary

defences all across the Sikkim border in the form of stone/
mud emplacements. Additionally, blasting activity was also
carried out to improve the existing road infrastructure in the
Chinese territory.

(d) *Mutual Build-up of Military Strength:* Incrementally, the PLA
built up its presence to a division plus size force, along with
150 tanks and guns stationed opposite Sikkim in the general
area of Phari Dzong in Chumbi Valley areas opposite North
Sikkim and beyond.

India also quietly matched the build-up, but due to a shorter
logistics line, it did not have to get troops close to the border.

On ground however cordial interactions took place at Doka
La on a daily basis between Commanding Officers from the
opposing forces wherein both sides reiterated their respective
stances.

From 14 August however, a thaw was gradually taking
place between the forces as diplomatic activity picked up pace.
Eventually, the disengagement took place on 28 August.

15

Defence: Good Start, Much to Do

In the three years plus that Modi has been India's Prime Minister, people have come to expect the unexpected from him. And that's exactly what he did on 3 September 2017.

That day, two hours before he was to leave for the BRICS summit in China and more importantly meet Chinese President Xi Jingping in a bilateral meeting, Modi was at the Rashtrapati Bhawan to witness the oath taking ceremony of newly inducted ministers. All eyes were however on the newly elevated ministers in his cabinet. Four of the better performing Ministers of State (MoS')—Piyush

Big shoes to fill: Nirmala Sitharaman takes over as Defence Minister from Arun Jaitley

PM chairs Combined Commanders Conference on board
INS Vikramaditya at Sea (15 December 2015)

Goyal, Dharmendra Pradhan, Nirmala Sitharaman and Mukhtar Abbas Naqvi—were being promoted to full Cabinet rank. That wasn't a surprise. What came as a bolt from the blue however was the appointment of Sitharaman as India's first full time woman defence minister!

Not a single political analyst had anticipated or predicted that Sitharaman would get the defence portfolio, considered one of the big four ministries—Home, Finance, External Affairs being the other three. This was as unexpected as plucking Manohar Parrikar out of Goa in November 2014. Parrikar however had a decade long record as Chief Minister behind him. Sitharaman on the other hand, was a relatively new entrant to the BJP, but clearly she has impressed the Prime Minister by her efficiency and quiet determination in tackling tricky issues in the Commerce and industry portfolio that she held before being elevated as Defence Minister.

Sitharaman has her task cut out. India's security challenges are mounting and the armed forces are in need of several urgent decisions and reforms. She will have to hit the ground running. Parrikar during his 28-month tenure as defence minister had brought a fresh approach to several legacy matters and resolved many knotty issues.

He and then Jaitley, have prepared the ground for Sitharaman to build on several far-reaching intiatives.

Despite frequent changes (first Jaitley, then Parrikar and again Jaitley as defence minister means Sitharaman is the fourth incumbent in the hot seat in less than four years) at the top, it must be said that measures to break the shackles of the past and shed the legendary hesitation in decisive action—elevated to an art form during Congress' AK Antony's long tenure as Defence Minister between 2006 and 2014—have been taken, thanks to the clear directives of the Prime Minister.

The Prime Minister began well by articulating his vision for India's armed forces. He wanted the military to be ready for future wars; to modernise themselves, to become leaner and make more efficient use of limited resources. His speech at the Combined Commanders conference in December 2015—held onboard INS Vikramaditya, breaking the tradition of always hosting it in Delhi—held out the hope that major reforms in ushering in the much-needed integration of the three services and appointing a Chief of Defence Staff (CDS), or at least a Permanent Chairman Chiefs of Staff Committee would be realised. The Prime Minister told top commanders, 'Above all, we look to our Armed Forces to prepare for the future. And, it cannot be achieved by doing more of the same, or preparing perspective plans based on outdated doctrines and disconnected from financial realities.

'In the course of the past year, I have seen progress, but I also feel that our forces and our government need to do more to reform their beliefs, doctrines, objectives and strategies. We must define our aims and our instruments for the changing world.'

'At a time when major powers are reducing their forces and rely more on technology, we are still constantly seeking to expand the size of our forces.'

'Modernisation and expansion of forces at the same time is a difficult and unnecessary goal.'

'We need forces that are agile, mobile and driven by technology, not just human valour.'

'We need capabilities to win swift wars, for we will not have the luxury of long drawn battles. We must re-examine our assumptions that keep massive funds locked up in inventories.'

'As our security horizons and responsibilities extend beyond our shores and borders, we must prepare our forces for range and mobility.'

'We must fully incorporate the power of digital networks and space assets into our capabilities. Equally, we must be prepared to defend them, for they will be the first targets of our adversaries.'

'And, networks must be seamless and integrated across agencies and forces, and are precise, clear and quick in response.'

'We have been slow to reform the structures of our Armed Forces. We should shorten the tooth-to-tail ratio.'

'And, we should promote jointness across every level of our Armed Forces. We wear different colours, but we serve the same cause and bear the same flag. Jointness at the top is a need that is long overdue.'

'Senior military leaders must have experience of tri-service commands, experience in technology—driven environment and exposure to the full spectrum of challenges—from terrorism to strategic.'

'We need military commanders who not only lead brilliantly in the field, but are also thought leaders who guide our forces and security systems into the future.'

Much to my surprise however, many of the points Modi made, are still a work in progress.

Moreover, why he allowed Manohar Parrikar—who was his unexpected yet correct choice in the first place—to go back to Goa in March 2017 is also intriguing to say the least.

To be fair, Arun Jaitley, the Prime Minister's 'go-to' man has stepped in both the times—for six months before Parrikar was brought in from Goa in 2014 and now again in 2017.

That said, the Prime Minister has been instrumental in taking some bold measures in defence.

Very early in his tenure, Modi made defence central to his 'Make in India' initiative. Speaking at the Aero India show in February 2015, he set out a broad roadmap for the MoD. 'Our defence industry in private sector is still small. But it already employs thousands of people. This is despite the fact that nearly 60 per cent of our defence equipment continues to be imported. And, we are spending tens of billions of dollars on acquisitions from abroad. There are studies that show that even a 20 to 25 per cent

The PM and Parrikar at Aero India 2015

reduction in imports could directly create an additional 100,000 to 120,000 highly skilled jobs in India. If we could raise the percentage of domestic procurement from 40 per cent to 70 per cent in the next five years, we would double the output in our defence industry. Imagine the impact in terms of jobs created directly and in the related manufacturing and services sector! Think of the spin-off benefits on other sectors in terms of advanced materials and technologies! That is why we are focusing on developing India's defence industry with a sense of mission.

'This is why it is at the heart of our Make in India programme. We are reforming our defence procurement policies and procedures. There would be a clear preference for equipment manufactured in India. Our procurement procedures will ensure simplicity, accountability and speedy decision making,' the Prime Minister told the assembled audience of top defence executives from around the world, and officials, vendors and smaller players in India's defence sector, in Bangalore. To achieve the objectives that he had listed, the Prime Minister could not have picked a better candidate than Manohar Parrikar.

To my mind, Parrikar's technical background (an engineer from IIT, Bombay) and sharp intellect not only allowed him to grasp the complexities of the important ministry, but also enabled him to put his own stamp on the daily functioning of the MoD. Undoubtedly, there were slip-ups and some embarrassments, but those can probably be attributed to well-entrenched vested interests who tried to undermine his authority. For instance, when Parrikar worked diligently to arrive at a definitive figure for granting the One Rank One Pension (OROP) to India's two million plus defence veterans, some civil servants—because of their traditional antipathy towards the military—dug their heels in and ultimately vitiated the process, leaving Parrikar to hold the can. The government in the bargain lost a good deal of goodwill it had earned by granting the OROP. Ultimately, the government could not overcome the bureaucracy's resistance resulting in a less than desirable implementation of the OROP.

I remember meeting Parrikar for the first time in February 2015 (before that, I had only heard of him as an unusual politician). One of the questions he had was, 'What, in your view, is the biggest challenge here (in the MoD)?'

At first, due to my lack of familiarity with him, I had thought of playing safe and given a standard reply, 'It is a large, sensitive and important ministry and therefore not easy to understand quickly.'

However, his easy manner encouraged me to be bolder and comment further: 'Your greatest challenge will be the status quo mind-set, which pervades the civil and military bureaucracy. Everyone will tell you that such and such thing cannot be done because there is no precedent to it. If you can overcome that trend, maybe then you will make a big start.'

I cannot judge if Parrikar took that input (not advice) seriously, but whoever I have come across since then—whether in the Services or in the defence industry—swore by Parrikar's efforts to re-energise the MoD and create greater accountability. This in itself is a big change because at the best of times, the MoD is a lumbering giant, slow to stir and act.

The MoD is not only entrusted with the defence of the country, but it is also the administrative machinery for India's nearly 15 lakh military personnel (the Army, Navy, Air Force and Coast Guard).

It also has one of the largest budgets in the government. For instance in 2017–18, it has been allocated Rs 359,854 crores ($53.5 billion).

Critics have quibbled over the comparatively low increase in the defence budget in 2017–18. But that is the least of the problems that the ministry faces.

The more important challenges for South Block have been reducing timelines for acquisitions, better and optimum utilisation of available resources, creating an atmosphere of greater accountability and transparency in the MoD's functioning, and making sure the most critical voids in India's defence preparedness are made up in quicktime.

Parrikar set out to achieve all that but the MoD saw to it that the Prime Minister's Make in India initiative receives the necessary impetus in defence production. Critics may point to the dismal Foreign Direct Investment (FDI) figures to debunk the Make in India initiative. However, there is another way to look at it. Many Indian companies are now getting more contracts. For instance, the Capital expenditure on procurement of defence equipment by three Services from Indian vendors has increased from Rs 31,575 Crores (47 per cent of total procurement value) in 2013–14 to Rs 41,873 crores (60.5 per cent of total procurement value) in 2016–17. In the last three financial years, i.e. 2014–15 to 2016–17, the Government has accorded Acceptance of Necessity (AoN) for 145 proposals worth Rs 3,99,800 crores approximately, out of which 103 proposals worth Rs 2,46,400 crores approximately have been approved under 'Buy (Indian-IDDM)', 'Buy (Indian)', 'Buy and Make (Indian)' and 'Make' categories of capital acquisition.

In fact, promulgation of the Defence Procurement Policy-2016 was the first step towards making fundamental changes in the way weapons platforms are acquired in India. The Buy IDDM (Indigenously Designed, Developed and Manufactured) category, introduced in DPP-2016, now gets the topmost priority among six categories that constitute the new DPP, which is the guiding document for all defence purchases in India.

In effect, this means all those Indian companies which have the ability to design and develop their products indigenously will get first preference from now onward in most purchases that the three armed forces undertake.

Under the new category for IDDM equipment, it will be mandatory for 40 per cent of the content to be sourced locally.

DPP-2016 contains a number of fresh ideas designed to accelerate defence acquisitions, while encouraging indigenous companies under the flagship programme of Make in India.

For instance, in order to cut down delays, the DPP henceforth mandates that all Acceptances of Necessity for a particular platform will be valid only for only six months, as opposed to the twelve-month deadline that it earlier had. Moreover, no AON will be notified until it is accompanied by a finalised RFP (Request for Proposal or detailed tender).

In essence, this eliminates one intermediate stage since notifying an RFP after an AON used to be inordinately delayed. Thereafter, prioritisation of projects was the first step. Defence acquisitions are expensive and since very little was purchased in the UPA II regime, the backlog just added to the problem.

The result of a review of proposed projects made over the previous five years found that the bureaucracy in the ministry—both civil and military—was sitting on some 400-odd big and small projects, which were critical to the three armed forces.

A thorough review revealed that nearly one-third of the 400-odd projects were now irrelevant. Hence, they were discarded.

About 50 projects were accelerated since they were of critical importance.

Next, important schemes across the three services that needed immediate funding and implementation were identified.

The effect of the spring cleaning is now visible. According to information given to the Parliament, the number and value of contracts is showing a healthy, positive upward trend.

In 2014–15 for instance, 18 contracts worth Rs 11,261.72 crores were signed with foreign vendors. In 2015–16, only 17 contracts were signed but their value went up to Rs 29,171.75

crores and in 2016–17, it shot up to a healthy Rs 81,129.62 crores for 23 contracts. The foreign companies are mainly from USA, Russia, Israel, UK, Germany, France and Sweden.

This was not an easy feat to achieve.

As Sudhansu Mohanty, who worked as Controller General of Defence Accounts and then as Financial Adviser, Defence Services, wrote in this perceptive piece on the website, *The Wire*, on Parrikar: 'He was a hands-on minister like no other. He was quick, but behind his quick decision-making lay a mind that had reflected long and hard on crucial aspects of the issue. He was a brainiac who would dissect procurement cases, and expatiate at length on the pros and cons in the Defence Acquisition Council (DAC) meetings as if he was slowly peeling off layers of an onion. But he granted every official their right of say, no matter how much he disagreed with them. He knew his every move was under the media scanner and the ubiquitous defence lobby, but he was firm and open in his conviction.

'But more than anything that I saw during my tenure was when the new defence procurement procedure (DPP) was a work-in-progress. Of the many discussions we had in meetings, including in the DAC, the meeting of eight-ten senior officers of the ministry and services headquarters that Parrikar called for us to hammer out the DPP clauses is etched in my memory. The meeting went on for a good six hours. What to my mind still rings loud is the new concept of evaluation that he brought to play on the 'essential and enhanced' parameters in the services qualitative requirements granting nuances to the progressive, pragmatic way for single vendor situations in the DPP.'

However, the biggest achievement of the Modi–Parrikar combine was to break the logjam that had ensued in the process to acquire new fighter jets for the Indian Air Force. The previous UPA regime had tied itself in knots over the procurement process and left behind a mess for the Modi government to deal with. Parrikar, with full support from Prime Minister Modi, spent a considerable amount of time in devising a way out of the impasse, and finally came up with what ultimately turned out to be a win-win outcome for everyone.

The process wasn't as simple as it sounds though. It was tortuous and inordinately long. To understand the background, it is essential to go back in time, to a period exactly a decade ago.

THE TORTUOUS MEDIUM MULTI ROLE COMBAT AIRCRAFT (MMRCA) SAGA

The competition to acquire 126 Medium Multi Role Combat Aircraft for the Indian Air Force began in 2007, after the government agreed with the IAF that it needed to replace the ageing fleet of MiG aircraft.

Six companies across the world were issued the tender papers. They were: EADS from Germany, manufacturers of the Eurofighter Typhoon; Lockheed Martin (makers of the F-16s) and Boeing (F-18 aircraft) from the USA; Sweden's SAAB (makers of Gripen); Dassault Aviation from France (the Rafale manufacturers); and Russia's Rosoboron Export (MiG-35).

India was looking for 18 aircraft to be bought off the shelf and 108 were to be manufactured in India (with a local partner, in this case, it was supposed to be the state-owned Hindustan Aeronautics Ltd). The required maintenance, repair and overhaul facilities were to be set up locally. The MMRCA contract was variously described as 'mother of all deals', 'most complex defence contract,' and so on in the media reports. And it indeed was.

According to official documents that I had a chance to read in 2012–13, the MoD had in 2011, benchmarked the Total Cost of Acquisition at Rs 163,403 crores. This, it must be pointed out, was different from the total cost of deliverables in the 126 MMRCA contract, which was benchmarked by the MoD at Rs 69,456 crores, excluding the offset loading cost, estimated to be anywhere between Rs 2,530 crores to Rs 5,060 crores.

All of this came after the six companies had submitted their techno-commercial bids in April 2008, followed by nearly eleven months of field evaluation trial (FET) held in the heat of the Rajasthan desert during peak summer months and in extreme cold conditions in the high altitude zone of Ladakh. The trials were completed in May 2010. The evaluation committee of the IAF shortlisted two aircraft—the Eurofighter Typhoon and the Rafale aircraft fielded by Dassault Aviation (DA)—and forwarded the recommendation to Defence Minister AK Antony. Antony took almost a year to accept the recommendation. It was already 2011. After prolonged internal discussions in two sub-committees (the Technical Oversight Committee-TOC and the Technical Offset Evaluation Committee-TOEC), a Contract Negotiations Committee (CNC) were formed in April 2011. By September of that year, the CNC had arrived at the benchmarking cost after applying escalation rates by averaging simple year-on-year escalation.

But it was not before July 2012, that the CNC activated four Sub-Committees, the 'Maintenance', 'Offset', and 'ToT' and 'Contract' Sub-Committees.

For the next two years, negotiations on Transfer of Technology, Offset and Maintenance went on at a leisurely pace. However, certain aspects related to the License Manufacture of 108 aircraft in India with HAL as the lead production agency could not be finalised. Major differences arose with regard to the matter of Man Hours that would be required to produce the aircraft from kits in India and who would take the responsibility for the entire lot of 126 aircraft. While DA maintained that 31 Million Man Hours that it had proposed should be sufficient to produce 108 Rafale aircraft in India, HAL was asking for a mark-up of Man Hours by 2.7 times.

This point became the bone of contention between the government and the French manufacturer.

Moreover, in the understanding of the MoD, the company that had emerged as the winner in the bid—Dassault Aviation—would have to sign a single contract with the Indian government. The French Company would then need to have back-to-back contracts with HAL and other Indian Production Agencies. Dassault Aviation would also be responsible for the delivery of the complete 126 aircraft to IAF and the single point responsibility for this contract rested with Dassault Aviation because the RFP was issued to them.

At that stage, the representatives of Dassault Aviation agreed to do their best in order to meet all requirements of the project as envisaged in the RFP.

However, Dassault Aviation did not fulfil the commitment given in the first meeting and there was an impasse in the matter of the responsibility for delivering 108 aircraft to be manufactured in India. Another hurdle came up on the point of work share of HAL. Dassault Aviation was asked to submit a 'Responsibility Matrix', clearly defining the role and responsibility of Dassault Aviation and HAL. The 'Responsibility Matrix' was to facilitate a back-to-back contract of Dassault Aviation with HAL. However, the CNC was unable to move the negotiations forward since the interpretation of those two fundamental aspects of the case by the French Company was not in line with the terms of the original terms in the tender.

The UPA government, under the overly cautious AK Antony, instead of imposing a deadline for the French manufacturer to comply with the terms of the RFP, dragged its feet and allowed Dassault Aviation to get away with obfuscation. Moreover, in an unusual move, Antony instructed MoD officials to bring the file back to him after concluding the CNC to re-examine the integrity of the process before proceeding to finalise the contract, creating confusion and doubt in the minds of the officials who were negotiating with the manufacturer.

Even as talks reached a complete standstill, the government changed in Delhi.

As the new political leadership was briefed about the impasse, MoD officials were told by the PMO and Jaitley to try and break the deadlock as soon as possible since the IAF's fleet of fighter aircraft was depleting alarmingly.

Thus, during a meeting of CNC on 25 September 2014, Dassault Aviation was directed to provide commitment on these two issues within ten days. The Company demurred. As no response was received from their end, another letter dated 31 October 2014 was sent to them seeking requisite commitment within a week. In their response dated 7 November 2014, Dassault Aviation did not provide the confirmations sought by the CNC.

On 10 November 2014, Parrikar took over as Defence Minister. While being briefed about the major pending projects and contracts, he realised that the MMRCA contract wasn't going anywhere. Yet he wanted to give the French company sufficient time to comply with the terms of the tender.

In December 2014, the French Defence Minister was visiting Delhi, and as was expected, he raised the issue of the conclusion of contract negotiations in the MMRCA case with Parrikar. The latter told him that the conclusion of the contract had been held up on account of the vendor not confirming compliance to the terms of the RFP. This was followed up by a formal letter from Parrikar to the French Defence Minister stating that it would be really useful for Dassault Aviation to confirm compliance with the terms of the RFP and the terms of the bid submitted by them at the earliest. It was further mentioned in the letter that the negotiations can be carried forward and concluded thereafter if Dassault Aviation could be asked to depute a fully empowered representative to discuss non-stop with CNC.

Another discussion with the delegation of Dassault Aviation was held on 12 February 2015. A clarification was sought from Dassault Aviation towards confirmation of compliance to the terms of the RFP and terms of the bid submitted by them specifically. The two crucial points, (i) the consolidated Man Hours (MH) based on which Dassault Aviation had been declared L-1 would be the same man hours required for license manufacture of 108 Rafale aircraft in India, and (ii) Dassault Aviation as the Seller under the contract for 126 aircraft for the IAF will undertake necessary contractual obligations as per RFP requirements.

The representatives of Dassault Aviation reiterated their stand on both issues and stated that while Dassault Aviation will be responsible only for delivery of 18 aircraft in a flyaway condition, they will not take ownership for the 108 aircraft to be manufactured by HAL as the Local Production Agency (LPA). On the issue regarding Man Hours, the Dassault Aviation representative stated that the company's stand has always been consistent with their previously stated position. The representative was of the view that the Man Hours indicated in their proposal correspond to the related tasks performed in French Industrial condition. He also mentioned that only HAL being the Lead Production Agency can talk about the factor of multiplication to be applied to these Man Hours to convert the same to the Man Hours required for license production of 108 aircraft in India. Clearly, Dassault Aviation was using the loophole in the original terms of the tender to get away with shirking its responsibility towards the quality of the 108 jets to be manufactured in India.

Exasperated at the obduracy shown by the French company, MoD issued an ultimatum on 20 March 2015, asking it to fulfill the commitment to and confirmation of the two aspects mentioned above, 'failing which MoD may be constrained to withdraw the RFP issued'.

However, Dassault Aviation, in its response dated 24 March 2015, did not commit to the two aspects mentioned above. Instead, the French Company stated that their estimate of consolidated Man Hours is to be used by HAL to prepare its own quotation with respect to the completion of its (HAL's) tasks under the MMRCA. The MoD realised that applying a factor of 2.7 on the Man Hours quoted by both Dassault Aviation and EADS (the company that had quoted the second lowest price), the Total Cost of Acquisition (TCA) as of November 2011 would undergo a material change, to the extent that Dassault Aviation would no longer remain L1 vendor (lowest bidder), and would instead become L2 vendor.

As the CNC members took the matter to Parrikar, he realised the process had been convoluted to such an extent that it would have been impossible to take it forward. Nevertheless, he knew from the IAF briefings that there was no time to lose in acquiring fighter jets. The number of effective squadrons was rapidly going down. The IAF leadership also told him that they were happy with the Rafale's performance and would rather have the fighter in its fleet than scout for other options. Parrikar realised that conducting a second round of MMRCA kind of competition would take an enormous amount of time and effort. Hence, he took the matter to the Prime Minister and briefed him about the necessity of procuring the fighter in a different manner. At the same time, Parrikar told Modi it would be legally untenable to go through with the MMRCA contract since the process had become completely vitiated thanks to Antony's indecisiveness and a crucial oversight in the original terms of the contract.

Under the circumstances, there was no alternative but to withdraw the original tender, Parrikar told Modi, since the CVC (Central Vigilance Commission) guidelines provide that negotiations cannot be held with the competitor who has come second in the contract (L2 vendor in officialese). The defence minister suggested that the only way left was to scrap the tender and buy a minimum number of Rafale jets off the shelf to fill a critical gap in the IAF's inventory. The Prime Minister agreed and decided to talk to the French President about such a possibility during his upcoming visit to Paris in April 2015. The Cabinet Committee on Security (CCS) also gave its approval to the new proposal before Modi left for Paris on 9 April 2015. Parrikar left for Goa that same morning, prompting later comments from uninformed commentators that he was not in the loop about Prime Minister Modi's subsequent announcement in Paris.

That evening, alerted by a source about the possibility of India scrapping the MMRCA tender and going in for off-the-shelf purchase of Rafale jets, I scooped the story on my blog *News Warrior* (www.nitinagokhale.blogspot.in), ten minutes to midnight on 9 April, almost 22 hours before Modi's announcement in Paris, of India deciding to buy Rafale jets off the shelf. However, I got the numbers wrong. My report said India would buy 63 Rafale directly from Dassault Aviation.

Once the Prime Minister's delegation landed in Paris, it was left to NSA Doval and PMO officials to negotiate with the French on the roadmap ahead to buy the Rafales off the shelf. It took them almost the entire day to agree on scrapping the MMRCA process and come to an understanding on the minimum numbers that India could procure.

Prime Minister Modi with the then President of France, François Hollande

Eventually, Prime Minister Modi announced in Paris that India would purchase 36 aircraft. Shishir Gupta of the *Hindustan Times* was more accurate (as far as numbers were concerned).

India's decision, announced at a joint Press Conference between Modi and the then French President Francoise Hollande on 10 April 2015, took everyone by surprise, but under the circumstances, the Prime Minister had chosen the best possible solution.

Once the in-principle decision was taken, it was left to Parrikar and his team in the MoD to negotiate the eventual price for buying the 36 jets. Their confidence bolstered by the PMO, the Parrikar-led MoD drove a hard bargain with the French. But it wasn't until another 15 months later—in September 2016—that India finally signed the contract and got the state-of-the-art fighters at a competitive price.

36 RAFALE VS 126 MMRCA PACKAGE COMPARISON

As the contract was signed, the inevitable comparisons in terms of costs that India was paying for the 36 jets and the 126 planes which the country would have supposedly bought under the MMRCA deal began.

The final negotiated price for 36 Rafale package, along with initial consignment of weapons, Performance-based Logistics

Defence Ministers of France and India sign the agreement on Rafale

(PBL), simulators along with annual maintenance, and associated equipment and services was fixed at 7,890 million Euros. The average unit cost of Rafale aircraft thus turned out to be 91.7 million Euros (going by the Euro-to-rupee conversion rate at the time of signing the contract, it meant each aircraft would cost Rs 688.30 crore and not Rs 1,500 or Rs 1,700 crore quoted by some analysts). In any case, officials involved in the nitty-gritty of the negotiations pointed out that the package cost of 126 MMRCA and 36 Rafale cannot be directly compared to work out per unit cost as the deliverables in the two cases were quite different. Obviously, the CCS, briefed in detail about the absolute necessity of procuring the Rafale jets for the IAF and the cost comparisons, did not hesitate for a moment to clear the proposal, as Parrikar remembers. 'I must give full credit to the negotiating team for having diligently worked out all the details to get a good bargain, and the Prime Minister's total trust in us,' Parrikar told me.

What the former defence minister doesn't mention however is his own steadfast belief that the cost had to be negotiated to India's advantage. A senior IAF official, involved in the hard bargain with the French, recalls: 'It was Mr Parrikar who backed us to the hilt and even held firm in the face of tremendous pressure applied by the French when their President (Francois Hollande) was in Delhi as the Chief Guest for the Republic Day Parade in January 2016. Mr Hollande was keen to sign the MoU, inclusive of the finalised price, with our Prime Minister while in Delhi. We negotiated through the night until 1600 hours, but the price Mr Parrikar thought was still high. So, he took the matter to the PM and requested him to sign the MoU without mentioning the final price, which Modi promptly did. On 26 January 2016, India and France signed a MoU for India to buy 36 Rafale fighter jets. Newspapers reports the next day said the 9 billion dollar deal would take some time to be finalised.'

It took another eight months for the contract to be signed. The team drove a hard bargain and obtained a hefty discount. As I wrote on my website, *www.bharatshakti.in*: 'The MoD-IAF negotiating team extracted many concessions and discounts to arrive at a price that is almost 750 million less than what was being quoted by the French side in January 2016, when the commercial negotiations had gathered pace, almost seven months after Prime Minister Narendra Modi announced India's intention to buy 36 Rafales off the shelf from France during his trip to Paris in April 2015.'

'To bring down the cost, the Indian team asked French officials to calculate the deal on actual cost (price as on today) plus European Inflation Indices (which varies like stock markets and is currently around 1 per cent per annum). The MoD has also capped the European Inflation Indices to a maximum of 3.5 per cent a year. In other words, if inflation indices go down (chances of it going down are more, looking at the current situation of European markets), India will have to pay less. Even if it goes up, India will not pay more than the 3.5 per cent increase.'

As my explanatory piece on www.BharatShakti.in pointed out: 'In the now scrapped process for buying 126 Medium Multi-role Combat Aircraft (MMRCA), confusion reigned supreme in calculating the cost of the contract. After the French Dassault Aviation—makers of the Rafale Jet—had emerged winners, the

UPA government agreed with French officials to calculate the price on the fixed cost formula that allowed the company to include an additional price of 3.9 per cent Inflation Indices from day 1 of the deal. So, had India gone ahead with the UPA deal and the European Inflation Indices had fallen (as it indeed has), India would have ended up paying an additional cost of Inflation Indices (@3.9 per cent) which had already been added at the initial negotiation stage.'

Apart from the lower price, the Rafales that the IAF operate will also have a weapon suite much superior to the ones proposed in the earlier case. They will include Air to Air weapons METEOR Beyond Visual Range Missiles with ranges more than 150 km, MICA-RF Beyond Visual Range Missiles with ranges more than 80 km and MICA-IR Close Combat Missiles with ranges more than 60 km. The Air-Ground weapons include SCALP missiles with a range in excess of 300 km. The induction of METEOR and SCALP missiles will provide a significant capability edge to the IAF over India's adversaries.

The Rafale for IAF will have 13 India Specific Enhancement (ISE) capabilities which are not present in the Rafale aircraft being operated by other countries. Three capabilities pertain to Radar enhancements which will provide IAF with better long range capability. One of the specific capabilities being acquired is the Helmet Mounted Display (HMD) through which the IAF pilots will be able counter many threats simultaneously. Another very significant capability enhancement is the ability to start and operate from 'High Altitude Airfields'. The 36 Rafale aircraft are to be delivered to the IAF within 67 months after the signing of the Inter-Government Agreement. This delivery schedule is better than the delivery schedule proposed earlier by the French side by five months.

Nevertheless, buying the aircraft is only the first step. After the initial purchase, the real measure of the effectiveness of any aircraft is in the speed with which it can be repaired and 'turned around', that is readied for another mission the moment it returns to base. In that respect, the IAF could not have negotiated a better deal.

In the MMRCA case, the initial PBL support was to be for five years for one squadron. In the case of the 36 Rafale, the PBL is for five years for two squadrons, along with an additional contractual commitment of another two years with the base year prices kept intact. In the previously proposed contract, the computation of PBL performance had considered cannibalisation of components from unserviceable aircraft. The Indian side was able to remove this clause without any additional cost. The PBL Agreement now stipulates that the company will ensure that a minimum of 75 per cent of the fleet will always be available for operations. Moreover, the Rafale has a lower turnaround time compared to other fighter aircraft available. The Rafale aircraft can do five sorties in a day in contrast to other twin-engine fighter aircraft available, which have a sortie generation rate of three per day.

The Rafale was the biggest of the complicated cases that the MoD resolved, but there are other crucial pieces of equipment that India needs and quickly at that. Therefore, all the hurdles in the purchase of artillery guns (M-777 howitzers from the US), attack and medium lift helicopters for the Army (Chinook and Apache helicopters from the US), frigates and mine counter-measure vessels for the Navy, and Akash missiles for the Air Force, were removed in double quick time.

These measures had to be prioritised due to the previous government's negligence even in the case of basic requirements. The previous Comptroller and Auditor General report tabled in Parliament made for grim reading.

'Stocking of ammunition even at "minimum acceptable risk level" was not ensured, as availability of ammunition as of March 2013 was below this level in respect of 125 out of a total of 170 types of ammunition,' the report stated.

Also, for 50 per cent of the total types of ammunition, the holding was 'critical'—insufficient for even 10 days of fighting, the report added.

This has now been corrected by making sure that ammunition for 10 days of intense fighting is always in stock. Once that objective is achieved, the ministry will look into the further replenishment of stocks. The delegated financial powers for the vice-chiefs of the three Services and army commanders have been enhanced to allow speedier purchases.

This is a big change in the notoriously slow and opaque functioning, which has historically besieged the MoD.

In another major decision, the government opened up the defence sector for FDI, allowing 49 per cent FDI through the automatic route and up to 100 per cent FDI on a case-to-case basis.

Also, the restrictions on what was 'state-of-the-art technology' have been reduced to 'modern technology'. This would increase the number of defence companies investing in India.

The procurement and modernisation of the three services apart, the biggest decision by the Modi government was to grant the One Rank One Pension scheme—a 40-year-old demand of the veterans. Although there have been some voices of disgruntlement on the issue, the fact is, this government showed the necessary political will and resolve to find a solution to a 40-year old mess. Prime Minister Modi also makes it a point to visit soldiers in remote frontiers and celebrate festivals like Diwali with them.

Remembers Lt Gen KJ Singh, then the Western Army Commander, 'Mr Modi's attention to detail is amazing. He came to visit soldiers during one Diwali. He visited two war memorials, one at Ferozpure and the other at Hussainiwala. At both places, he wanted to know the details of the battles fought there. Even when we organised the 1965 War exhibition, he wanted us to reach out to the common people and let them know more about the exploits of our soldiers.'

On the eve of Diwali 2016, concerned about the normal lives of soldiers in India Modi launched a campaign wherein people across the country could send their wishes and messages to soldiers for Diwali, who are miles away from home and their families, protecting the people of this nation so we can celebrate the festival in peace.

'I sent my #Sandesh2Soldiers. You could also do the same. Your wishes will certainly make our forces very happy,' he tweeted. The PM also shared a video in which he said 'we should make

our soldiers from the Army, Navy, Air Force, Central Reserve
Police Force (CRPF), Border Security Force (BSF), feel that we are
grateful for what they do for us,' said Modi.

According to data available with the PMO, over 3.5 lakh
messages were received from different people and 7.5 lakh tweets
were noticed following the PM's appeal.

As Richard (Rick) Rossow, senior advisor and Wadhwani
Chair in US–India Policy Studies at the Center for Strategic
and International Studies in Washington DC observes, 'On the
defence front, the Modi government seems to have put its imprint
on three priority initiatives. First, freeing up the private sector,
including augmenting foreign equity limits. Second, introducing
One-Rank, One-Pension (OROP). And third, revising India's
Defense Procurement Policy (DPP). The procurement process
still seems torturously slow, and other widely-anticipated decisions
like creating a "joint chiefs" role, remain on the horizon—good
initiatives for the reminder of Mr. Modi's first term, or perhaps, for
a potential second term in office.'

However, in spite of the Modi government's good intentions,
a toxic legacy left behind by a decade and more of lethargy and
timidity under AK Antony, it will take sustained efforts to ensure
that the MoD effectively discharges its duties towards securing the
nation.

Through various measures and focused attention, the three
armed forces and the notoriously slow and inefficient Defence
Research and Development Organisation (DRDO) have also been
spurred into action to improve their performance.

STRENGTHENING MISSILE POWER

Policy changes in acquisition and procurement apart, the Modi
government has consciously refocused its attention on defence
diplomacy and self-sufficiency in indigenously developing and
manufacturing missiles. One of the visible success stories for the
DRDO in the past twenty years has been its Integrated Guided
Missile Development Programme (IGMDP), an initiative of APJ
Abdul Kalam, who went on to become India's 11th President.

The success is all the more creditable when seen in the context of several technological sanctions that had been imposed by Western countries on India, following the 1998 nuclear tests. India had built its missiles on the basis of its own technological strength, unlike Pakistan, which is completely dependent on other countries.

Like its predecessor, the current government has also provided the much needed thrust for the strategic defence programmes. In fact, given the deteriorating situation with China and continuing tensions with Pakistan, the government has speeded up the effort to attain self-sufficiency in Missile systems and technologies. These include navigation, control and guidance systems seekers, propulsion and materials which have been developed indigenously. Today, India has the capability to develop any kind of missile system with indigenous technology, through full support from the domestic defence industry. Dr G. Satheesh Reddy, Scientific Adviser to the Raksha Mantri, who is also the Director General of Missiles and Strategic Systems, is of the opinion that India is now capable of producing several hundred missiles of different types in a year, thanks to the government's emphasis on the Make in India programme in the defence sector, particularly with reference to Missiles. He further reveals that funding has increased substantially for both R&D in missiles and their production, along with increasing participation from the private sector.

In fact, it is based on the success of the indigenous missile production initiatives that for the first time the government is encouraging the export of missiles to friendly countries for their self-defence, a right step towards the nation becoming economically prosperous and politically powerful. Although India has 'no first use' policy in the nuclear domain, it has developed a strong suit of strategic weapons. While the long range strategic missiles Agni 1, 2, 3 and 4 have been already inducted into the services, Agni 5 with a range of over 5,000 km is now ready for induction. Though neither Dr Reddy nor others in the know are willing to talk about the development of India's nuclear triad, information available in public domain suggests that India's nuclear-capable underwater missile systems are well on their way to be fully developed and inducted into the Navy sooner than anyone expects.

BALLISTIC MISSILE DEFENCE (BMD)

Given that both China and Pakistan ostensibly have hostile attitudes towards India, and both possess missiles capable of hitting key targets like big cities and critical infrastructure assets in India, New Delhi has for years sought to establish a Ballistic Missile Defence system. Such that any incoming threat can be intercepted either at the boost (launch) point, mid-course (flight through space), or terminal phase (during atmospheric descent).

The BMD is a two-tier fully automated system that comprises overlapping network of early warning and tracking radars, reliable command and control posts, as well as land and sea-based batteries of advanced interceptor missiles.

DRDO tested its first interceptor missile in 2006. Since then, at least a dozen tests have been carried out, three of which have failed. The previous government had given a deadline of 2014 to operationalise the BMD for Delhi by 2014. However, the DRDO failed to meet the deadline. After the current government took over, DRDO was directed to rectify the shortcomings and get the system in place. Hence, after a couple of years of extensive rectification, two successive tests were carried out in February and March of 2017. In February 2017, the exo-atmospheric PDV (Prithvi Defence Vehicle) interceptor missile directly hit a ballistic target and destroyed it at an altitude of about 100 km. In March 2017, the Advanced Air Defence (AAD) endo-atmospheric interceptor missile destroyed the incoming ballistic target at an altitude of about 15 km with pinpoint accuracy. This achievement has put India in the elite league of four nations—US, Russia, Israel and China—which have the capability to neutralise ballistic missile targets at both endo and exo-atmospheric altitudes.

The BMD apart, the DRDO has undertaken several new projects to boost India's defensive, as well as offensive capabilities. These include: The Quick Reaction Surface to Air Missile (QRSAM), Smart Anti-Airfield System (SAAW), Astra Beyond

Visual Range Air-to-Air Missile System (BVRAAM) and Guided Bombs.

The QRSAM focuses on the enhanced capability to search and track targets on the move, with a range of around 30 km. DRDO scientists say the system has an on the move 360 degree all round coverage, giving it a rapid scan and neutralisation capability against an incoming threat.

Meanwhile, the DRDO claims that the Indian Air Force's (IAF) search for a beyond visual range capability in air-to-air combat has been fulfilled with the development of the Astra BVRAAM. The Astra missile has a range of 80 to 110 km and is capable of being fired from the IAF's frontline fighters such as the Su-30. After completing a series of successful trials in 2015–16 and demonstrating repeat performance in engaging live targets under various aircraft flight conditions, the Astra missile has bolstered the confidence of the user, remark the DRDO scientists and IAF test pilots alike. The government has since then given clearance for limited series production of the missile to be inducted into the IAF.

In another development, the DRDO has developed winged and non-winged guided bombs to provide long standoff capability for tactical employment by the IAF. Both bombs have been developed for multiple roles and multiple platform applications. A series of trials conducted during 2015–16 from Su-30 aircraft have proved to be very accurate for the intended range between 30 and 90 km. Both glide bombs are now ready for production.

DRDO's most successful programme is in missiles

The DRDO has also developed a Smart Anti Airfield Weapon (SAAW) to be used against enemy airfields. The air launched weapon was recently released from a Jaguar aircraft. During the December 2016 trials, it reached the target with accuracy. The DRDO now expects the 125 kg SAAW weapon to be a vital part of the IAF's arsenal.

Meanwhile, the DRDO's previous programmes of developing Surface to Air Missiles (SAM systems) is still on track. It has much to do with the requirement of replacing the costly imported arsenal of SAMs already operated by the Indian armed forces. Working from first principles, the DRDO has been successful in developing a fully functional SAM system, the Akash Missile System that boasts of a complex network of sensors, data links and a fire control system. The system is capable of effectively engaging a variety of airborne threats through real time decision making.

'The Akash missile, a medium range SAM, has successfully entered production stage in the last three years, with total support and encouragement from the present political leadership,' the Dr Satheesh Reddy said. The system has been inducted into the Indian Air Force and Indian Army post successful user trials in April 2016. It has paved the way for self-reliance in defence systems with a considerable amount of indigenous content sourced from the Indian industry. Following the success of Akash, the government has now given the go-ahead for induction of more squadrons into the IAF to replace the existing imported SAMs. The decision to induct more regiments of Akash into the Indian Army will mean more growth and opportunity for indigenous defence industries.

Medium range Surface to Air missile with a range of 70 km and very high manevouring capability has been deployed by DRDO in collaboration with Israel. Both the Naval and Air force versions have been tested against multiple scenarios of live targets. Now, the government has sanctioned MRSAM project for Indian Army also at about 17,000 crores.

There are a couple of other success stories that the DRDO can be justifiably proud of. Take for instance, the Guided Pinaka system. The DRDO has upgraded the multi barrel rocket launch system with a control and guidance system, giving it both pinpoint accuracy and an increased range of 90 km. The upgraded Pinaka system's effectiveness was successfully demonstrated during the flight tests conducted in January 2017. The upgraded system will mean one such rocket can achieve the objective in place of several unguided rockets.

Similarly, the fire and forget Nag and HeliNa ATGM (Anti-tank Guided Missiles) adds a much needed operational superiority to the anti-tank capabilities of the Indian Army. The 3rd generation ATGM Nag has been proven successfully this year. The IIR seeker technologies have been improvised to meet the complete requirements including the range. Target acquistion by the seeker and missile range were demonstrated during the the trials from the Advanced Light Helicopter (ALH) in June 2014. After several such trials, it is now certain that the large anti-tank missile requirements of the country can be met indigenously.

INDIAN NAVY ON A ROLL

While the Indian Army is by far the biggest of the three armed forces, in view of China's increasing forays into the Indian Ocean and the Bay of Bengal over the past decade, the role of the Indian Navy has increased in India's strategic decision-making. And for once, the government is putting its money where its mouth is. Since 2014, the Modi government has moved swiftly to plug gaps in India's maritime sector and pushed the navy to do more bilateral exercises and send additional ships for overseas deployment in comparison to previous governments.

For instance, there were seven overseas deployments, Operational Turnarounds (OTS) and surveillance of Exclusive Economic Zones (EEZ) for friendly countries such as Mauritius, Seychelles and Maldives in 2014. That number quickly doubled in 2015 and 2016.

New Delhi has also reached out to the Indian Ocean littoral states, allocated more resources for bilateral and multilateral naval exercises and finalised the development of two islands for future Indian military bases in the smaller but strategically located countries—Mauritius and Seychelles—besides bolstering the development of military and civil infrastructure of its island territories, the Andaman and Lakshadweep islands.

In March 2015, Prime Minister Modi decided to undertake a three-nation tour of the Indian Ocean countries starting with Sri Lanka and then to Mauritius and Seychelles. The intention was to further strengthen India's long-standing ties with all the three countries, but in a little known fact at that time, Modi's team had also decided to finalise the lease of two islands—one each in Seychelles and Mauritius—that had been under negotiation for some years. Located in the Western Indian Ocean, these small islands are now being developed with required infrastructure needed for naval ships transiting through the waters of the western Indian Ocean. This is part of India's plan to help the Indian Ocean littorals in strengthening their maritime domain awareness capabilities.

During the Modi visit—again a first by an Indian Prime Minister in more than three decades—four agreements, including one on maritime security, were signed.

India and Seychelles also declared that India will be leasing Assumption Island, one of the 115 islands that comprise the Seychelles. It is an uninhabited island, near the northern end of the Mozambique Channel. Along with the Suez Canal, the Mozambique Channel is one of the two main routes for shipping between the Pacific and the Atlantic Oceans. Naval observers have noted that New Delhi's plans in the Western Indian Ocean are in response to the increasing Chinese forays into the Indian Ocean and hiring Djibouti as the PLA Navy's first overseas military base (see Plate 23).

Modi also inaugurated the first of the eight Coastal Surveillance Radar Systems (CSRS) that India is setting up. Soon after Modi's visit, the Indian Navy began survey and preliminary work on the island. Later the Seychelles President revealed the details in a media interview. President James Michel of the Seychelles told The Hindu: 'This is a joint project between India and Seychelles involving our two Defence Forces in enhancing our mutual security along our western seaboard. Seychelles is absolutely committed to the project.'

In Mauritius too, India already has a foothold. Both the security adviser and the head of the Mauritian Navy/Coast Guard have been Indian Naval officers for decades, India had for long resisted basing Indian Military hardware on the Island. That is about to change.

'Modi's visit to Mauritius included an announcement that India will upgrade airfield and port facilities at North Agalega Island, located some 1000 km northeast of Madagascar, for use by the Indian military. This has long been discussed, but never acted upon. Using Agalega as a staging point will substantially help India's maritime reconnaissance efforts throughout the western Indian Ocean,' wrote a naval expert, immediately after the Prime Minister's visit. Dr David Brewster, working with the Strategic and Defence Studies Centre at the Australian National University, where he specialises in South Asian and Indian Ocean strategic affairs, observes that 'India's moves also reflect an instinctive view among many in Delhi that if the Indian Ocean is not actually India's Ocean, then in an ideal world it ought to be.'

The Indian Navy is accordingly gearing up for the upcoming strategic competition with the PLA Navy. Several new plans—from speeding up infrastructure building in Andaman and Lakshadweep islands to acquiring more assets and inducting more personnel— are now taking off (*see Appendix III*).

India's annual joint naval exercise with the United States— Exercise Malabar—is now officially a trilateral one with Japan joining the manoeuvre in the 2017 edition. India's signing the LEMOA (Logistics Exchange Memorandum of Agreement) in August 2016, after years of hesitation, was a breakthrough moment in Indo-US military ties. On the discussion table for at least 11 years, the previous government was unwilling to take the plunge for fear of being branded 'pro-US', but Prime Minister Modi and his national security team appears to have overcome the hesitation and signalled an unequivocal shift towards a greater defence, especially maritime, cooperation with the United States and its allies.

The LEMOA, specifically drawn up for India, takes care of many concerns that critics have had about the US gaining access to Indian Naval bases and the Americans using Indian facilities to launch a war in the region, dismissing them as unfounded. A Press release issued by the Indian Ministry of Defence states: 'LEMOA is a facilitating agreement that establishes basic terms, conditions, and procedures for reciprocal provision of Logistic Support, Supplies, and Services between the armed forces of India and the United States.'

Contrary to apprehensions expressed by critics about the intrusive nature of the pact, the LEMOA does not authorise establishment of any bases or provide for basing arrangements. Neither does the agreement create any obligations for either India or the US to carry out any joint activity.

The Congress and Left parties had their reservations though. The Congress said it will jeopardise India's national, geopolitics and strategic interests, while the CPI (M) stressed it 'has compromised on Indian sovereignty and surrendered its strategic autonomy'.

The Modi government however decided to overcome the hesitation and went ahead with the signing of the LEMOA, which it insists is an enabling agreement and not a war pact.

Defence Ministry officials point out that the terms in the agreement are very clear on this count. 'Logistics support for any other cooperative efforts shall only be provided on a case-by-case

Growing naval cooperation: Indian, US and Japanese naval personnel during exercise Malabar in 2017

basis through prior mutual consent of the Parties, consistent with their respective laws, regulations and policies,' said a part of the media statement in August 2016.

Part of the reason to go ahead and clinch the LEMOA is also perhaps New Delhi's way of signalling to Beijing that India is willing to go further than it has gone so far, in maintaining a balance of power in Asia and disallowing China a free run in the geo-politics of the continent. In that context a tailor-made agreement for India, the diluted LSA, now called the LEMOA, is just the right message to China in the on-going tussle for influence in Asia.

The clarifications notwithstanding, the implementation of LEMOA will be watched keenly by long-time India ally Russia. Moscow has been wary of the increasing India-US bonhomie for the past decade. Consequently, it has made its displeasure clear at being displaced as India's primary military hardware supplier by the US a number of times. How it will react to the new development will be a matter of interest within the country and to the rest of the world.

As I had written in the wake of the signing of the agreement, 'The upswing in the defence ties has been the centre-piece of improved India–US relationship. With LEMOA it has gone up a step.'

Prime Minister Modi has done well to ensure a turnaround in the way the defence ministry functions, but many critical voids need to be made up quickly and the military made agile and ready for future wars, as he himself said to the top brass onboard INS Vikramaditya. That should be his major task in the remaining time that he has in the current term and a second one IF he wins another, the likelihood of which seem almost certain as of September 2017.

Appendix I

Indian Missile Tests since 2017

S.No.	Mission	Date	Remarks/ Achievements
1.	SAAW	31 Oct 2017 02 Nov 2017	Maiden Launch of SAAW missile from A/c. All Range sensor tracked missile and all data handed over to project.
2.	BrahMos	22 Nov 2017	Maiden Air Launch of Brahmos missile. All Range sensor tracked missile and all data handed over to project
3.	Akash MK-1S	05 Dec 2017	Maiden Launch of Akash MK-1S missile against Banshee Target. All Range sensor tracked missile and target. Interception was captured and all data handed over to project
4.	Prithvi	21 Feb 2018	Maiden night launch. Mission was successfull and desired data provided to project.
5.	PDV	23 Sep 2018	Maiden night launch. Mission was successfull. All Range sensor tracked missile and target. Interception was captured and all data handed over to project.
6.	Prithvi	06 Oct 2018	Maiden night launch. Mission was successfull and desired data provided to project.
7.	Agni	30 Oct 2018	Maiden night launch. Mission was successfull and desired data provided to project.
8.	Dhruvastra (Helina)	07 Feb 2019 08 Feb 2019	Maiden Lunch from LC-III. All Range sensor tracked missile and all data handed over to project

S.No.	Mission	Date	Remarks/Achievements
9.	SFDR (Solid fuel Ducted ramjet)	08 Feb 2019	Maiden Lunch from LC-III. All Range sensor tracked missile and all data handed over to project
10.	PDV MK-II (A-SAT Mission)	27 Mar 2019	Maiden lunch of PDV MK-II against low earth orbit satellite.LEO Satellite was killed by MDV MK-II Missile. Interception was captured and all data handed over to project
11.	Nirbhay	15 Apr 2019	Low Level Flight, Flight over land of Nirhay mission was conducted. Last leg of Nirbhay has done sea skimming at 05 m altitude. Event was monitored in real time by EOTS sensors and CDS activation was captured by EOTS. All Range sensor tracked missile througout the profile and all data handed over to project
12.	SANT-03	02 May 2019	Maiden Lunch from LC-III. All Range sensor tracked missile and all data handed over to project
13.	Abhyas	13 May 2019	First Successful Lunch of Non Expandable Aerial Target ABHYAS from LC-III. ABHYAS has flown thro all pre defined waypoints. All Range sensor tracked the target and all data handed over to project

Appendix II

NATIONAL INVESTIGATION AGENCY MINISTRY OF
HOME AFFAIRS GOVERNMENT OF INDIA,
NEW DELHI – 110 001

CHARGESHEET
(Under Section 173 CrPC)

IN THE HONOURABLE NIA SPECIAL COURT MOHALI

State (NIA) v/s
Maulana Masood Azhar (A-1) and Others

1.	Name of the Police Station	National Investigation Agency New Delhi
	FIR No.	RC-03/2016/NIA/DLI
	Year	2016
	Date	04.01.2016
2.	Charge Sheet No.	11/2016
	Date	19-12-16

SECTIONS OF LAW

Sections 120B,121,121 A,302, 307, 364, 365, 367, 368, 397 IPC; Sections 16, 18, 20, 23, 38 Unlawful Activities (Prevention) Act, 1967; Section 25 Arms Act, 1959; Section 3(b) Explosive Substances Act, 1908; Section 4 Prevention of Destruction to Public Property Act.

Infiltration into the Indian Territory

Investigation further revealed that the four heavily armed terrorists infiltrated into the Indian territory on 30 December 2015 from Pakistan, after illegally crossing the Indo–Pak international border through the forest area near the Simbal Border Outpost of the Border Security Force. Empty food packets manufactured in Pakistan and other food articles from Pakistan were recovered from the forest area near the Simbal Border Outpost of the BSF. The date of manufacture of the milk packets was 16 November 2015. Two witnesses who had earlier attended training camps of JeM, also identified the milk cream packet made in Pakistan, stating that similar 'Malai' packets manufactured by Nestle Pakistan Ltd, 308, Upper Mall, Lahore, were given to them by their handlers while they were being sent to J&K to carry out terror attacks. Unidentified shoe prints were also noticed in the nearby fields in Bamiyal village which is close to the Simbal Border Outpost of the BSF. Further, the audio intercept of the conversation of one of the four terrorists, with a lady, whom he addresses as his mother, also revealed that the four of them had infiltrated into the Indian territory for carrying out the instant terror. At around 0400 hours on 1 January 2016, the terrorists reached the village Akalgarh near the Air Force Station, Pathankot. They tied Rajesh Verma and brutally slit his throat with an intention to kill him and abandoned him and the vehicle in the fields at around 0400 hours. The terrorists, thereafter, moved towards the Air Force Station, Pathankot, on foot. Meanwhile, the victim managed to untie himself and rushed to the nearby village, Akalgarh, for help. The FIR of the case, the recovery from the vehicle and the statements of the victims clearly establish the chain of events and the complicity of the slaint errorists.

As per the forensic report, the DNA profile of the genetic material lifted from the Red Bull can recovered from the Mahindra XUV vehicle matched with that of one of the deceased terrorists. The DNA profile of the genetic material lifted from the dagger recovered from the possession of another terrorist matched with that of the victims. Similarly, the DNA profile of the genetic material lifted from the handle of the dagger matched with that of another terrorist. The nylon rope recovered from the perimeter wall of the Air Force Station matched with the rope recovered from the Mahindra XUV vehicle. The seat belt of the Mahindra XUV was cut and used to tie one of the victims. As per the forensic report, the seat belt pieces recovered from the forest area, where the terrorists had dumped Salvinder Singh and his cook, Madan Gopal, matched with the remaining seat belt pieces of the Mahindra XUV vehicle. One walkie-talkie set belonging to the terrorists and one slip written in English were recovered from the Mahindra XUV vehicle.

The terrorists had left that slip in which it was written, *Jaish E Muhamad Zindabad Tanghdar se le kar Samba Kathua Rajbagh Aur def hi tak Afzal guro Shadeed Kay Jan nisar Tum ko meltay rahege. lnsha Allah. A.G.S. 25-12-1511.* Two 500 rupees Indian currency notes taken by the terrorists from the wallet of the victim were also recovered from the body of the terrorists. The iPhone of one of the victims, which was snatched by the terrorists was recovered from the 'nallah' near the perimeter wall inside the Air Force Station where the terrorists had hidden before carrying out the terrorist attack.

The Truecaller names for all the numbers with which the terrorists communicated reveal that all these numbers belong to Pakistan. The Call Data Records of the snatched mobile phones revealed that the terrorists were continuously communicating over phone with their handler, Kashif Jan, and other senior operatives of the Jaish-e-Mohammad in Pakistan during the execution of the terrorist attack. As per the data collected as evidence, when the terrorists were on their way to the Air Force Station, at around 0331 hours on 1 January 2016, they received a call from the Pakistani mobile number. The analysis of the said call established that the caller, who had called from Pakistan, appeared to be a senior member of the Jaish-e-Mohammad directing the attackers, the latter respectfully addressing him as '*Ustadji*'. The recorded conversation revealed that they had discussed details about the planned route, the route actually being taken, and an alternate plan to attack a police station in case of extraordinary delay in reaching Pathankot. The person who had made the call also reassured, motivated and encouraged the terrorists to accomplish the planned terrorist attack. The terrorists kept seeking instructions from the 'Ustadji' and senior leaders/operatives of the Jaish-e-Mohammad in Pakistan all the time. Investigation revealed that the number was associated with Kashif Jan.

Attack at the Air Force Station Pathankot

Investigation revealed that after abandoning the Mahindra XUV vehicle, the terrorists moved to the western side of the Air Force Station on foot. The terrorists forced their entry into the Air Force Station, Pathankot, after cutting the wire fencing over the western side of the perimeter wall and then crossed it and entered the airbase on 1 January 2016, early in the morning. As per the forensic report, the marks of the cutting tool recovered from the terrorists matched with the marks on the cut fencing wire. Also, the climbing rope recovered from the perimeter wall matched with the rope recovered from the Mahindra XUV vehicle. A glove and a woollen cap, similar to those recovered from the terrorists, were recovered entangled with the wire fencing over the perimeter wall. Further there were marks of climbing over the eucalyptus tree just outside the perimeter wall panel and also on the other side of the perimeter wall.

Investigation revealed that after getting inside the Air Force Station, the terrorists hid themselves inside the *nallah* and the dilapidated MES Store sheds till the time they had launched the assault. As per the forensic report, the shoe prints lifted from the *nallah* matched with the shoes of a terrorist. Also the iPhone of one of the victims, which was snatched away by the terrorists and used to communicate with the handlers and senior leaders/operatives of the Jaish-e-Mohammad, was recovered from the *nallah*. Further there were signs of forced entry into the MES Stores shed as its door was broken and the fence wire was cut or manipulated at many places.

Intercepts of Calls between the Terrorists and Pakistan Numbers

Investigation revealed that while the terrorists were hiding inside the Air Force station, at about 0840 hours on 1 January 2016, one of the terrorists, identified by the name 'Nasir', tried calling the Pakistan telephone number (redacted) in Pakistan using the snatched Indian mobile number but could not converse. The name of the user of the Pakistan phone number is Khayam Bhatti @ Khayam Rasool @ Babar Bhatti. He runs a local merchandise shop (*kirana*) shop in Rum, Sialkot, Pakistan. Most of the numbers in the contact list of this person belong to Pakistan which shows that the user, Khayam Bhatti, is a native of Pakistan. He is also addressed as Babar during the conversation between Nasir and the lady on the other side whom he addresses as his mother.

Investigation further revealed that, at about 0920 hours on 1 January 2016, the terrorist, Nasir, called the Pakistan telephone number, using the snatched Indian mobile. In this conversation, the terrorist, Nasir, disclosed the names of his other three associates as Major, Abu Bakar and Umar.

Then again at 0922 hours on 1 January 2016, the terrorist, Nasir, called up the Pakistan number and expressed his desire to the person on the other side to talk to a lady whom he addressed as his mother. The person took the phone to her and Nasir talked to her in detail for around 18 minutes. Nasir told the lady that they had infiltrated into the Indian territory at 'do baje' on Wednesday (which was 30 December 2015). He further told her that he had killed two persons referring to the deceased Ikagar Singh and the injured victim (Rajesh Verma) whose throat was slit by the terrorist but happened to survive. He also spoke to his brother/cousin who is referred to by the name Babar, and to another person who is referred to by the name Munna. While speaking to the lady addressed as his mother, Nasir asked her to record his conversation on the mobile set. During his conversation with her, Nasir mentioned about one 'Ustad' who was supposed to come to her with his 'Wasihat' after his death. Nasir also asked her to host a 'dawat' (feast) for his 'derawala friends' after his death. The terrorist, Nasir, had also taken the names of some of the members in his family/relatives, viz., Mudassir, Mariyam, Altamash, in the conversation. Nasir also disclosed that they were hiding inside the Air Force Station (referred to as Camp in conversation) and waiting to carry out the terror attack which was part of the larger conspiracy of the Jaish-e-Mohammad and its operatives to wage war against the Government of India...

The statements of the witnesses, recoveries from the scenes of crime, and material and documentary evidence establish that the terrorists carried out the terrorist attack at the Air Force Station, Pathankot, killing and injuring innocent persons and destroying public property.

During the course of investigation, it was established that the terrorists were heavily armed with sophisticated weapons and explosive devices. The scientific evidences gathered during the investigation established that lkagar Singh was murdered by the same terrorists who attacked the Air Force Station, Pathankot. It was also established that Salvinder Singh, and his co-passengers were abducted by four terrorists. They used his vehicle to reach a village near the Air Force station. The terrorists even wounded one of the passengers very badly, with the intention to kill, but he miraculously survived. Oral, documentary and scientific evidence such as the DNA profiling reports has established the presence of four terrorists at the scene of crime.

The expert opinion of CFSL, regarding the charred/burnt mass, having pieces of clothes and parts of a pitthu-bag, which were recovered from a residential billet, by the armed forces, was inconclusive, as far as revealing anyone's identity, age, origin, or number of persons is concerned. As per the report 'These burnt mass materials belong to Human Male. It could not be possible to establish the identity of burnt male remains as under reference'. Due to the absence of any recovered arms from the aforementioned billet, its residential nature and the inconclusive DNA analysis report of the charred mass, the presence of any other terrorist could not be established till date and hence the investigation regarding this aspect is continuing under section 173(8) of CrPC.

Appendix III

INDIAN NAVY: CAPABILITY BUILDING, OVERSEAS DEPLOYMENTS AND FUTURE PLANS

INS Sardar Patel. An Indian Naval base at Porbandar, INS Sardar Patel, was commissioned on in May 2015.

INS Vajrakosh was commissioned in September 2015. The unit is located at approximately 25 km from Naval Base Karwar and spread over an area of approximately 580 acres. The primary aim of the unit is to enable delivery of missiles to ships on the Western Seaboard and establishing state of the art testing/maintenance facilities for new generation missiles.

INS Vishwakarma was commissioned as a training establishment in November 2015. The establishment is the alma mater of Naval Architect Officers, Shipwright Officers, HA sailors and civilian design officers/staff of constructor cadre of the IN. On an average, the unit undertakes training of about 35 officers and 260 sailors in a year.

An Indian Naval base, INS Karna was commissioned by the Chief of the Naval Staff at Visakhapatnam on in July 2016. INS Karna will serve as the operational base for the Marine Commandos on the East Coast.

Two Naval Detachments (NAVDET) at Androth and Bitra in Lakshadweep are in the process of being set up. A Forward Operating Base (FOB) at Tuticorin has been sanctioned. Operational Turn Round (OTR) Bases at Kamorta and Campbell Bay have been given a sanction in April 2016. OTR Port at Dicilipur. The 'Go-ahead' sanction for consultancy was accorded in March 2016 and the preparation of DPR is in progress.

For Andaman & Nicobar Command

Renewed impetus has been accorded to creation of Marine infrastructure especially in A&N Islands. Approval of MoD has been obtained for the following Marine Infrastructure cases:

(i) Sanction for Construction of Wet Basin and Refit Jetty at NSRY Port Blair.

(ii) Sanction for Jetty Extension for berthing FDN-II at NSRY (Port Blair).

Capital Acquisition Contracts

Indian Navy has signed 68 capital acquisition contracts with Indian and Foreign vendors, amounting to Rs 71,820.20 crores since May 2014. The major contracts include procurement of seven P-17A Frigates, 22 Harpoon missiles, MLU of Kamov 28 helicopters, four P81 Boeing Aircraft, 12 Dorniers for Coastal Security, 16 Advanced Light Helicopters, Deep Submergence Rescue Vessels and augmentation of Repair Facilities at Naval Dockyards.

Important Operations

Search and Rescue Operation of Missing Malaysian Aircraft. Malaysian Airlines Aircraft MH 370 was reported to be missing on the night of 7–8 March 2014, during the transit from Kuala Lumpur to Beijing. The search and rescue operation by the IN was undertaken (Operation Sahayata) from 13–17 April 2014 by INS Kumbhir, Kesari and Saryu. Operation Haystack for the same incident was undertaken by INS Saryu, Bangaram and Battimalv from 19–26 April 2014. P-81 maritime surveillance aircraft of the Indian Navy were also deployed for search operations.

The IN is continuously deploying one ship in Gulf of Aden on anti-piracy patrol duties since October 2008. The IN ship escorts merchant ships through the 490 nm long Internationally Recommended Transit Corridor (IRTC). So far, 63 IN ships have been deployed on anti-piracy patrol duties. These have safely escorted 3,348 merchant ships manned by nearly 24,500 seafarers. No ship under escort by the IN has ever been hijacked.

- **Assistance to Maldives—Op Neer.** On 5 December 2014, Maldives reported an acute shortage of water in the island country due to a fire in control panel and cabling of the generator supply to the distillation plants. INS Sukanya, which was deployed at sea, was diverted to proceed to Male and INS Deepak sailed from Mumbai with 800 tonnes of water. INS Sukanya arrived Male on 5 December with 70 tonnes of water prior to departing on 7 December. INS Deepak remained in Male for week and provided 2016 tonnes of fresh water to the Maldivian authorities.

- **Evacuation of Indian Nationals from Yemen:** Op Rahat. As a consequence of the volatile security situation in Yemen in March 2015, the Government of India issued an advisory for Indian nationals to leave Yemen. This was followed by a decision to evacuate Indians from Yemen. In the wake of the Government's decision, IN ships Mumbai, Tarkash and Sumitra, were deployed for Op Rahat from 30 March to 19 April 2015. During the operation, the ships undertook nine evacuations from three ports in Yemen, viz. Aden, Hodeidah and Ash Shi'hr. The evacuees were transported to Djibouti for onward passage to India by IAF/ Air India aircraft and merchant vessels Kavaratti and Corals. A total of 3,074 personnel, including 1,783 Indians and 1,291 foreign nationals were evacuated by IN ships from Yemen.

Overseas Deployments

(a) *Op Capella:* INS Mysore was deployed in the Persian Gulf from end June to July 2014 and was on standby undertake evacuation of personnel from Iraq.

(b) *Eastern Fleet OSD:* IN ships Shakti, Ranvijay and Shivalik were deployed in the South China Sea, Sea of Japan and Western Pacific Ocean in July–August 2014. The ships undertook two major exercises, viz., INDRA 14 with the Russian Navy and in Malabar 2014 with the US Navy.

(c) *Eastern Fleet Overseas Deployment (OSD):* IN ships Satpura, Kamorta, Ranvir and Shakti were deployed in South China

Sea, Sea of Japan and Java Sea in May and June 15. The Indian Navy participated in SIMBEX-15 in the South China Sea with the Singapore Navy and also carried out PASSEX with the navies of Indonesia, Australia, Thailand and Cambodia.

(d) *Western Fleet OSD:* IN ships Deepak, Mumbai, Talwar and Teg were deployed in the Southern Indian Ocean in October-November 2014 and visited Antisiranana, Mombasa, Dar-es-Salem, Simon's Town, Cape Town, Port Louis, St Denis, Port Victoria and Nacala during the OSD.

(e) *OSD of Training Squadron.* IN ships of 1st Training Squadron visited Abu Dhabi and Muscat as part of training for sea cadets.

(f) *Western Fleet Overseas Deployment (OSD):* IN ships Delhi, Deepak, Tabar and Trishul were deployed to Persian Gulf as part of Western Fleet OSD in September 2015. In addition, IN ships Beas and Betwa undertook a deployment to Iran in August–September 2015.

(g) *OSD of Training Squadron:* IN ships of 1st Training Squadron (1 Training Ships) visited Indonesia, Singapore, Malaysia, Bangladesh, Sri Lanka in March 2015 and, Mauritius and Seychelles from September to November 2016 as part of sea training of cadets. During the visit of one Training Ship to Mauritius, INS Sujata also participated in the exercise.

Cyclone 'Roanu' had caused widespread floods, damage and loss of life in Sri Lanka. The Sri Lankan Government requested for flood relief related HADR stores from Indian Government. In response to the request, IN ships Sutlej and Sunayna were deployed for flood relief operation at Colombo from 21–23 May 2016. In addition to transfer of relief and medical stores, the ships also conducted a medical camp.

Hydrographic Survey for Foreign Countries

Indian Naval Hydrographic ships and survey units have assisted the following countries since 2014 for undertaking survey of various ports, approaches to harbours, etc., based on requests received from the host governments:

(a) Mombassa, Kenya.

(b) Dar-es-Salem & Zanzibar, Tanzania.

(c) Sittwe, Myanmar.

(d) Port Victoria, Seychelles.

(e) Port Louis, Mauritius.

Assistance in Hydrography. In addition to the assistance provided in Hydrographic surveys, IN also trains officers and sailors of foreign navies/concerned organisations in hydrography related subjects at the Naval Institute of Hydrography, Goa.

Material Assistance to Vietnam Peoples Navy (VPN)

An IN Technical Team was deputed to Vietnam in November 2015 for undertaking defect rectification of various VPN equipment based on request from the host Government. In addition, training on yard processes, upkeep and maintenance of ship-borne systems was also conducted for VPN personnel. Further, in accordance with Composite Training Plan (CTP), 119 personnel from Vietnam People's Navy have been trained at Naval Dockyard, Visakhapatnam, INS Eksila, INS Kalinga and Naval Armament Depot, Visakhapatnam in different groups.

Provision of Advance Light Helicopter (ALH)

IN has provided one ALH to Maldives in April 2016. The aircraft is deployed at Kadhdhoo island in South Central Maldives and being extensively tasked for medical evacuation, search and rescue and other humanitarian tasks.

Fast Interceptor Boats

India has delivered 11 Fast Interceptor Boats (FIBs) to Mauritius Coast Guard in March 2016. The craft were built by M/s GSL under Indian Navy's supervision.

Delivery of Mauritius Coast Guard Ship

The first of the two Water Jet Fast P Vessel built by Goa Shipyard Limited Mauritius Coast Guard, was delivered in 16 September.

Construction of the ship, named 'Victory', was overseen by the Indian Navy.

Fire Assistance at Antsiranana, Madagascar

A major fire broke out at Ambilobe, Madagascar in September 2016 which affected more than 5,000 people. Based on a request received from the host Government, teams from INS Trikhand were deployed to render timely assistance by donating victualling stores, medical and surgical material to the local civil authorities.

Marine Infrastructure

The Indian Navy is playing a key role in the creation of marine infrastructure in the following countries:

(a) *Mauritius:* One officer has been posted at Mauritius for developing Marine infrastructure/Jetty since January 2016.
(b) *Seychelles:* One officer is being deputed to Seychelles as part of the team for infrastructure development and presently attached to E-in-C Branch.
(c) *Maldives:* IN representatives visited Maldives in July and October 2016 as part of MoD delegation for discussions on development of marine infrastructure.

Between 2014 and 2017, IN has deputed Mobile Training Teams to Mauritius, Sri Lanka, Oman, Bangladesh, Myanmar, and Maldives.IN is also exploring feasibility of deputing similar teams to UAE, Tanzania, and Qatar.

Courtesy: Indian Navy

About the Author

Nitin A. Gokhale is a media entrepreneur, strategic affairs analyst and author of more than half a dozen books on military history, insurgencies and wars.

One of South Asia's leading strategic analysts, Gokhale started his career in journalism in 1983. In the past 36 years, he has led teams of journalists across print, broadcast and web platforms.

A specialist in conflict coverage, Gokhale has lived and reported from India's North-East for 23 years, been on the ground at Kargil in the summer of 1999 and also brought us live reports from Sri Lanka's Eelam War IV between 2006–2009.

An alumni of the Asia-Pacific Centre for Security Studies in Hawaii, Gokhale now writes, lectures and analyses security and strategic matters in Indo-Pacific and travels regularly to China, Europe, South and South-East Asia to take part in various seminars and conferences.

Gokhale is a also popular visiting faculty at India's Defence Services Staff College, the three war colleges, India's National Defence College, College of Defence Management and the IB's intelligence school. He now owns and runs two important portals, bharatshakti.in and Strategic News International (sniwire.com).

બાલચંદ